# The Path To Pelini

The Stories Behind The Shakeups
That Led Nebraska Back To Bo

Memorial Stadium was filled to the brim on the night of Sept. 15, 2007, when top-ranked Southern Cal came to town for the first time since 1969. (Gwyneth Roberts)

Published by Lincoln Journal Star Books
926 P Street
Lincoln, Nebraska 68508
(800) 742-7315

Copyright © 2008
Lincoln Journal Star Books
www.journalstar.com

First edition

ISBN: 978-0-615-24007-7

Editor: Julie Koch

Research and production: Denise I. Matulka

Cover and page design: Clark Grell

New commentary: Steven M. Sipple

Contributing writers: Brian Christopherson, Todd Henrichs, Colleen Kenney, Cindy Lange-Kubick, John Mabry, Curt McKeever, Kathryn Cates Moore, Brian Rosenthal, Steven M. Sipple.

Photos from the Lincoln Journal Star

Photo editor: Ted Kirk.

Contributing photographers: Robert Becker, Eric Gregory, Heidi Hoffman, Ted Kirk, William Lauer, Michael Paulsen, Gwyneth Roberts.

Photo techs: Loren Rye and Jay Benson

Introduction

Path to Pelini full of twists, turns

What if?

What if Steve Pederson had hired Bo Pelini as head football coach in 2003? Where would the Nebraska football program be if Pederson and chancellor Harvey Perlman had handed the keys to Pelini after Frank Solich was fired?

Hard to say, but it definitely makes you wonder.

It's been a wild ride for Husker football fans since Tom Osborne stepped aside as head coach after the 1997 season. The winds of change have been gusting through Memorial Stadium ever since.

Despite their campaign to "Restore the Order," Bill Callahan and Pederson were unable to make it happen for the long haul. It actually took an old friend, Osborne, to bring a sense of calm back to the program.

Osborne, in turn, chose Pelini to bring the fire back to Nebraska football, and the rest is history that has yet to be written.

I remember a phone visit with Southern Cal coach Pete Carroll after Pelini was hired by Solich to be NU's defensive coordinator. Carroll, considered by many to be the top coach in college football, was to-the-point in his praise for Pelini, who had worked with Carroll in the NFL.

"They'll be so much better than they were before, you won't believe it," Carroll said. "He'll do all the right things."

I also remember a phone visit with Solich the night Pelini interviewed for the position. Solich was trying to get us meddlers at the Journal Star to back off. He wanted to keep it quiet because he didn't want anything to jeopardize the deal.

As Solich and Pederson learned, sometimes painfully, keeping things out of the media is no easy trick.

As you might imagine, relations between the Journal Star and the NU athletic department were strained during the 2003 season.

I always felt like I had a good professional relationship with Solich, but he wasn't happy when I wrote a column suggesting he might not be able to save his job, regardless of how well the 2003 season ended. "I'll talk to anyone else from your paper, but not you," he said after NU's victory against Kansas.

Solich and I spoke briefly to clear the air a few days later, but that was just about the time things really got messy.

When the decision was made to run the story about plans for Solich's dismissal, I was charged with the task of getting a quote from Pederson, who was attending a basketball game at the Devaney Sports Center. When I found him at courtside and told him what was happening, he was in shock. Pederson knew that the story would make his life extremely difficult, and of course, it did.

In that brief visit, Pederson looked toward the heavens and said something about how this wasn't the way Nebraskans treated each other (referring to the Journal Star's treatment of him). Many held the opinion that the firing of Solich fit into the wrong-way category, and Pederson never seemed to live that one down.

Nebraska winters don't pack a chill as icy as what I felt in the radio booth at Folsom Field before the Colorado-Nebraska game on Nov. 28, 2003. I walked into the room to do a quick interview, and guess who was in the same cramped space? Pederson himself.

Awkward to say the least.

If the Huskers had just lost to Colorado that day, Pederson's job would have been so much easier. But Frank and Bo and the rest of the fellas wouldn't have it. It was a memorable victory, but it was also one more uncomfortable moment in a long line of them.

I won't forget the fun of having Perlman compare the Journal Star to a broken clock (has to be right at least twice a day) or Benard Thomas angrily grilling Pederson during the Sunday news conference a day after the firing.

And I certainly won't forget the postgame interview sessions after Pelini and the rest of Solich's staff led the Huskers to an impressive 17-3 Alamo Bowl win against Michigan State.

The coaches were miffed that Pederson waited until that day to tell them how much he appreciated their work during the interim period, when most of them knew they probably would be out of work when the season ended. They were asked to try to keep it civil in their public comments after the game.

Some did. Others couldn't hide their frustration. The last coach I interviewed that night was Marvin Sanders, now back on the staff with Bo in 2008.

"I hope this is not about one man's ego," Sanders said that night.

And that, my friends, is why you don't just take what they give you on the official sports information-issued quote sheet.

Wish I could say "I told you so" about Pederson, but that is not the case. For some real entertainment, please read the column I wrote when Pederson was hired as athletic director (Page 11). Here's a quick excerpt:

Go ahead, try to find something wrong with this hire.

Really? I wrote that?

Whoops.

It seemed like the perfect fit. Osborne was pushing for Pederson's return. Perlman's search committee never met. That's how much of a no-brainer it was.

"It's my extraordinary pleasure," Perlman said, "to announce this morning that effective Jan. 1, 2003, the new athletic director of the University of Nebraska-Lincoln will be Steve Pederson."

Tami Pederson said "there was something that told me, and told Steve also, that it was just time, time to go home."

JOHN MABRY

As it turned out, the Pedersons felt more at home in Pittsburgh, so it was fortunate for them that Steve had the opportunity to go back after his NU dismissal.

Pederson was meant for Pitt, and Bo was meant for Big Red. Or at least that's what Husker fans are hoping as Pelini prepares for his first season as Nebraska's head coach.

Just to be clear, this book is not a Bo Pelini biography. There's plenty about Pelini on the following pages, but the mission for this book was not to tell his life story. Rather, this book is about the journey of change that led the Nebraska football program back to Bo.

We didn't want to fill every page with stories from the past. That's why Steven M. Sipple has provided new commentary throughout the book. No journalist has been more in touch with the Nebraska football program since Pelini first came on the scene in 2002. I think you will find Steve's insider views very enlightening. I did.

Many thanks to Steve, book editor Julie Koch and all of the outstanding journalists at the Journal Star who covered these events so thoroughly. What a journey it has been.

So, back to wondering. Would Pederson still be here if he had hired Pelini in 2003? Was Pelini ready for the job then? Is he ready for the job now?

Time to find out.

John Mabry, product development manager for the Lincoln Journal Star, was the Journal Star's sports editor from November 1997 to January 2007.

Chapter 1: Out with the old, in with the new (kind of)

The winter of our discontent

Nothing overly drastic occurred at the University of Nebraska-Lincoln in December of 2002. Yep, it was just your average holiday season in Lincoln.

Husker head football coach Frank Solich gutted his defensive staff following a 7-6 regular season.

STEVEN M. SIPPLE

Steve Pederson took over as the school's athletic director. Also, as NU prepared to play Mississippi and Eli Manning in the Independence Bowl, Solich hired then-35-year-old Bo Pelini as defensive coordinator.

Yeah, a nice, quiet December in Lincoln.

Amid the tumult, Solich somehow gathered his thoughts long enough to capture the essence of Pelini.

"He's very demanding of his players, but he's demanding in a way that people want to play for him," Solich said at the time.

Perfect.

With Pelini in command in 2003, the Nebraska defense tied a school record by forcing 47 turnovers in 13 games, helping the Blackshirts lead the nation in turnover margin. In finishing 10-3, the Huskers also topped the nation in pass-efficiency defense and ranked second in scoring defense.

Former Nebraska player and assistant coach Monte Kiffin, currently defensive coordinator of the Tampa Bay Buccaneers, recommended Pelini to Solich. However, it should be noted that Solich also consulted with several other colleagues before settling on Pelini.

Indeed, Solich obviously did his homework well in finding a replacement for Craig Bohl.

Solich's second choice was

Frank Solich's decision in December of 2002 to hire Bo Pelini as the Huskers' defensive coordinator turned out to be a good move. But who would have known that Pelini, and Solich, would last only through the 2003 season. (Journal Star archives)

highly regarded Jon Tenuta, now an assistant head coach and linebackers coach at Notre Dame. In 2002, Tenuta was in his first year of what would become a successful six-year tenure as defensive coordinator at Georgia Tech. In 2001, Tenuta had guided a North Carolina unit that led the Atlantic Coast Conference in total defense and pass defense.

Tenuta was interviewed on the Nebraska campus. He ate lunch with one of Solich's staff members at a popular downtown Lincoln restaurant. Tenuta and Pelini were the only candidates who visited Lincoln.

However, Solich also had a few telephone discussions with then-University of Pittsburgh defensive

coordinator Paul Rhoads, a native of Ankeny, Iowa. In 2002, the Panther defense ranked among the top 25 in seven statistical categories. Following the 2007 season at Pittsburgh, Rhoads became the defensive coordinator at Auburn.

Of course, history shows Solich hit a home run with the hiring of Pelini. At the time, neither Pelini nor Tenuta (nor Rhoads, for that matter) were at the tips of people's tongues when discussing "hot" defensive coordinators.

My initial impression of Pelini turned out to be accurate. In my first phone call to Green Bay, Wis., as the Journal Star chased the ongoing story of Bohl's replacement, I was immediately struck by Pelini's blunt, honest and confident

nature.

You could tell he hadn't hit the big time because he always answered his own office phone.

At any rate, you have to credit Solich for maintaining focus during a tumultuous period in program history. The 2002 season obviously was extremely difficult for all involved. Then came Pederson's hire on Dec. 21. The news was greeted with utter glee in all corners of Huskerville — well, almost all corners.

From the very start, there was concern among at least a few prescient members of Solich's staff that Pederson would make dramatic changes at Nebraska much the way he had done as athletic director at Pittsburgh.

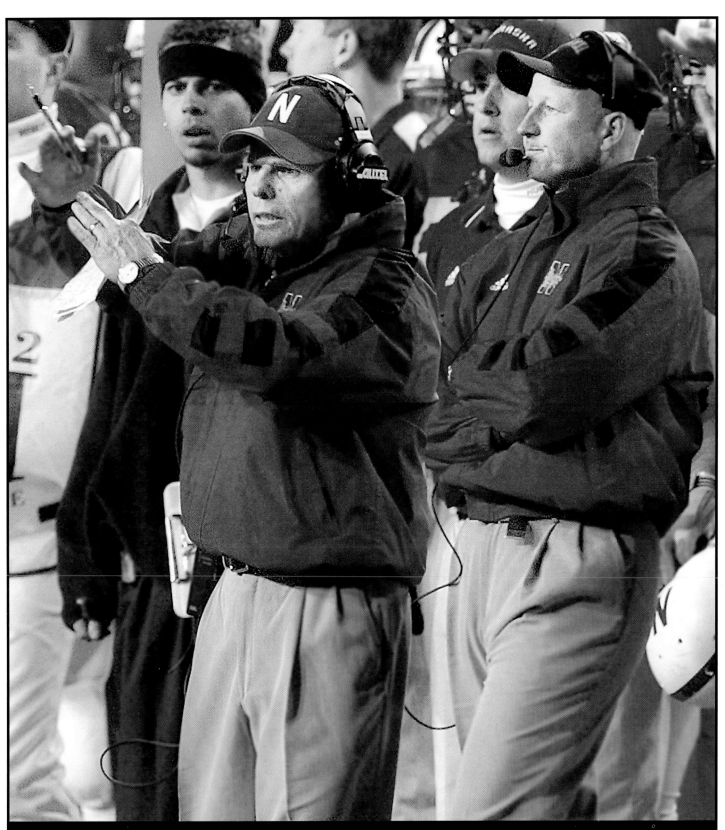

The 2002 season was a tough one for Nebraska football coach Frank Solich. His team went 7-7, and he fired defensive coordinator Craig Bohl (right), rush ends coach Nelson Barnes and secondary coach George Darlington. (William Lauer)

Whether those are the right changes or not, we needed change.
— NU rush end Trevor Johnson

Sometimes loyalty is put aside

There isn't a person around who hasn't at some point in his or her life had to pass a test of loyalty. Frank Solich was so sworn to what Tom Osborne believed in that his boss left the University of Nebraska football team's fortunes in his lap five years ago.

But for all his unfailing faithfulness in Osborne, Solich

By CURT McKEEVER

never would have been handed the crown jewel of college football if his boss didn't think that was in the program's best interest.

No wonder Monday turned out to be gut-wrenching for Solich.

While Craig Bohl, George Darlington and Nelson Barnes may have been just as devoted assistants, Solich felt compelled to cut the cord with them because he lost his trust in their ability.

Compassion may have tugged at him when he was deciding their futures, but not nearly so much as his instinct to survive. Right now, Solich is no different than one of those reality-show contestants. He's trying not to get voted off the island.

"We will do whatever it takes," he said in regard to returning Nebraska to the nation's elite.

Since that equation includes replacing himself as offensive coordinator, I'd say Solich's intentions are serious. But NU's meteoric decline this season leaves him with a huge crater to crawl out of — and you have to doubt whether he can guide the Huskers back to the top.

Monday's announcement caught no one who follows Big Red by surprise. Nebraska was fifth in the Big 12 in total defense each of Bohl's three seasons as defensive coordinator.

Solich's handling of the situation, though, was right out of Rip-

DeAntae Grixby talks with members of the media after the announcement that NU head coach Frank Solich had fired defensive coordinator Craig Bohl, rush ends coach Nelson Barnes and secondary coach George Darlington. (Journal Star archives)

ley's Believe It or Not!

In one day, he fired as many coaches as Osborne did in 25 years. Yet, the event was deemed so insignificant that Nebraska officials didn't even call a news conference. Instead, reporters who'd gotten wind that something was brewing waited outside the South Stadium offices until Solich appeared and courteously announced he would speak with the electronic media outside and the print media upstairs in the football team's main meeting room.

During the latter session, Solich steadied himself while working his way through a line of questioning he hopes he'll never have to hear again. Because, barring a retirement or two after Nebraska's bowl game, he knows the next time someone is talking about major changes in the Husker coaching staff, it'll be the athletic director announcing Solich is being replaced.

NU's current AD, Bill Byrne, promised Monday that "we're go-

ing to get this turned around." I'm just not sure whether he meant the situation at Nebraska or the one at Texas A&M, where he looks to be headed and faced with hiring a replacement for the just-fired R.C. Slocum.

Don't think Solich doesn't understand how that might affect his standing, either.

Without Byrne (or maybe even with him), if the Huskers' head man had given Bohl and his secondary and rush ends coaches enough rope to last another season, they might've all hung together.

Solich appears as comfortable as someone can be sitting on a horse, with his head in a noose.

His hopes of survival revolve around becoming more involved with the defense, having a bigger presence in recruiting, and taking care of administrative duties. Rather than coach any one area, Solich is taking on a CEO approach.

He hopes to have his new co-ordinators in place for the

Huskers' bowl game, which will likely be the Independence Bowl in Shreveport, La., 24 days from now.

Whoever the new coaches are, Nebraska's philosophy will still be to stop the run on defense and establish a dominant ground game on offense. Those in charge, Solich promised, will have a lot of flexibility.

Really, though, what choice does he have?

"It's a day that I don't believe anyone ever plans for, (or) feels comfortable about," Solich said.

No, in an ideal world, or at least in Nebraska's for the past 33 seasons, you could think loyalty would be enough to keep these kinds of things from happening.

But now, even the Huskers can see that good friends sometimes must part ways.

"Whether those are the right changes or not," said junior rush end Trevor Johnson, "we needed change."

Changes jolt Nebraska program

At 3:29 p.m. Monday, players were scurrying into the Nebraska football office.

While most probably had a clue why they'd been summoned for a 3:30 meeting with Coach Frank Solich, some weren't entirely certain.

"I don't know," junior fullback DeAntae Grixby said, "but I know today is not the day to be late."

Said senior wingback Ben Cornelsen, passing through a throng of reporters:

"I don't know, but it must be something big if you guys are all out here."

About 15 minutes later, Cornelsen exited South Stadium, shaking his head.

"Get your pens ready," he said.

Shortly thereafter, other players began emerging, many whipping out cell phones.

They were spreading the news to friends and family that three of their coaches had been fired.

Suddenly, Nebraska's reputation for continuity among its coaching staff had taken a hit.

"I guess that's done now," senior I-back Dahrran Diedrick said. "They won't be able to use that in recruiting anymore."

Solich, whose 7-6 team suffered its worst regular season since 1961, fired defensive coordinator Craig Bohl, secondary coach George Darlington and rush ends coach Nelson Barnes.

"It's just really shocking to me ... one bad season," Diedrick said. "Nebraska's been good for 30 years, then you have one bad season, and all of the sudden everything has to change."

Other players, however, weren't as surprised.

"Just from listening to other people, you knew it was going to happen," senior rush end Chris Kelsay said. "It was just kind of inevitable."

Kelsay expressed sympathy for the departing coaches, but said he backs Solich's decision 100 percent.

"Coach Solich, he felt these changes were necessary to get back on top, keep this team rolling and get things going again next year," Kelsay said.

Sophomore linebacker Barrett Ruud said

he'd heard so many rumors that he wasn't surprised by Monday's announcement, either.

"When you go 7-6, it's probably a combination of coaches and players," Ruud said. "There's something wrong, definitely. That's not just something where you get unlucky every game. Something had to be done."

Said senior rush end Justin Smith:

"We've been on top for a long, long time, and when you have a year like this, there needs to be something done.

"I respect Coach's decision. It was a hard decision for him, but he did what he needed to do."

Ruud, though, admitted that as a player, he felt somewhat responsible for the coaches' demise.

He wasn't alone.

"I know I do," Kelsay said. "They always commend us for our coaching staff. That's what Nebraska's football program has really been known for. Then you have an off season like we've had, and everybody's pointing the finger at them.

"A lot has to do with the players, and the attitudes and mentality this team had overall, and how we kind of stood by the wayside a lot of times and just kind of watched this team crumble."

As for Barnes and Bohl, the two coaches Kelsay worked with the most?

"There's things that I love about each of them, and there's other things that I might not agree on," Kelsay said. "But I respect both of them very much. I'll never be one to point a finger at a coach for mistakes on this team. I feel it's kind of a culmination of things."

Said Ruud about Bohl, who also served as linebackers coach:

"He was always a good guy, somebody that I was never really angry with. I thought he was a good X's and O's guy. I don't know, sometimes things just didn't work out."

None of the fired coaches attended the meeting, which Ruud described as somber.

"People weren't saying much," he said. "It was Coach Solich talking and people listening."

Freshman I-back Cory Ross agreed.

"Everybody was just wondering," he said.

"When Coach Solich says he just wants to meet with the players, and everybody else had to leave, we knew it was serious."

Solich also told the team he'd relinquished his duties as offensive coordinator and would hire a replacement soon.

"It's not going to hurt," junior quarterback Jammal Lord said. "I'm not saying he was a bad offensive coordinator, but sometimes you need some help to pick you up.

"In the flow of the game, some things went right, some things went wrong. It's not really his fault, it's not really our fault. It's a mixture of things."

By **BRIAN ROSENTHAL**

Having Solich concentrate on his duties as a head coach, Lord said, will benefit the whole team.

"Now he's like a rover," he said. "He can see the whole field, see how everybody plays."

One Nebraska recruiting prospect said the changes wouldn't affect his decision, but was surprised at the moves.

"Yeah ... that's weird," said defensive back Ron Ellis of Palm Bay, Fla., who wasn't aware of the news.

"I didn't know about that. I don't have too big of a reaction. It's kind of a shock, I guess.

"The head coach is still there, right?"

Ellis, who's scheduled to visit Nebraska the weekend of Dec. 13, said the firing of a head coach would be the only move that would cause him to rethink a school.

As for current players, most said the staff changes wouldn't be a major distraction to the Huskers, who return to practice later this week in preparation for a bowl game.

Already this season, Nebraska has weathered player suspensions, one resulting in I-back Thunder Collins' departure, along with the end of several streaks, most notably the string of nine-win seasons.

"This season's been so up-and-down, that this fits right into place," Kelsay said. "If it's not one thing, it's another. I don't think another distraction like this is going to hinder this team any more than what it's already been hindered."

Dec. 7, 2002

From powerhouse to punching bag

Husker fans, it's time for a talk.

Log off that Husker chat room a minute, walk down those red-carpeted stairs to your Husker basement, move aside the Husker media guides and the autographed book on Eric Crouch.

Now lie back on that Big Red couch.

By COLLEEN KENNEY

The one over there beneath the five national championship posters.

Cry, if you want.

It's OK.

I'm OK. You're OK. Now take a few deep breaths and repeat: This state is going to be OK with a football team that's no longer on top.

With a team that's just finished its worst season in 41 years.

With a team that's fumbled away the state's self-esteem in one 7-6 season of discontent.

And disbelief.

It's OK.

Now let's talk about your issues.

Why does this state care so much about whether a bunch of boys win or lose each autumn Saturday on a little plastic-grass field? Why does this state make football so very important on a social, political, economic, psychological and even spiritual level?

Why does this state care so much about a game?

Call it one big red inferiority complex.

"Nobody cares about corn, steaks or soybeans," said Husker fan Bryan Smith of Omaha, who thinks about the Huskers "365 days of the year."

But everybody cares about a winner.

And the Huskers, he said, are the state's one source of collective pride because they've always seemed to be among the best.

Fireworks light up the sky in celebration of the 250th consecutive sellout at Memorial Stadium after NU's game against Utah State on Sept. 7, 2002. A record crowd of 78,176 watched as NU won 44-13. (Eric Gregory)

The Huskers rank in Smith's heart right behind his wife and kids.

"If it weren't for Nebraska Cornhusker football, many people in this country couldn't give a hoot about Nebraska," he said. "So every time the team steps onto the field and into the limelight, they are representing me, my state and all Nebraskans."

Scott Daehling of Lincoln says that before each Saturday in the fall, his blood pressure rises ... by Wednesday.

He and his friends schedule their entire weekends around The Game.

"We don't have any big cities that people are going to fly into to experience some once-in-a-lifetime event, like New York or L.A. or Chicago," he said. "We don't have any pro teams that would garner national press. We don't have much in the way of in-state tourism. No beaches. No mountains. No hugely historic sites.

"But what we do have is a population of mostly poor to middle class, hardworking Midwesterners who still open doors for people, who really care about what's going on in their communities.

"When the team that represents your state on a national stage is the only thing you got that lets the outside world know what all of Nebraska stands for — well, you live it. You love it. You're born with it. And you die with it."

Hmmmm. Tell me more.

"It's more than a sporting event," Husker fan Joe Carter said. "Nebraska football is a cultural event.

"It's our identity."

Carter lives in Scottsbluff. But he feels like he's just down the block from Memorial Stadium because the football team unites the state. And in a state of stoic Midwestern types, it gives people something to talk about besides the weather.

"For us men," Carter said, "you can't talk about your feelings, but you can sure talk about the Huskers — like , 'That sure was one hell of a hit on blah-blah-blah, wasn't it?'"

Unlike Iowa or Kansas, he said, there's no State U in Nebraska that divides fan loyalty. Each game day is like one big statewide holiday.

Carter's wife, Trish, hates sports. She hates football. But she loves the Huskers.

"It's our pride," said Joe Carter, who runs bighuskerfan.com, one of dozens of Husker Web sites.

"We're so tired of hearing in the media about the 'hicks from Nebraska' and that we're all 'just a bunch of farmers.'"

I'm sensing anger

Dr. Richard Dienstbier is a social psychologist at the University of Nebraska-Lincoln. His specialties are stress and emotion.

This season, he's seen a lot of both

"You see a lot of anger from fans," Dienstbier said. "And that anger is exactly what you'd expect if someone were to have insulted them personally."

Many Husker fans, he said, have lost a sense of self-worth. The state, he said, has a collective lack of confidence.

Dienstbier came to Lincoln in 1969 from the East Coast. Immediately he noticed it — Nebraskans apologizing for Nebraska.

"That is a shame because Nebraska is a very interesting and important state," he said. "Lincoln is a wonderful town.

"But people here have a kind of inferiority complex about being here rather than living on the coast, and perhaps that is one reason they put so much investment in this business of being fans for a winning team."

Another guy with a fancy psychology degree has his take on it. You might have heard of him.

Dr. Tom Osborne.

"The game of football matches the psyche of the state," Osborne said. "We tend to be from pioneer stock, fairly hardy people. And football is basically a Spartan type of game. It's a very tough game. And so it seems to have captivated Nebraskans more than baseball or basketball or some other sport."

Because most Husker players over the years have been corn-fed Nebraska boys, he said, NU fans have felt more of a personal investment in the team.

"Almost every little town you go to has a guy who maybe is 40

Some diehard Husker fans stuck it out until the bitter end of Nebraska's loss to Oklahoma State in Stillwater, Okla., on Oct. 19, 2002. It was the Cowboys' first win against Nebraska in 41 years. (Journal Star archives)

years old now," Osborne said. "But everyone in town can point out that guy and say, 'He went down and played at the university.'"

Most fans keep it in a healthy perspective, Osborne said. But it's his professional opinion that a Husker loss affects 90 percent of the state.

He remembers all the letters after a loss.

"One Monday morning we got this letter from this guy who you could tell had spent all day Sunday drawing this picture — this pretty much obscene picture that was very uncomplimentary. And I thought, 'Why in the world would you spend most of your day on Sunday doing that?'"

Tell me about your mom

Well, she loves the Huskers. Dad loves the Huskers. Even Grandma loves the Huskers.

Nebraskans love their Huskers because they're socialized to love them by the people they love.

Parents buy their boys Husker jerseys and their girls Husker cheerleader outfits.

"It starts from the time you are born," said Husker fan Robert Kroll of Auburn. "It starts with all the memories you keep from your childhood — growing up watching the Huskers with that special someone. Your dad. Your mother. Whoever.

"It's brought down from family member to family member. And you end up with a long tradition of Husker fans in your family."

Carter, of Scottsbluff, says everyone remembers that first trip to Memorial Stadium for a game. He was 12. He was with his father. He had never seen so many people. Or so much red.

It was almost spiritual.

"I can remember after the game, you'd come home and play football in the school yard. And you were Jeff Kinney or Johnny Rodgers ..."

Who am I talking to?

This is Johnny Rodgers.

"If you want to follow winners,

you follow the University of Nebraska because we've been winners," said Rodgers, the 1972 Heisman Trophy winner. "It's had a positive psychological effect on the state, it's almost spiritual. We're sending good energies and we've expected to do so well over the years."

There's always been such positive energy at Memorial Stadium, Rodgers said. He felt it back in the early '70s when he was waiting for the ball to come down on each punt return. The fans knew he could score. He felt that energy. He's felt it in the stadium ever since. But this season, Rodgers sensed something new.

Doubt.

It started with the blowout losses to Colorado and Miami that ended last season.

"When the team runs onto the field, everybody's cheering and thinking good thoughts. So when now you get a bunch of people with mixed feelings, then there's not as much energy going in your direction. You can feel that physically.

"This season, everybody is not sure. You stand up and you hope. You don't stand up and know."

Osborne attended most home games this season. He sensed apprehension.

How would Husker fans react to a losing season?

"This year, you kind of caught a glimpse of it," he said. "But my sense is that two or three down years in a row would be pretty hard on the state. I would hope it wouldn't be. But I'm afraid it might."

But Husker fans still have hope.

"It's been hard," said Carter. "But in Nebraska, there's always that feeling of — just wait until next year. We're going to make changes, do the right things and be right back in it."

OK. Let's go with that.

Dec. 10, 2002

" Until a formal offer is made, there's not much to tell you. When the time is right, and things develop, I'll give you everything you need. — Bo Pelini "

Coach says he's talked with NU

Bo Pelini, believed to be the leading candidate to become Nebraska's defensive coordinator, said Monday he has spoken with Husker head coach Frank Solich "a couple of times" within the past week about the job.

"We're talking," said Pelini, the Green Bay Packers' linebackers coach.

By STEVEN M. SIPPLE

"No formal offer has been made. We'll see where it goes from here.

"For now, that's about as much as I can say. Until a formal offer is made, there's not much to tell you. When the time is right, and things develop, I'll give you everything you need."

In addition, sources close to the situation said Solich also has been in contact with University of Pittsburgh defensive coordinator Paul Rhoads, a former assistant at Iowa State. Rhoads, in his third year at Pitt, was on the road recruiting Monday night and couldn't be reached for comment.

Solich last week announced the firing of three defensive assistants, including coordinator Craig Bohl. In stumbling to a 7-6 regular-season record, Nebraska ranked 55th nationally in total defense, allowing 361.7 yards per game.

Solich immediately contacted Green Bay head coach Mike Sherman, seeking permission to interview Pelini. A 34-year-old native of Youngstown, Ohio, Pelini is in his third season with the Packers and his ninth in the NFL.

Asked Monday whether he's had a formal interview with Solich, Pelini said, "I don't know if you'd call it that. There's been conversation, and that's as far as it's gone. There's been discussion on both sides, trying to figure out what each other is all about."

Pelini, a three-year starting

Frank Solich (right) hired Green Bay Packers linebackers coach Bo Pelini to replace Craig Bohl as the Huskers' defensive coordinator in December of 2002. (Ted Kirk)

free safety at Ohio State, began his coaching career in 1991 as a graduate assistant at Iowa under Hayden Fry. He also has been a defensive assistant with the San Francisco 49ers (1994-96) and New England Patriots (1997-99). He joined the Packers' staff in February of 2000.

Asked Monday if he aspires to coach in the college ranks, Pelini said, "To me, coaching is coaching, no matter the level. It's not about specifically wanting to

coach in the pros, or specifically wanting to coach in college. It's about being around good people and good organizations."

Pelini said he has high regard for Nebraska's program, which won three national championships during the 1990s.

"Nebraska's not just any school," Pelini said.

Pelini said he's trying to stay focused on his current job. With a 10-3 record, Green Bay has clinched a playoff spot, meaning

the Packers' season could extend well into January.

"I have a lot of commitments here (with the Packers), and I have to be respectful of everything we're doing here," Pelini said.

Pelini declined comment when asked about reports that Solich flew into Green Bay on Thursday to interview Pelini.

"Let's just say this: I'm happy with my present job," Pelini said. "To be honest, taking another job is the furthest thing from my mind."

There was something that told me, and told Steve
also, that it was just time, time to go home.
-- Tami Osborne Pederson

Dec. 21, 2002

Husker homecoming for Pederson

This is a big pickup, my friends.

I don't know how we could have done much better.

I haven't been to the symphony in several years, but it looks as if Lincoln got one heck of a violinist in Tami Osborne Pederson.

Nice of Tami, a member of the Pittsburgh Virtuosi String Ensemble, to bring the mister along, too. Steve's not a bad throw-in.

Mrs. Osborne Pederson is not related to the famous football coach who helped make this deal happen, but she is very much related to the biggest sports story in town.

When Steve, Tami, their three children and enough family and friends to fill the Coliseum showed up for Friday's news conference at Memorial Stadium, it was obvious this was not your average news day in Husker land.

You know it's big stuff when the Big Red machine breaks out the fancy acrylic lectern. No cheap folding tables for this occasion.

You can talk all you want about Bo Pelini and Curt Dukes and Tommy Zbikowski and all the buzz on the football front, but none of it compares to Steve Pederson's return to Lincoln.

Go ahead, try to find something wrong with this hire. You'll have more luck finding a parking spot this morning at Whatever-itscalled Shoppingtown Gateway.

Pederson is from North Platte. He is a Nebraska grad. He is funny. He is bright. He knows how to make friends and influence wealthy people.

And besides all of that, he is the mastermind behind the Tunnel Walk at Memorial Stadium.

What more do you need to know?

Harvey Perlman knew it was a no-brainer. Check out the chancellor's introduction of his new athletic director Friday:

"It's my extraordinary pleasure to announce this morning that effective Jan. 1, 2003, the new athletic director of the University of Nebraska-Lincoln will be Steve Pederson."

Extraordinary? Yes, extraordinary. That's what Perlman said, and this is what I'm guessing he thought:

Finally, praise the heavens, something has gone right for me in this job from hell.

Harvey pulled a big rabbit out of his hat Friday. Not that it was a big surprise that he

North Platte native Steve Pederson returned to the University of Nebraska as athletic director in December of 2002. (Ted Kirk)

got the North Platte native to return to Nebraska, but that he got Pederson to return so quickly.

And what a relief for a university chief who hasn't delivered a whole lot of good news lately.

Interim athletic director Joe Selig, initially a candidate for the permanent job, praised Perlman for his handling of the situation.

"I assumed that Steve would be in the mix, and if he was in the mix, he was going to be a very credible candidate," Selig said. "In those situations, I try to put myself in Harvey's shoes and think what he's thinking.

"I really respect what Harvey's done in expediting this process and making it happen."

It seems like only yesterday Perlman formed that star-studded search committee to find a successor to Bill Byrne.

Jim Abel. James O'Hanlon. Jo Potuto. Rhonda Revelle. Turner Gill.

I guess you can forget about the annual search committee reunion party.

"I don't know," Selig said. "I don't think you can have a reunion unless you've been together."

Speaking of reunions, Selig and Pederson go way back, more than 20 years, to their mail-sorting days in the NU sports information department.

"I was the assistant mail guy," Pederson said. "That meant I only got to do the mail when Joe Selig went out of town."

From mail room to board room.

It's clear the mere thought of Pederson scared off all the top candidates across the country. All of them except Bob Burton, an NU senior associate athletic director and the only other known candidate for the job.

By JOHN MABRY

Burton would have been a strong challenger had he not been up against Godzilla.

Pederson has spent his whole life preparing for his dream job, and now he has it.

The sense of humor. The ambition. The enthusiasm. It's always been there.

"What you see right now is the way he always was," said his father, state Sen. Don Pederson. "He's very ambitious. He has no problem contacting and talking with anybody.

"He wasn't planning on imminently leaving (Pitt) at all. It was only as a result of this change that I'm sure that he gave consideration to leaving."

Pederson is ready to get started now. He will be in the house when NU faces Creighton in an important men's basketball game at the Devaney Sports Center, a building named for Pederson's first boss in college athletics.

"I'd like to shake hands with all 15,000 people who are coming to the game tomorrow night," he said.

See what I'm talking about. He's already planning to add a bunch of seats and sell more than 3,000 tickets before tonight's 7:05 tip-off. That's getting after it.

Steve and Tami Pederson are ready for this challenge. They are right for this challenge.

It's just the way it had to be.

"Something just in my heart," Tami said. "There was something that told me, and told Steve also, that it was just time, time to go home."

Dec. 24, 2002

"I think Bo's as good as it gets. He's the kind of guy who'll go very far in this profession." -- Frank Solich

Pelini wants defense to play hard

SHREVEPORT, La. — Green Bay Packers linebackers coach Bo Pelini didn't see Nebraska play much this season.

He managed to take a few glances at the Huskers playing on television. He's watched no film of NU.

Anyway, it matters little, Pelini said. Because, as of Monday, everybody on the Nebraska defense started with a clean slate in his mind.

By STEVEN M. SIPPLE

"I'm really into the here and now," said Pelini, who was officially named the Huskers' defensive coordinator Monday. "Everyone will start fresh. The players can learn about me as I'm learning about them. And they'll know exactly what's expected of them."

The 35-year-old Pelini will remain with Green Bay throughout the rest of its NFL season.

Although the lion's share of Pelini's attention will be directed toward the Packers, he's already formed a mental image of what he wants from the Husker defense next season.

"It'll be a defense that plays hard," Pelini said from Green Bay. "It'll be a defense that plays together and plays on the same page. The guys will know exactly what they're doing. They'll be asked to play harder than they've ever played in their life."

Nebraska coach Frank Solich announced Pelini's hiring as the Huskers continued preparation for the Independence Bowl game against Mississippi.

At an evening news conference, Solich said he hired Pelini for a combination of reasons. For one, Solich said, Pelini is an excellent X's and O's coach. Plus, the fact Pelini's coaching background involves mostly linebackers and defensive backs will serve him

Members of the state's media were eager to get to know Bo Pelini after he was hired by Frank Solich. Unlike many of the other Solich hires after the 2002 regular season, Pelini didn't have any ties to Nebraska. (Journal Star archives)

well as a coordinator, Solich said.

Solich also likes Pelini's enthusiasm.

"He's very demanding of his players, but he's demanding in a way that people want to play for him," Solich said.

Solich said Pelini was recommended to him by former Nebraska player and assistant coach Monte Kiffin, currently the defensive coordinator of the Tampa Bay Buccaneers.

"I think Bo's as good as it gets," Solich said. "He's the kind of guy who'll go very far in this profession."

This season, the Husker defense ranks no better than 35th in any of the five major categories. NU is 57th in scoring defense, allowing 25.7 points per game.

However, the Blackshirts are relatively young, as six juniors, two sophomores and six freshmen played extensively this season.

Next season, NU will be led by a first-year defensive coordinator.

"I'm not concerned about that," said Pelini, who worked under head coach Pete Carroll with the New England Patriots (1997-99) and under head coach George Seifert with the San Francisco 49ers (1994-96). "I have a tremendous amount of experience working with great coaches. I've had a lot of input.

"For me, this is the next logical step. I have a plan, and I know exactly how I want to go about things."

Pelini said he will employ "a variation" of the 4-3 defense, which Nebraska has used for the last decade.

Solich said that Pelini will use a combination of packages, and that Nebraska will line up "in a couple different fronts."

"His scheme is uncomplicated, and I think it'll fit our players well," Solich said.

Until the Packers' season is finished, Pelini will be expected to make calls to recruits, Solich said.

"But he certainly has an obli-

gation to the Green Bay organization," Solich said.

Pelini sounded excited to get started at Nebraska.

"It's a heck of an opportunity," he said. "It's a chance to work as a coordinator and run my own show, and do it at a place with a lot of tradition. To me, Nebraska is one of the top five programs in America."

Pelini seemed unconcerned about the Huskers' recent struggles.

"I have a heck of a job right now," he said. "I wouldn't have considered doing this unless Nebraska had a first-rate, top-notch program."

Pelini's respect for the program will make recruiting players an easy task, he said.

"Recruiting is all about being able to sell a product," he said. "It's not difficult to see the benefit of going to Nebraska. Recruiting is a matter of getting along with people and telling them what Nebraska has to offer."

> There's a lot of work to be done here in a short amount of time. I'm just concerned about getting the job done.
> -- Bo Pelini

Feb. 23, 2003

'Outsider' settles into Husker job

Yeah, he's the staff "outsider." But Bo Pelini has no time to ponder the distinction.

Nebraska's new defensive coordinator has a system to install as spring practice looms just more than a month away.

Of course, Pelini would've liked to coach with his brother Carl, whom NU head coach Frank Solich bypassed in favor of ex-Husker Jimmy Williams for the job as linebackers coach. Of Nebraska's six new full-time coaches, five had previous ties to the program.

Then there's Bo.

What's done is done, Pelini says. He's moved on. That's how he operates. No messing around. No B.S. He has a house in south Lincoln. His wife and two children arrived in town last weekend. He's here, OK. He's working. He's adapting. He's a Husker.

Nonetheless, some predict Pelini will leave town after a couple of seasons, maybe even after the coming season. After all, he's regarded as an up-and-comer.

"Time will tell, I guess," Pelini said.

But he said a short stint in Lincoln "isn't my intention."

As for being the staff "outsider," Pelini said, "I can't worry about that at this point. To me, that's something that can distract you, and there's a lot of work to be done here in a short amount of time. I'm just concerned about getting the job done."

It's a daunting task, indeed. Nebraska's defense ranked 55th nationally as the Huskers stumbled to a 7-7 record in 2002. Intrigued by the challenge, and impressed by NU's tradition, the 35-year-old Pelini was lured from the Packers to replace the fired Craig Bohl.

It's become clear that Pelini possesses a hard-edged, no-nonsense attitude — just what Nebraska's defense needed. Pelini is nothing if not succinct. He gets to the point more quickly than a Nolan Ryan fastball, and Pelini can be as intimidating as one of Ryan's high-and-tight heaters.

Pelini now has had time to watch film of Nebraska's defense in 2002. Well?

"They were 7-7, so they didn't play well enough," he said flatly.

However, Pelini said, he's careful to avoid judging his players individually based on last season's performance.

"That would be unfair because I don't know exactly what they were being asked to do," Pelini said. "I wouldn't want to put anybody in the doghouse before I see how he responds to the new system and the new style of coaching."

Pelini declined to offer detail about the "new system," though he did say Nebraska's base alignment will remain a 4-3. However, there apparently will be significant changes elsewhere.

By STEVEN M. SIPPLE

"From what I've seen on film, it'll be dramatically different," Pelini said. "To the naked eye, I don't know how dramatically different it'll look. But it's a different system — that's all I want to say."

Pelini is careful to avoid dwelling on Nebraska's struggles in 2002. "I can't concern myself with that at all," he said. What's more, Pelini insists he didn't harshly criticize the 2002 Husker defense last month when he and his fellow defensive coaches met with the defenders for the first time.

"It was a short meeting to let them know exactly what's expected."

And that is?

"Excellence, top to bottom, in everything they do," Pelini said.

Pelini, meanwhile, is getting used to the lay of the land. For instance, he now has a decent understanding of the Blackshirt tradition. But he said those coveted black practice jerseys signifying first-team status won't be handed out liberally. Last August, Bohl awarded 15 players with the jerseys.

"I don't know if we'll give out that many or not," Pelini said. "From what I understand, it's something you have to earn."

In 2003, Husker fans will demand improvement. Patience will be in short supply.

Pelini commands respect with his stern and confident demeanor and his coaching background. Remember, he was hired at age 25 as a secondary coach with the San Francisco 49ers. In 1994, his first season with the Niners, they won the Super Bowl.

Pelini seldom wears his title ring.

"I'm not much of a jewelry guy," he said.

Somehow I'm not surprised.

Guess I'm getting to know the "outsider."

Bo Pelini (left) and his brother Carl were both on Frank Solich's staff in 2003. And they're together again in 2008. (Ted Kirk)

Chapter 2: Goodbye, Frank

The end came quickly for Solich

It was a Saturday night that goes down as a memorable part of Nebraska's rich history.

At 7:29 p.m. on Nov. 29, 2003, Husker head coach Frank Solich parked his SUV and walked through the front doors of South Stadium, having been summoned by his boss, athletic director Steve Pederson. Solich walked up the stairs to his office and grabbed a notebook and pen, mindful of the magnitude of the situation. He then locked his office door and walked back down the stairs and into Pederson's office.

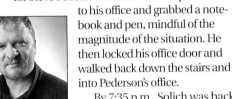

STEVEN M. SIPPLE

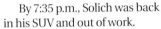

By 7:35 p.m., Solich was back in his SUV and out of work.

Solich's daughter, Cindy Dalton, immediately phoned the Journal Star with the news.

The firing was the most dramatic moment in a season of tension in the Nebraska football program. Thick tension. The tension actually began in earnest in July when Husker assistants refused to report to work one day because they were angry about Pederson's proposal for their contracts. One of the sticking points involved how long the assistants would be paid if Solich were fired.

"We felt betrayed," said one coach, speaking in December of 2003 on the condition of anonymity. "There was a grim feeling that Pederson had a plan to fire the whole staff.

"You don't bring in a whole staff and change the whole structure of how contracts had previously been done here."

The contract situation eventually was resolved, but tension in the program that season never really subsided much, even though Nebraska's defense — guided by first-year defensive coordinator Bo Pelini — helped push the Huskers to a respectable regular-season record of 9-3.

Tension escalated dramatically Nov. 1 in Austin, Texas, where the Longhorns hammered Nebraska 31-7 using an explosive running attack to complement a defense that held the Huskers to 53 rushing yards. Several of Big Red's big-money athletic boosters were on hand. As the game began to turn ugly, Pederson stood in a hallway outside the press box staring toward the heavens, his frustration evident.

The following week, Solich was conspicuous by his absence as Pederson unveiled plans for a $50 million facilities upgrade at an elabo-

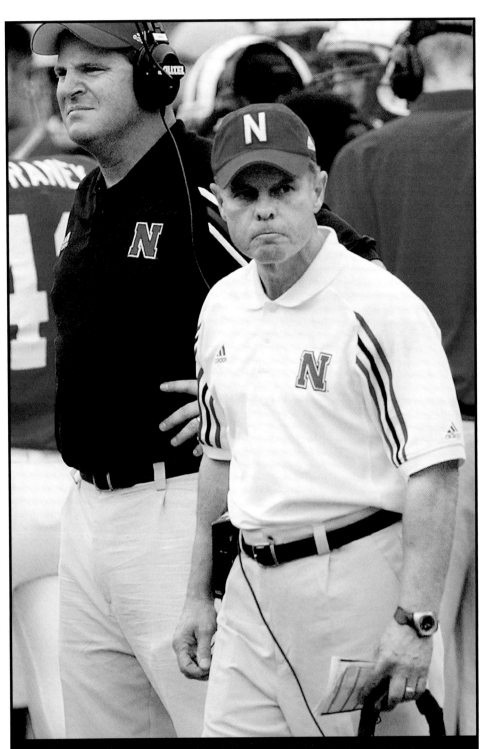

Nebraska football coach Frank Solich was fired by athletic director Steve Pederson on Nov. 29, 2003, one day after the Huskers completed a 9-3 regular season with a 31-22 victory at Colorado. (Ted Kirk)

The 2003 Nebraska football coaching staff: (Front row from left) Turner Gill, Ron Brown, Bo Pelini, Frank Solich, Barney Cotton; (back row from left) Tim Albin, Jimmy Williams, Scott Downing, Marvin Sanders and Jeff Jamrog. (William Lauer)

rate on-campus news conference. In fact, Solich and his staff only learned about the project the week it was announced. "We had no say, no input," said one former staff member.

Tension in the program was palpable Nov. 23 when, eight days after Nebraska's 38-9 home loss to Kansas State, the Journal Star published a story in which three anonymous boosters said Pederson planned to try to persuade Solich to retire after the Colorado game.

Nebraska practiced Nov. 23, the day of the Journal Star article. One staff member remembers "a very somber" meeting that Sunday morning. Tom Osborne addressed the coaches, telling them, "I'll do what I can for you. I think you're doing a great job."

Pelini to this day expresses pride in the way Nebraska players practiced during the week leading to the Huskers' Nov. 28 game at Colorado. Staying focused amid the turbulence surrounding their head coach, the Huskers beat the Buffaloes 31-22, setting off a loud locker room celebration. A few bowl officials mingled with smiling Big Red coaches.

Meanwhile, Pederson was nowhere to be found, choosing to remain in his stadium suite.

I'll always remember a troubling scene after the Colorado game: As Nebraska players and coaches celebrated the win in an area near the locker room, two of Pederson's high-ranking athletic department staff members — Marc Boehm and Paul Meyers — looked on with stern glares. They basically were the only people affiliated with NU who weren't smiling. At that point, it seemed clear Solich had coached his last game at Nebraska.

The next night, soon after his brief meeting with Pederson at South Stadium, Solich instructed a staff member to remove some important files from what used to be his office.

The next day, Dec. 1, Pelini was named interim head coach, and the Huskers began preparations for the Alamo Bowl.

Of course, the tension in the program remained thick even during the days leading to the bowl game.

"You can't ever get comfortable in this business," Pelini said then. "If you get too comfortable, you're going to get run over."

Tension was thick before Alamo Bowl

You want tension?

Consider Steve Pederson's meeting with the Nebraska coaches a few hours before the 2003 Alamo Bowl.

According to recollections of two former Husker staff members, Pederson gathered the coaches to thank them for their hard work during the month leading to the bowl game. He told them he had no new updates about NU's open full-time head coaching job, and that he hadn't contacted any candidates (it was later learned Pederson spoke via cell phone to then-Kansas City Chiefs offensive coordinator Al Saunders during halftime that night).

Jimmy Williams, the Huskers' linebackers coach at the time, apparently didn't like what he was hearing during the pre-game meeting. He told Pederson, "You haven't told us anything we didn't already know."

Williams then illustrated his displeasure with the situation using three of Pederson's favorite tenets: Teamwork, tradition and integrity.

"Teamwork? You're a one-man show, Steve. You've hardly associated with the coaches this month. Tradition? You've ruined it here. This isn't the Nebraska I know. Integrity? You haven't shown one bit of it. This whole thing has been badly mishandled."

— Steven M. Sipple

Aug. 30, 2003

We've been working hard all through summer, all through fall camp. I can't even explain how excited I am.
— NU linebacker T.J. Hollowell

Huskers ready to unveil new look

By BRIAN ROSENTHAL

It's finally here.

Perhaps the most highly anticipated, hotly debated season opener in the modern history of Nebraska football is upon us.

And not a moment too soon.

It's been 247 days since Nebraska ended its most dismal season in 41 years — a 7-7 record that caused civil unrest throughout the state.

Big-time changes followed. Long-time assistant coaches retired. Frank Solich revamped his staff, hiring former Husker great Barney Cotton as offensive coordinator and plucking Bo Pelini from the NFL ranks to lead a downtrodden defense.

Nebraska alum Steve Pederson took over as athletic director and immediately turned his attention to soothing relations with Big Red faithful. He's declared this the year of the fan, trying to re-create a sense of togetherness in what he's labeled Husker Nation.

Pederson's even brought past Husker football players into the mix. More than 800 former letterwinners will take the field prior to the game, likely to send Memorial Stadium's 256th consecutive sellout into a silly frenzy.

As if that's not enough to create mega-interest for a home opener, there's also today's opponent: No. 24 Oklahoma State.

It's a Big 12 Conference game, and the Cowboys beat Nebraska for the first time in 41 years last season, winning 24-21 in Stillwater.

"We've been waiting for this since the end of the game last year," Nebraska linebacker T.J. Hollowell said. "We've been working hard all through summer, all through fall camp. I can't even explain how excited I am."

Oklahoma State won six of its final seven games in 2002, and enters this season with high hopes. With the likes of quarterback Josh Fields, wide receiver Rashaun Woods and running back Tatum Bell, the Cowboys feel they're on track to make some noise in the Big 12 South.

"We'll have to find out how confident and wide their swagger is come (Saturday)," Oklahoma State coach Les Miles said.

NU, meanwhile, is trying to re-establish its swagger. The Huskers dropped three of their last four games last season. They haven't won since beating lowly Kansas on Nov. 9, 2002.

By Nebraska standards, that's a long time between victories. Too long.

Former defensive coordinator Charlie McBride (left) and legendary coach Tom Osborne were among the more than 800 former Husker players, coaches, etc., to attend NU's 2003 game against Oklahoma State. (Ted Kirk)

"We've got to come out and get ourselves back on track and get Nebraska where it's supposed to be," Husker captain Demorrio Williams said.

Even at Memorial Stadium, where the Huskers are 95-5 over the past 14 years, that won't be easy against Oklahoma State.

A task for the Huskers today: Finding a way to stop the Cowboys' offensive trio of Fields, Woods and Bell.

"Their offense, it isn't too complicated," Hollowell said. "They like to do a lot of shifting and motioning. The main things we've got to do, when they shift and motion, just be able to line up to it and adjust. Our coaches have done a good job with us in practice on working on handling their shifts and motions."

Bell ran 33 times for 182 yards last year against the Huskers and finished the year with 1,096 rushing yards. Woods, regarded by many as the best receiver in college football, holds OSU records for season receiving yards (1,695), season receptions (107), career recep-

tions (216) and game receiving yards (226).

"It always starts with stopping the running game," Pelini said. "That's what good defense starts with. But, obviously, when you have a tremendous football player and All-American like Rashaun Woods sitting out there, you can't ignore him either."

How Pelini will go about defending the Cowboys, and particularly Woods, is anybody's guess. He's never been a coordinator before, and the Nebraska coaching staff has been very secretive throughout fall camp.

"They're going to play man and zone," Miles said. "They'll play two and three and one. They'll play a three over here and a one over there and a standup guy over here.

"There's only so many ways they can line up. I'm certain that he's going to have them prepared. I'm sure they'll do better than they did a year ago."

A victory today could set the tone for a turnaround year for Nebraska.

"They'll be so much better than they were before, you won't believe it. He'll do all the right things.
— USC coach Pete Carroll

Aug. 31, 2003

Plan shows Pelini knows defense

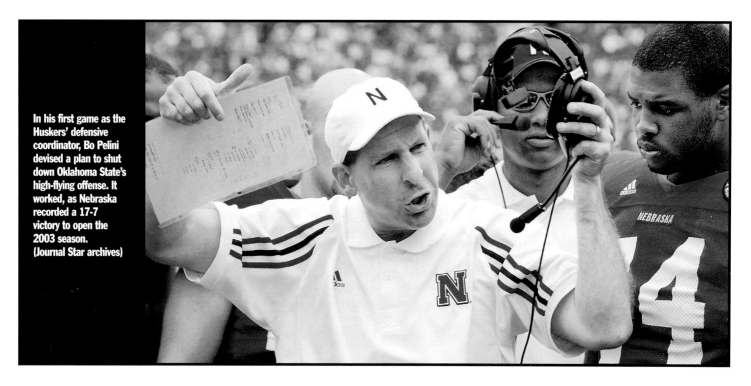

In his first game as the Huskers' defensive coordinator, Bo Pelini devised a plan to shut down Oklahoma State's high-flying offense. It worked, as Nebraska recorded a 17-7 victory to open the 2003 season. (Journal Star archives)

I didn't know Nebraska's Demorrio Williams played defensive end. And I'm betting neither did the offensive tackle he went past like a blur before putting a lick on Oklahoma State quarterback Josh Fields during the second quarter of Saturday's season opener.

I didn't know the Huskers, even with all their returning defensive players, could hold a unit with as much play-making talent as you'll see enter Memorial Stadium this season to just one score.

I'm not even sure if NU's 17-7 come-from-behind win against the nation's 24th-ranked team is something to build up or bemoan.

But I am starting to understand one thing: Pete Carroll is right about the unassuming man behind the Husker defense, Bo Pelini. The guy has a plan, and knows how to make it work.

"They'll be so much better than they were before, you won't believe it," Carroll said of Pelini. "He'll do all the right things."

This was two weeks ago, when Carroll — who hired Pelini while head coach of the NFL New England Patriots, and also served with him on the San Francisco 49ers' staff — was preparing his Southern California team to play at No. 6 Auburn. The Trojans, by the way,

pitched a shutout.

Carroll would be just as impressed with what Pelini orchestrated against the quick-draw Cowboys, who, after driving 52 yards for a touchdown on their first possession, spent the rest of the afternoon shooting blanks.

Fields, who came in regarded as the top returning quarterback in the Big 12, left with his lowest passing total (97 yards) as a starter.

It happened, thanks in large part, because of the punches thrown by Pelini.

If he wasn't moving weakside linebacker Williams up to the line, he was mixing in man-to-man coverages with zone looks at a rate that left Fields dizzy.

"The players are the same," OSU's All-America wide receiver Rashaun Woods said of the Huskers. But "their schemes are different."

Woods didn't like them, either.

Woods scored Saturday on a 4-yard grab just in front of NU cornerback Pat Ricketts. But thereafter, he was limited to three catches for 15 yards.

Even the tough guy from Youngstown, Ohio, shook his head at that stat.

"I've been away from college ball for so long, I wasn't sure how we would stack up,"

Pelini admitted. "We made some right calls ... other times, guys just made plays. It's a credit to what they've learned."

Although wary that the Cowboys could change the game's tone with one big play to Woods, or 1,000-yard rusher Tatum Bell, Pelini's group never flinched.

"No one panicked, and everyone responded the way I thought they would," said Pelini.

Funny, how on Friday night he was harping on how they'd have to stay after it if Oklahoma State came out and "hit them in the face" with an opening-drive TD.

"We weren't scared," middle linebacker Barrett Ruud said. "They'd line up and we said, 'We're going to do this.'"

Control the game they did.

After Oklahoma State's third series, which ended with a blocked field goal, the Cowboys made it into Husker territory on just one other drive.

"We're going to keep setting the bar higher," Pelini said. "Our defensive players, they're men of great character, and they'll keep raising it."

By CURT McKEEVER

Oct. 1, 2003

'Hopefully, he's not going to take a head coaching job any time soon. I'd like to see him stay around at least a few more years.
— NU linebacker Barrett Ruud'

He's head coach material, but when?

It's all about getting your body in the right position.

Bo Pelini means that only in regard to playing successful football. But his No. 1 rule also would seem to apply to sharp, 30-something assistants who want to become head coaches at big-time programs.

Pelini is one of those guys, and with the way his Nebraska

By CURT McKEEVER

defense is playing, he's definitely positioned for a fast track toward achieving that dream.

How fast? Well, John Mackovic barely had time to clean out his office after getting fired at the University of Arizona on Sunday before Pelini's name surfaced in an SI.com story that tackled who the Wildcats might seek as a replacement.

Of course, it's all just speculation. But it's still good to be on the list, especially if you've only been a defensive coordinator for four games.

"Four games is pretty quick," said linebacker Barrett Ruud, grinning as he talked about the unwanted attention the article brought Pelini. "But being around the guy, you knew right away he knew what he was talking about. Hopefully, he's not going to take a head coaching job any time soon. I'd like to see him stay around at least a few more years."

A few years? Isn't it a hard and fast rule that if you come to Nebraska you stay until you need assistance to walk the sideline? Oh, yeah, I forgot. That applies only to Big Red's old-school, continuity-is-best line of thinking.

These are different times, even for the Huskers. So you shouldn't bank on the 35-year-old Pelini, a Youngstown, Ohio, native, sticking around long enough to get senior rates on the local golf

Kiffin sees Pelini as gifted teacher

TAMPA, Fla. — Monte Kiffin is 1,500 miles and 27 years removed from Nebraska.

But once a Husker, always a Husker.

On football Saturdays, the Tampa Bay Buccaneers' defensive coordinator reaches for the television remote to fulfill his duty to his native state.

Whether at home or in a hotel awaiting a Bucs' road game, the pride of Lexington scans TV channels in a furious search for Big Red football.

"When I watch Nebraska play on TV, and I hear that fight song play, I still get chills," said Kiffin, who played offensive and defensive tackle for NU from 1959-63 before coaching at his alma mater for 11 seasons, until 1976.

Kiffin's interest in Nebraska football is at its peak this season. After all, it was Kiffin who recommended Bo Pelini to Frank Solich when Nebraska's head coach was searching for a defensive coordinator last winter.

Pelini eventually grabbed the job and has been given a lot of the credit for Nebraska's 7-2 record. The Blackshirts struggled early in a 31-7 loss to Texas on Saturday, but the NU defense has been ranked among the nation's elite all season.

"I'm not going to recommend a guy if he's not good," Kiffin said. "But (Pelini's) exceeded even my expectations."

And what makes Pelini so good?

"It's all about teaching — getting people to follow you and believe what you're telling them," Kiffin said. "Coaching is just like being a history or math teacher. If you lose your students, they're just going to be twiddling their thumbs for two hours."

Kiffin had only met Pelini in passing, and the two had never coached together. So why recommend him?

The link is Pete Carroll. Kiffin asked the Southern Cal coach and longtime friend if he knew of any coaches fit for the Nebraska job. It took all of about five seconds for Pelini's name to surface.

Carroll, considered a defensive mastermind in the coaching ranks, had been on the same staff as Pelini with both the San Francisco 49ers and New England Patriots.

"Pete said, 'Monte, you could not find a better guy than Bo. He's enthusiastic and he'll get players to play for him,'" Kiffin said.

Before Kiffin could suggest Pelini to Solich as a possible hire, though, he wanted to see if the man serving as the Green Bay Packers' linebackers coach was even interested in the job.

So Kiffin phoned Pelini and sold Nebraska football like he was talking to a prized recruit.

"Some people in pro ball might not be interested in going back to college, but I tried to tell him what a great experience I had there," Kiffin said. "I said, 'You're not going to work for a better guy than Frankie. He's going to let you run the defense and have full control of it. Just get it going again.'"

He compared Nebraska's proud football history to that of Ohio State, where Pelini played his college ball.

"Nebraska was coming off a tough year, and people were tough on Frankie. Bo had to consider all that, and you don't go from Green Bay to just anywhere," Kiffin said. "But I told him the people in Nebraska are just as passionate as Ohio State fans. You win there, and they'll love you forever."

— Brian Christopherson

courses. Unless ... he would one day succeed Frank Solich?

"You never know what's going to happen in this business," said Pelini, in a tone that would make you believe his only thoughts were on developing a game plan to slow Nebraska's next opponent, Troy State. "I don't try to think in the future. I don't try and plan for it. I don't think you can

approach things that way.

"If you start worrying about it, then you start getting distracted."

Pelini has been going at a whirlwind pace since late December, when he accepted Solich's offer to run the Husker defense over staying with the Green Bay Packers as linebackers coach.

His efforts have led to NU fielding the nation's top-ranked

defense.

And to Solich fielding questions about how long Pelini might stick around.

"It's never a negative if you have the right guy in the program," said Solich, who is all for his assistants "to reach whatever goals they have."

The question is: Could he afford to lose Pelini after just one

Bo Pelini commends Husker defenders Barrett Ruud (38) and Trevor Johnson (88) as they come off the field after a three-and-out series against Troy State on Oct. 4, 2003. Pelini's defense shut out the Trojans 30-0. (Ted Kirk)

season? Or better yet: Will there even be a job come open that Pelini deems worth investigating? He said he has no interest in Arizona and has turned down plenty of other opportunities, including a "significant" promotion.

Solich declined to say whether he asked for a specific time commitment from Pelini. But having seen the way Pelini operates, I doubt he would have agreed to such a proposition, anyway.

For starters, Solich wasn't exactly standing on concrete entering the season, so anything beyond a year would have put them in a gray area. And with Pelini, everything is spelled out in black and white. That's why when he says Nebraska is a good fit for him right now, we

should believe him. Never mind that "right now" leaves him with a wide-open window.

"It comes down to what your goals are and when opportunities arise to reach your goals," said Solich, who's thankful to have Pelini and the other new assistants on his staff but warns about making too much of their part in NU's turnaround. "I hope it's becoming obvious we do have a good group of athletes.

"What you're coaching matters. ... You can have the greatest athletes in the world and get outcoached. But you can also be the greatest coach in the world — you'd still better have some players."

The ones mostly responsible for making the Huskers into a force to contend with in the

Big 12 — those under Pelini's guidance — should hope their leader hangs around.

"I don't feel like I've achieved anything yet. I don't really think about it," Pelini said. "Whatever happens, happens. It's a crazy business."

Just the same, it'd be funny if he showed up at next week's news conference wearing an Arizona cap.

"It's always been a goal of mine. Most people in the business want to be a head coach," Pelini said. "I think when the time comes, I'll be ready."

Remember, it's all about getting your body in the right position.

Nov. 7, 2003

NU unveils stadium expansion plan

By **TODD HENRICHS**

Are you "N?"

If you're a Husker fan, that's the question you'll no doubt be hearing from Steve Pederson over the next two months.

In a bold step to put Nebraska football back into the lead when it comes to facilities, Pederson on Thursday unveiled long-anticipated plans for a new athletic complex, including a new locker room, weight room and indoor practice area, and the addition of 5,000 seats to Memorial Stadium.

The price tag of the two-phase project is estimated at nearly $50 million, NU's athletic director said, or 33 percent more than it cost to construct the skybox addition to West Stadium in 1999.

Memorial Stadium was built at a cost of $450,000 in 1923.

"We're going to call on every Nebraskan to help, just as they did in 1923,"Pederson said. "This is going to be an all-out, grass-roots campaign. We really believe that Nebraskans will step up as they always do."

Pederson spoke at a news conference inside Schulte Field House, an area which will be renovated and expanded into the Tom and Nancy Osborne Athletic Complex.

Completion of the project will depend on fund-raising efforts, but Pederson said he hopes to have the additional seats in place for the 2005 season.

The Huskers could move into their new locker room in 2006.

Nebraska has been in its current locker room since 1973, a sub-standard area in South Stadium that NU coaches won't even show to recruits.

"From the moment I took over as football coach, I did ask that a few things get improved," Frank Solich said. "Those few things were never met, and I'm glad to see we're taking steps to make some improvements that were long overdue."

Billed as America's finest football facility, Pederson offered to pick up recruits and drive them to the front door once it's complete.

From sketches Pederson first drew on napkins flying back to Pittsburgh after being introduced as Nebraska's athletic director last December, the conceptual drawings released Thursday showed a street-level, 17,600-square foot weight room graced by Schulte's venerable windows.

The upper floors would house Nebraska's new locker room, offices and meeting rooms for the football staff and athletic department administrators.

The addition of the new seats will stretch North Stadium to 107 rows and allow for a concourse level with restrooms and concession areas. Two new stairwells will provide fans better access to and from their seats.

The new strength training and medical facilities will be used by athletes from all of Nebraska's 23 varsity teams, so not only football will benefit.

NU's soccer team, which currently plays its home games at the Abbott Sports Complex in extreme northeast Lincoln, will move to the infield of the Ed Weir Track once the project is complete.

"Playing at Abbott has been great," soccer coach John Walker said. "At the same time, for the players, to have the chance to play on campus, in front of their peers, the other students, that's naturally what they would want."

Phase one of the project involves the $40 million transformation of Schulte. Once the additional seats are sold, plans are to use ticket revenues to construct the $9 million indoor workout facility next to Nebraska's two grass practice fields. Doors would roll up to make it an open-air venue.

Nebraska would continue to utilize Cook Pavilion, an indoor facility built in 1987, giving Husker teams two substantial weather-protected areas to work out.

Nebraska's baseball and softball teams will lose their existing indoor batting cages inside Schulte.

"We've been assured we're going to be a big part of things," baseball coach Mike Anderson said. "We're talking about the Cook and the new facility. We've got four or five options."

Peterson kept the long-rumored plans secret for several months, unintentionally building momentum for the project.

Paul Garnett of Beatrice, a member of the executive board of the Husker Athletics Fund, received a phone call from NU officials once Thursday's news conference ended. Garnett predicted Husker fans would step up to keep Nebraska's tradition strong.

"My guess is that if there was ever a time and place that it could succeed, it's now," Garnett said. "And if ever there was a person to pull it off, it's Steve Pederson."

UNL chancellor Harvey Perlman also predicted success. Thursday's joint announcement detailed plans for Nebraska's athletic department to turn over its current office complex at South Stadium to the College of Computer Science and Engineering. The existing NU locker room would be maintained for use by visiting teams.

"I'm excited about any part of the University that has large ambitions, and large visions and pursuits," Perlman said. "Football is extremely important to the state of Nebraska and extremely important to this University. It holds this state together."

From his first news conference at Nebraska, Pederson called on the support of the 1.7 million and more inhabitants of the Husker Nation to help get NU's football program back out front.

For years, Nebraska was known for having the biggest and best weight room, the college stadium with the first video screens and FieldTurf.

In the past, other schools copied Nebraska's work, but Peterson plans on keeping them out of the new facility.

"Nobody's coming in to look at this one," Pederson said. "Once this is done, we're not going to show it off.

"We'll show it off to our fans and the people who want to come here and play."

> *Any time people see the program moving forward, it's always great for recruiting.*
> — Frank Solich

Solich's focus on team, not hoopla

More than a couple of people, including yours truly, wondered aloud where the head coach of the Nebraska football team was hiding during Thursday's facilities festivities.

Some found it odd Frank Solich didn't stop by to at least smile and say hi while athletic director Steve Pederson detailed plans to build a new athletic complex. The one that will house Solich and his football team in a couple (?) of years.

Then a Nebraska sports information official pointed out what should've been most obvious.

Solich was a little busy. Coaching football practice.

Duh.

OK, I suppose that's a good enough excuse to be absent.

Boy, is it a good excuse.

Solich, you see, has a football game to win this weekend in Kansas. And a couple of more, at least, to win after that.

I didn't say play. I said win.

Last I heard, you don't raise $40 million by getting walloped by Texas.

My guess is Pederson wasn't too excited about the whole timing of this announcement. Sure, it's nice to have these plans drawn in time for a big recruiting weekend on Nov. 15, when the Huskers face Kansas State in Lincoln.

But coming on the heels of a 31-7 loss in Austin? Yikes.

I don't exactly hear pocketbooks creaking open across the state.

Let's face it. These are big plans. Monumental. State-of-the-art. They'll put Nebraska back on top of the football facilities world, where it belongs. People will notice.

"Any time you make a commitment and show that commitment, make an investment —

Athletic director Steve Pederson announced in November of 2003 plans to add seats to the north end of Memorial Stadium and build new facilities to house the NU athletic department offices, a new football locker room and an indoor practice facility. The project was finished in 2006. This photo is from the 2008 Spring Game. (Ted Kirk)

parents, recruits, it means a great deal to them," Solich said following Thursday's practice. "Any time people see the program moving forward, it's always great for recruiting."

And $40 million, especially given the state of our economy, isn't piggy bank change.

So Pederson is counting on Big Red faithful everywhere to pitch in. Many will — some now, others later.

It's the "some now" that will help Pederson get this party started soon. (Remember, he wants fans sitting in those 5,000 extra seats by 2005).

And it's the "some now" who will likely begin writing out checks once they're convinced the Huskers are back on the win-

ning track.

Are they? Last weekend's game certainly raised some doubts, at least in some givers' eyes.

A strong finish to the 2003 season — nine or 10 wins, maybe a Big 12 North title, or a bowl victory, or all of the above — will suffice, thank you.

But what if Nebraska enters a tailspin?

Yep, here we are again. The onus is on Frank.

Has it ever not been? From the moment Solich took over for Tom Osborne, to the changes that followed last year's season, to today's announcement ... it's like everything falls back on Frank's shoulders.

Thursday, he brushed off any notion that perhaps the heat's now been turned up a notch.

"I never feel extra pressure for reasons beyond what I can control," Solich said. "I feel good with an AD that's ready to help in regards to moving your program forward, help in establishing things for our athletes and future athletes here."

By BRIAN ROSENTHAL

Truth be told, the pressure's on Solich to finish this season strong, with or without a $40 million fundraising drive on the horizon.

But this project would likely get off to a better, quicker start with some victories to whet a donor's appetite.

So it's probably a good thing we didn't see Solich with his smile after all.

> If you get too comfortable, you're going to get run over. You have to keep working to get better all the time.
>
> — Bo Pelini

Pelini unaffected by NU detractors

Nebraska defensive coordinator Bo Pelini has seen it all before. After all, who's more cut-throat than the Boston media?

It was the late 1990s. Pelini was a linebackers coach for the New England Patriots, who had just lost in the playoffs. Even so, pundits were calling for head coach Pete Carroll's job.

By STEVEN M. SIPPLE

"It's the nature of the business," Pelini said Tuesday.

For the second straight season, negativity swirls around the Nebraska football program. Internet message boards and radio call-in shows are jammed with fans calling for head coach Frank Solich's job. Some people express skepticism about the direction the program's headed.

Pelini, in his first season at Nebraska, hears the talk and mostly ignores it. Consider the source, he says. And job stability? Well, that's for guys in businesses other than football.

"If I have to pick up my family and move on, we'll move on," said Pelini, the married father of three. "I'm ready to do that at any time. If they don't want me here, we'll go somewhere else, that's fine. My kids are young. They'll bounce back.

"If that's the case, so be it. That'll be Nebraska's loss, not mine."

Pelini said he feels good about the program, that the Huskers' 8-3 record shows progress. He said he enjoys work every day.

Oh, but Pelini was angry Saturday after Nebraska's 38-9 loss to Kansas State. He rushed toward Wildcat head coach Bill Snyder, the two meeting at midfield.

Pelini shouted an expletive, fuming because Snyder kept his starters in the game until the end.

So, one could say Pelini's honeymoon in Lincoln is over. Never-

Bo Pelini reacts to early success by his Blackshirts during the Nov. 15, 2003, game against Kansas State at Memorial Stadium. Pelini wasn't happy later, when KSU coach Bill Snyder kept his starters in until the end of the game. The Husker defensive coordinator rushed toward Snyder shouting an expletive after KSU's 38-9 victory. (Ted Kirk)

theless, the 35-year-old Ohio native retains the confidence and hard-edged demeanor of a gunslinger on the prowl.

"You can't ever be comfortable in this business," Pelini said. "If you get too comfortable, you're going to get run over. You have to keep working to get better all the time. You can't ever be satisfied about anything."

As for Internet and media speculation about Solich's employment status, Pelini said, "I don't give a damn about that. I can't control that. I only deal with things I can control."

Asked how he feels about the direction the program's headed, Pelini said, "Well, we're 8-3. Everybody has their feelings about where the program's headed. I don't know ... I wasn't here before.

"I'm just doing my job. If peo-

ple want to make comments about Frank or the staff, so be it — I really don't care. Why would it bother me? Everybody deals with it in a different way.

"I focus on what we have to get done."

For now, that's defeating 5-6 Colorado on Nov. 28 in Boulder. The Buffaloes have beaten the Huskers each of the last two seasons.

Pelini has heard about Nebraska's 62-36 loss two years ago in Boulder. Since then, the Huskers are 14-12 against Division I-A opponents and 1-8 against ranked foes. Many trace NU's current struggles to that 26-point setback in 2001.

"That was a different time, a different place, different circumstances," Pelini said. "It won't happen again, I can tell you that."

Pelini said he won't watch tape of the 2001 loss to Colorado, in-

sisting it's irrelevant. Indeed, Pelini constantly preaches the importance of moving forward. That's why he's forgetting Saturday's loss to Kansas State, in which the Wildcats accumulated 561 yards of total offense.

Nebraska ranks 15th nationally in total defense, allowing 305.1 yards per game, and fifth in scoring defense (14.8), major improvements compared to last season. The Huskers have forced 42 turnovers and lead the nation in turnover margin at plus 1.64.

But in Nebraska's three losses, it's allowed an average of 499.0 yards and 36.6 points. Even so, Pelini said he feels good about the defense's progress.

"I'm really proud of our guys," he said. "I think they've come a long way. We're in this together, and the kids believe in what's going on."

It's suggested that perhaps Nebraska players may lose intensity since many of their goals are now out of reach.

"Our job isn't finished," Pelini said. "Our kids will respond. I feel good about that."

Meanwhile, the buzz persists. Will Solich be back in 2004? If not, what would happen to all those assistants he hired in the offseason? Pelini shrugs it off.

"I just sort things out in my own mind and deal with it on my own," Pelini said. "I really don't care what other people think. I think we'll go in there (to Boulder) and play our butts off, and whatever happens, happens.

"I feel like that every year. Then I make an evaluation at the end of the year and either move on or move on to the next season where I'm at."

Pelini said he plans to be at Nebraska in 2004 but leaves open the possibility he won't.

"You never know," he said. "We'll see. Time will always tell."

Steve (Pederson) has to do this with some class and grace. (The boosters) want Frank to be able to bow out with some dignity. — unnamed Husker booster

Nov. 23, 2003

Huskers' Solich may be forced out

Athletic director Steve Pederson wants Frank Solich out as Nebraska's head football coach, according to three sources close to the situation.

Pederson will try to persuade the sixth-year head coach to formally announce his retirement following NU's Nov. 28 game at Colorado, offering him a job in the Nebraska Athletic Department and a lucrative buyout package, said the sources, who agreed to talk on the condition they not be identified.

"He wants Frank gone. He's made up his mind," said a longtime, out-of-state booster with close ties to the department.

The sources said Nebraska's first-year athletic director reached his decision eight days ago, after watching fans stream for the exits early in the fourth quarter of Nebraska's 38-9 loss to Kansas State, its worst home defeat in 45 years. The blowout, NU's second on national television this month, appeared to bore ABC sportscasters before the network cut to a more competitive game. It also came on the heels of Pederson's Nov. 6 news conference announcing a $40 million fundraiser for new athletic facilities.

"Texas and Kansas State weren't competitive games. They were the straws that broke the camel's back," said a booster from Texas, also with strong ties to the Husker program. After the K-State game, the source said, Pederson walked to the skyboxes to reassure boosters that "we're going to do something, don't get upset."

Pederson denies he's spoken to anyone about a plan to force Solich's retirement, and some of the program's biggest boosters deny they've ever heard that plan. Former coach Tom Osborne said he hasn't spoken to Pederson about such a plan.

"I am on the record as saying I have not discussed this matter publicly or privately," Pederson said at the Devaney Sports Center on Saturday night, where he was attending the NU men's basketball season opener. The athletic director declined to comment further. Solich also declined to comment.

"I haven't heard anything about it," Osborne said from Washington, D.C., on Saturday morning.

"I swear on a stack of Bibles that Steve has never given me any indication at all about what he'd decided as to what he's going to do

Nebraska's Frank Solich (left) and Texas coach Mack Brown share a light moment before their game in Austin, Texas, on Nov. 1, 2003. (Ted Kirk)

with Frank Solich," said Dan Cook, a longtime booster and benefactor for Cook Pavilion, NU's indoor practice field.

The three sources who spoke to the Journal Star tell a different story.

In the last week, the athletic director has met privately with a select few millionaire boosters to gauge support for his decision, they said. They also believe Pederson has arranged Solich's buyout package but hasn't yet presented it to the head coach, who makes $1.1 million annually in a contract that runs through the 2005 season.

The only thing left for the athletic director to do is to get Solich to accept his own retirement, the sources said.

If the 59-year-old coach refuses to go quietly, Pederson may not be willing to fire him, they said. The situation could be complicated by pro-Solich boosters who contribute heavily to the program and may balk at the firing of a man who entered the program in 1962, Bob Devaney's first year as head coach.

"Steve has to do this with some class and grace," said the booster from Texas. "(The boosters) want Frank to be able to bow out with some dignity."

Solich's retirement would come quickly after the Colorado game to minimize damage to NU's recruiting efforts, the sources said. They didn't know how Solich's job situation would affect his assistants, including first-year coor-

dinators Barney Cotton and Bo Pelini.

Retirement would end a quarter-century coaching career at Nebraska and a six-year head coaching stint marked by early success and marred by last season's 7-7 campaign, NU's worst since 1961.

Solich has a 57-19 career record as a head coach. He won 49 games during his first five seasons, more than either Devaney or Osborne won in their first five campaigns, and his 2001 team played for the national championship in the Rose Bowl.

By MATTHEW HANSEN

The Husker coach's .754 winning percentage during those five seasons ranked him sixth among all active coaches.

NU also has lost nine of its last 12 games away from Memorial Stadium under Solich and is 15-12 overall since Thanksgiving weekend, 2001. This year, the Huskers have lost three games by a combined 70 points, including the 29-point home loss to Kansas State.

Coach Bill Jennings was fired after NU's 1961 season and Devaney was hired, ushering in a new era of Nebraska football.

The failure to sustain what Devaney created is what drives Pederson's decision, a Lincoln booster close to the situation said.

"It's more than wins and losses," he said. "Frank does not instill the confidence in Pederson that he'd like to see."

That assessment of Solich's tenure doesn't sit well with Osborne, who hired Solich in 1979 and handpicked his longtime assistant to take over following Osborne's retirement after the 1998 Orange Bowl.

"I would certainly think Frank will coach two more games and be there next year," Osborne said.

Solich will undoubtedly coach one more game, but the outcome against Colorado won't change Pederson's mind, the sources said.

In fact, a Colorado win could actually help Pederson convince Solich that he should retire on a high note, they said.

Otherwise, Solich may fight harder to stay, convinced he's being shoved out unfairly, according to the longtime, out-of-state booster.

And if he does fight?

"Things could get ugly."

Nov. 24, 2003

> *The only thing that seems clear is that head football coach Frank Solich is on shaky ground with his boss.*

Pederson facing high hurdles

Tradition. Teamwork. Integrity.

Those are the three principles of Steve Pederson's Husker Nation.

Right now, the last one is the biggie for NU's athletic director.

Integrity.

There is a contradiction between what's being said by Pederson and what was said in the Sunday

By JOHN MABRY

Journal Star by three anonymous boosters.

I know they were anonymous sources, which makes some readers uncomfortable with our integrity, but regardless, someone's got some explaining to do.

The only thing that seems clear is that head football coach Frank Solich is on shaky ground with his boss.

The talk is everywhere, so much so that if Pederson really had Solich's back he would have to come out and say so at this point.

Pederson has maintained his stance on the matter. He has made it clear he would not comment on Solich until the end of the season.

But at some point, don't you have to say, "Enough is enough. This is my man. Give it a rest."?

And now we're led to believe Pederson is leaking information to boosters, after announcing that he had not discussed his plans for Solich publicly or privately.

I have had no cause to question Pederson's integrity, and I don't know enough to question it now. We'll just have to see how this all plays out.

What I do know is if Pederson wants Solich to go, he might want to place a call to Washington.

Tom Osborne, you will recall, was the man who told Pederson it was time to move back to Nebraska and lead the Huskers back to

greatness.

You might also recall Osborne picking Solich to be his successor.

Earlier this month, Pederson made a big production of his plans to name "The Tom And Nancy Osborne Athletic Complex" after the greatest coach-and-wife team in college football history.

Pederson thinks Osborne is just about the greatest human being on the planet, and Osborne loves the Nebraska-bred Pederson, too.

But what if they don't see eye-to-eye on Solich?

Osborne said Saturday he expects Solich to be back for another season. And on Sunday, the congressman said he sort of ex-

pected a little heads-up if Pederson planned a coaching change.

Yikes.

Oh, and here's another dilemma.

A lot of outstanding assistants are on Solich's staff, bright young minds assembled with Pederson smack dab in the middle of the hiring process.

Give Solich his due for putting together a strong group of assistants, all of whom appear to be in the dark right now.

I like the mix of personalities, from a coaching standpoint as well as from a recruiting perspective.

You have your hard-core businessmen (Bo Pelini, Jimmy Williams).

You have your not-too-high-not-too-low types (Barney Cotton, Turner Gill, Jeff Jamrog).

And you have your high-energy guys (Tim Albin, Ron Brown, Scott Downing, Marvin Sanders).

I know Sanders, NU's secondary coach, is going to be a head coach someday. You can just see it in some guys. Albin's the same way.

Those are the guys I really wonder about. How would you like to be in Albin's shoes right now? He pays his dues as a graduate assistant for three years and gets his dream job as running backs coach at Nebraska only to find out it might be a one-year gig. That doesn't seem right.

Can you make a change at the top without overhauling an entire staff? Unless you promote from within, I don't think it can be done.

That leads to all kinds of speculation about Gill or Pelini, the kind of speculation normally reserved for the time when there is actually a head-coaching vacancy to speculate about.

All I know is Solich is still the head coach and Pederson, well ...

Steve Pederson established three principles of Husker Nation when he was hired as Nebraska athletic director: Tradition, teamwork and integrity. (Eric Gregory)

SUNDAY, NOVEMBER 30, 2003
LINCOLN, NEBRASKA

LINCOLN JOURNAL STAR

www.journalstar.com

56 30

Details: 8B

★★

Solich fired

Husker players stunned by AD Pederson's move

Frank facts

Frank Solich was hired as head coach for the University of Nebraska Dec. 10, 1997, the same day Tom Osborne announced his retirement effective after the 1998 Orange Bowl game. Solich was fired Saturday after compiling a 58-19 career record. Here are some of his milestone wins and losses:

BIG WINS

■ **Oct. 3, 1998:** Improved to 5-0 in his first season with a 24-17 win over Oklahoma State in Kansas City, Mo.

■ **Nov. 26, 1999:** Defeated Colorado in Boulder, 33-30 in overtime.

■ **Dec. 4, 1999:** Avenged a loss earlier in the season to Texas in the 1998 Big 12 Championship Game with a 22-6 victory.

■ **Sept. 9, 2000:** Defeated Notre Dame 27-24 in overtime in South Bend, Ind. It would be Solich's only road win over a ranked opponent.

■ **Oct. 27, 2001:** Defeated No. 2 Oklahoma 20-10 in Lincoln.

■ **Aug. 30, 2003:** After a disappointing 7-7 season in 2002, the Huskers opened the season with a 17-7 win over Oklahoma State.

■ **Nov. 28, 2003:** Nebraska closed out the regular season with a 31-22 win over Colorado.

TOUGH LOSSES

■ **Nov. 14, 1998:** Lost to Kansas State 40-30, the first loss to the Wildcats by the Huskers since 1968.

■ **Oct. 28, 2000:** Lost to Oklahoma 31-14 in Norman after a 7-0 start.

■ **Nov. 23, 2001:** Lost to Colorado 62-36 after an 11-0 start.

■ **Jan. 3, 2002:** Lost to Miami in the Rose Bowl 37-14.

■ **2002 season:** Seven losses during the year at Penn State, at Iowa State, at Oklahoma State, home vs. Texas, at Kansas State, home vs. Colorado and Mississippi in the Independence Bowl.

■ **Oct. 11, 2003:** Lost at Missouri 41-24.

■ **Nov. 1, 2003:** Lost at Texas 31-7.

■ **Nov. 15, 2003:** Fell to Kansas State 38-9 at Memorial Stadium.

TED KIRK/Lincoln Journal Star
Frank Solich at Folsom Field in Boulder, Colo., where the Huskers defeated CU to go 9-3 this season.

BY STEVEN M. SIPPLE
Lincoln Journal Star

Nebraska football Coach Frank Solich was fired by Husker athletic director Steve Pederson Saturday night in a meeting at South Stadium.

Pederson called Solich into the athletic director's office at 7:30 p.m. and told him of the decision, according to Solich's daughter, Cindy Dalton.

"Pederson told Dad that he really hadn't made up his mind until five minutes before Dad walked through the door," Dalton said. "Dad said he couldn't believe that Pederson had the nerve to say that to his face."

Solich, 59, was fired one day after leading Nebraska to a 31-22 win over rival Colorado in Boulder. That gave the No. 25-ranked Huskers a regular-season record of 9-3 overall and 5-3 in the league.

Solich becomes the first Nebraska head coach to be fired since Bill Jennings after the Huskers finished 3-6-1 in 1961.

"Dad told us that Steve fired him and that he wasn't going to coach the bowl game," Dalton said.

She said her father was at her home Saturday night contacting his assistant coaches. Solich declined an interview with the Journal Star.

Dalton said her father earlier this season tried to verify information about his assistants' contracts with Pederson. Dalton said Pederson "left a nasty note under Dad's office door."

She said Solich tried to talk to Peder-

PEDERSON

son Monday about his job status. Solich was told he would need to e-mail Pederson.

First-year Nebraska defensive coordinator Bo Pelini reportedly will be named interim assistant coach. Reached Saturday night, Pelini said, "I don't know that."

Pederson reportedly will do a national search for a new head coach but has set no time table for that search.

The athletic department will hold a news conference today at 1 p.m.

First-year Husker offensive coordinator Barney Cotton said he was unsure which assistants would be coaching the bowl game.

"Frank just called me and said that it's over, and Steve Pederson would be con-

See SOLICH, Page 2A

Contract terms

Within 30 days, the University of Nebraska must pay nearly $800,000 to fulfill the terms of Frank Solich's contract. In addition, NU would be forced to pay eight assistant coaches more than $1.5 million if Solich's successor replaces them with a new staff.

Solich was fired Saturday with 31 months remaining in his multiyear deal, which was to run through June 30, 2006. The contract called for Solich to be paid liquidated damages at termination equal to his current monthly salary multiplied by the number of months remaining in his deal.

Solich's annual base salary paid by the athletic department was $295,010. His total compensation package amounts to more than $1.1 million a year.

Solich's assistants were making a combined $1,005,000 in annual base salary in contracts to run through June 30, 2005.

— Todd Henrichs

Shocking news spreads through downtown bars

BY COLLEEN KENNEY
Lincoln Journal Star

Husker Nation felt the shock of one of the biggest coaching bombshells in Husker history Saturday night: the firing of a Nebraska football head coach.

A 9-3 coach.

A coach coming off a victory at Colorado.

A nice guy, to boot.

"Happy Thanksgiving, Frank — by the way, you got fired," fan Derek Clarke said at Brewsky's Food & Spirits, 201 N. Eighth St.

People interviewed on the streets and in the downtown Lincoln bars Saturday night felt Solich should have been given another year or two to see how his new assistant coaching staff did, especially after the victory at Colorado on Friday.

"I personally don't think he did a bad enough job to get fired," said Rob Heuer, a University of Nebraska-Lincoln student.

"I didn't believe the story in the paper

that he would get fired because of all the anonymous sources outside the Athletic Department.

"I figured it was just a bunch of boosters talking like they had a lot of control but didn't.

"This is surprising. Especially since it's still the middle of the season."

"Are you talking about Frank?" His friend, Scott Layher, another UNL student, walked over.

"Don't tell me it happened."

Yes.

"I didn't have a clue."

He wasn't sure how he felt. Stuff goes on behind the scenes that fans don't know about. He trusts the Athletic Department and the first-year athletic director.

"I'll go with what Steve Pederson says."

Six friends at Brewsky's did not agree with Pederson.

See REACTION, Page 2A

Nov. 30, 2003

Players have hard time believing

Current and former Nebraska football players expressed shock and disbelief Saturday night upon learning that Frank Solich had been fired as the Huskers' head coach.

Sophomore wide receiver Ross Pilkington was so upset he lost composure before finishing a phone conversation, in which he praised Solich.

"I don't know, man. I mean, I think it's ridiculous," said Pilkington, speaking from his home state of Colorado, where the Huskers defeated the Buffaloes 31-22 Friday.

By BRIAN ROSENTHAL

Little did players know it would be the last game for Solich, who finished his sixth season with a 58-19 career record.

"Honestly, I'm pretty upset. I'm shocked," Pilkington said. "I don't know what to expect. I guess this is like losing part of your family."

Pilkington spent Saturday evening with a group of other Husker players. He said the guys had just been talking about the recent rumors concerning Solich's doubtful future and were wondering aloud how weird it would be without him as their coach.

"He was awesome," Pilkington said. "He's always positive. No matter what, he's always there for us."

Heisman Trophy-winning quarterback Eric Crouch, who led the Huskers to their only Big 12 championship and only appearance in a national championship game in Solich's tenure, was slow to believe the news of Solich's firing.

When finally convinced the news was true, and not rumor, Crouch seemed befuddled.

"I'm in complete shock," Crouch said. "I was kind of in the mind-frame that the rumors were just flat rumors, and that there was really no justification to fire a coach that could go 10-3 (with a bowl win).

"It's tough for me to talk about it right now. I'm kind of in disbelief."

Crouch reflected on his first year playing with the Huskers in 1998, which was also Solich's first season as NU's head coach. Nebraska finished 9-4 that season, then rebounded with a 12-1 record the following year, when NU won the Big 12 title.

"I think we learned a lot about each other as people, and we developed a relationship between coach and player that become more

Cody Volk (from left), Benard Thomas, NU assistant athletic director Marc Boehm, DeAntae Grixby, Lannie Hopkins, Jammal Lord (in blue) and athletic director Steve Pederson were in the same elevator at Memorial Stadium after a news conference announcing the firing of head coach Frank Solich. (Ted Kirk)

like a friendship," Crouch said.

"No matter what happens with Frank, I'm always going to be a supporter in his corner. No matter what. He's going to be a friend of mine through thick and thin. I'm 100 percent sure he knows that."

Crouch said he's "not in the circle" and not certain of Nebraska athletic director Steve Pederson's thought process in firing Solich.

"I don't know what Frank's and Steve's relationship is. I don't know what it's based on. I don't know," he said. "Steve has to make a decision based on the best interest of the program. ... It's tough. It's real tough."

Nebraska freshman Ryan Schuler, a prom-

ising offensive lineman who redshirted this season because of medical problems, was saddened by news of Solich's departure.

"That's news to me. It's a tough situation," Schuler said. "He's a great person and takes a personal interest in his players' lives, and that's something I respect a lot about him."

Said senior linebacker Demorrio Williams: "I just heard about it, and I ain't gonna comment on none of it."

Sophomore running back Cory Ross was involved in a three-way telephone conversation, discussing the news with friends, and had only one quick comment: "This is crazy."

> I hope I can count on Nebraska fans to support the decision and help us bring a great coach in here who can have tremendous success. — Steve Pederson

Dec. 1, 2003

AD: It's time NU returns to elite

The day after Steve Pederson broke up a 29-year union of Frank Solich and Husker football signaled the end of his own honeymoon as Nebraska's athletic director.

Pederson had championed his role as every fan's AD since returning to Nebraska last December. But Saturday night, amid growing turmoil and swirling speculation, he took the bold step of firing Solich, thereby placing the future of Husker football in his own hands.

It wasn't a committee decision, nor a decision based on any input from influential boosters, Pederson said Sunday.

And it surely wasn't a popularity contest.

But it's a decision, Pederson said, that should unify Husker fans who he says have been torn in recent years over whether Solich was the right man for the job.

"The truth is, this has been polarizing our fan base probably for a number of years," Pederson said. "I wasn't here, but certainly it escalated to high proportions a year ago. And I don't see that that's changed right now.

"I hope I can count on the people of Nebraska and Nebraska fans to step behind and support the decision and help us bring a great coach in here who can have tremendous success. It is time for us to rally together."

Pederson made his only public comments on Solich's dismissal at a Sunday afternoon news conference that began not with an explanation of the decision or tribute to Solich's service, but with a terse defense of the athletic director by UNL chancellor Harvey Perlman.

He said it was a "fair decision" and that he had "full confidence" that it was reached without any outside influence.

"Make no mistake about it, Steve Pederson and only Steve Pederson is running the athletic department," Perlman said.

Perlman's comments were in reference to a story published by the Journal Star last week in which three anonymous sources, identified as boosters, said Pederson would try to persuade Solich to retire after Friday's game against Colorado.

Pederson said he understands those who will question firing a coach with a 9-3 record whose program has played for a national championship more recently than Bob Stoops' or Bobby Bowden's. But until recently,

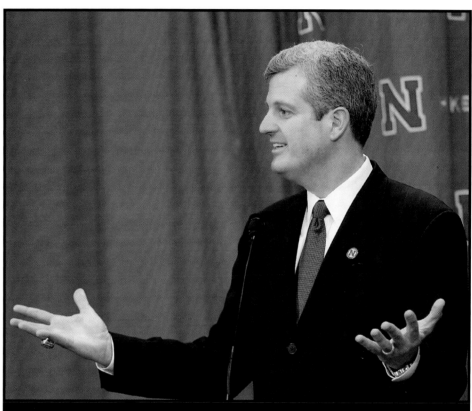

Nebraska athletic director Steve Pederson responds to a question during a news conference called Nov. 30, 2003, to announce the firing of Frank Solich and officially name Bo Pelini as the Huskers' interim head coach. (Ted Kirk)

he said he's never had his integrity challenged.

Pederson's oft-stated policy is to not comment on coaches' performances during the season.

"At no time have any one of these donors ever put me on the spot about the situation with the head football coach," Pederson said. "And nobody has offered a donation with strings attached because I think they know enough about me to know I wouldn't take it anyway. That's not how we run this program."

Pederson said the decision to fire Solich came down to an evaluation of recruiting, management and coaching against where Nebraska needs to be to compete against Big 12 powerhouses Oklahoma and Texas.

At different times in his 30-minute question-and-answer session, Pederson called Nebraska "the best place in the country," its followers "the

best fans in the country," and Solich's vacated post "the best job in the country."

First-year defensive coordinator Bo Pelini will serve as interim head coach while Pederson conducts a national search for a successor.

No timetable was laid out, just as Pederson said there was no specific time at which he decided Solich was no longer right for the job.

By TODD HENRICHS

Before Saturday, Pederson's most public moves at NU were to reduce football ticket prices and unveil $50 million worth of facilities improvements that would include an expansion of Memorial Stadium, moves that earned the AD plaudits, not the rancor caused by firing a coach with 58 career wins in six seasons.

Dec. 1, 2003

You have to hire a guy who'll make people say, 'Hey!'. You don't fire a guy who goes 9-3 and turn around and hire a coach from the WAC.
— Trev Alberts

Pelini's the man for NU, for now

By STEVEN M. SIPPLE

Steve Pederson noted the enthusiasm and energy of Nebraska's defense and decided first-year defensive coordinator Bo Pelini would be the right man to lead the Husker football team in the short term.

And perhaps the long term.

The 35-year-old Pelini on Sunday was introduced as interim head coach in place of Frank Solich, who was fired Saturday.

Pederson, Nebraska's first-year athletic director, has known Pelini since the late 1980s, when Pelini played defensive back at Ohio State and Pederson worked there as recruiting coordinator.

"He was a smart, aggressive, decisive player, and I feel like right now, in an unusual situation, Bo will do an excellent job of handling this program," Pederson said.

Said Pelini: "One-hundred percent of my effort and focus will go toward our players and giving them the best experience possible in the bowl game, because they have earned that.

"They've shed a lot of blood, sweat and tears to get to 9-3."

Although Solich was fired Saturday night, his staff of assistant coaches remained intact to prepare the team for its yet-to-be-determined bowl game.

Meanwhile, Pederson on Sunday began an "open" search to find Solich's permanent replacement. Pelini, the former Green Bay Packers linebackers coach, is a candidate for the job, Pederson said.

Nebraska assistant head coach Turner Gill also expressed interest, Pederson said.

Pederson said he had contacted nobody outside the program about the position. He said he didn't have a timetable to hire a head coach, but would move "as quickly and prudently as possible."

Pederson said he always has a list in mind of possible candidates for any job, just in case.

"When you find the right person, you know it," Pederson said. "Certainly we want a great coach who can take us to the very highest level."

Former Nebraska linebacker Trev Alberts, now a college football analyst for ESPN, said Pederson needs to hit a home run with his hire.

"You have to hire a guy who'll make people say, 'Hey!'" Alberts said. "You don't fire a guy who goes 9-3 and turn around and hire a coach from the WAC."

Pederson said he will avoid further comment regarding the coaching search until the day he names the new head man. The head coach will have the opportunity to choose all of his own assistants, Pederson said.

Will the fact Pederson fired a coach with a 9-3 regular-season record scare away potential applicants?

"Anybody who doesn't want to win the national championship shouldn't bother applying for this job," Pederson said. "I understand we aren't going to win the championship every year. But I believe we should be playing for, or gaining on the championship, on a consistent basis.

Bo clearly bucking for promotion

I've come to a difficult realization.

It's becoming abundantly clear I do not have the support of the athletic director.

It's also clear NU's offensive coaching staff is in the same boat.

That's unfortunate, because Barney Cotton and the gang haven't had much of a chance to prove their worth.

Steve Pederson appears to have chosen a side by picking defensive coordinator Bo Pelini as interim head coach over assistant head coach Turner Gill.

Perhaps Pelini meant no harm, but he gave a one-side-of-the-ball take on how he expected the Huskers to play under his leadership.

"I believe this team will play exactly the way our defense has played all year," he said, "with passion."

Pelini's frankness is at once refreshing and frightening.

"I know I'm ready to be a head coach," he said.

You're nuts if you think Pelini is OK with just filling a headset while Pederson looks elsewhere to find a replacement for Frank Solich.

Pelini was asked Sunday what traits make him a good head coaching candidate.

"I'm going to win," he said. "We're going to win."

Pederson loves that stuff. Pelini has the fire. He has the vision.

He might have a short fuse at times, as Bill Snyder found out, but Pelini's enthusiasm is a hit with players.

After T.J. Hollowell made a huge fourth-quarter interception Friday in Boulder, Pelini ran out on the field and hugged his senior linebacker like a son.

It was neat to see. Pelini can be rough around the edges, but the players seem to love him.

You have to believe recruits pick up the same sort of vibes.

Pelini has that NFL experience that kids go ga-ga over, and he has had great mentors in the business. He's worked for a couple of the best in Pete Carroll and George Seifert.

Carroll, now the head coach at No. 2 Southern Cal, thinks the world of Pelini.

"Bo and I worked together for five years," Carroll said Sunday, "and it was very obvious that he had what it takes to be a head coach.

"His tenacity is contagious. He has a great football mind, and it's no surprise how he turned Nebraska's defense around."

I think Pelini is a solid candidate to replace Solich, but his lack of head-coaching experience could be an issue.

Also at issue is Pederson's fondness for surprising people. He likes to wow folks with the unexpected.

His hiring of Northern Arizona's Ben Howland as men's basketball coach at Pittsburgh was a shock to many Panther fans, but it turned out to be a brilliant move.

Another of Pederson's hires at Pittsburgh, football coach Walt Harris, has been mentioned as a possible replacement for Solich.

Don't bank on that one, and whatever you do, don't bet against Bo.

— John Mabry

Athletic director Steve Pederson (center) and UNL chancellor Harvey Perlman watch as Bo Pelini addresses the media after being named interim head football coach of the Huskers after Frank Solich's firing. (Ted Kirk)

"I don't feel like currently we are playing for, or gaining on, the championship."

Among the names being tossed around as possible candidates for the Nebraska job are Walt Harris of Pittsburgh, Rich Rodriguez of West Virginia and Urban Meyer of Utah.

Meyer seemed taken aback that Nebraska fired a coach whose team went 9-3 this season.

"Could you believe they did that?" Meyer told the Salt Lake Tribune on Sunday. He added, "I'm very happy with what I'm doing and where I'm doing it, and I'd be very leery (about the NU job) with everything that's happened there."

Pederson met with Nebraska assistants Sunday morning.

"I understand if opportunities arise for them that they'll have to take a look at them," Pederson said. "They'll have my full support and whatever help I can give any of them. But there are really no guarantees for anybody,

and I think everybody knows that."

As expected, Pederson said, the Husker assistants expressed "a wave of emotions" during the Sunday morning meeting.

By Sunday night, Nebraska offensive coordinator Barney Cotton was ready to focus on bowl preparation. He said he was in the midst of calling players to discuss Solich's firing.

Cotton said he's confident the players will keep their focus on the field.

"I only have one thing to go on, and that was a pretty big distraction that occurred last week," Cotton said, referring to a Nov. 23 Journal Star story that reported that Solich would be forced into retirement.

Despite the story, Nebraska prepared well and defeated Colorado 31-22 on Friday in Boulder.

"I think this team has a lot of character," Cotton said.

There was speculation Sunday that Gill might not be retained as an assistant coach.

In selecting Pelini as interim head coach, Pederson bypassed Gill, a 12-year Nebraska assistant and former Husker standout quarterback.

Pederson described Gill as "one of my favorite people." However, Pederson simply thought Pelini was better suited for the interim role.

"I don't want anybody to read anything into this," Pederson said of Pelini's new position. "I've made no commitments to Bo, and Bo's made no commitments to me."

Asked whether he's ready to become a head coach, Pelini said, "I'm standing right here before you, aren't I?"

Pelini added, "I know I'm ready to be a head coach. Time will tell what the circumstances are. A lot goes into the hiring of a head coach."

Pelini — who has never been a head coach at any level — stressed the "interim" part of his position.

Dec. 16, 2003

There've been so many wounds opened, and every-
one wants those wounds to close by hiring Coach
Pelini.
-- Husker player

Husker players discuss boycott

A players-only meeting Monday afternoon ended with members of the Nebraska football team uncertain of how to handle their frustrations over the school's two-week search for a head coach.

Two players, speaking on the condition of anonymity, said the team discussed possible ways of voicing their concerns that interim head coach Bo Pelini hasn't yet been named a permanent replacement.

By BRIAN ROSENTHAL

Among the options was a boycott — of either practices, the Dec. 29 Alamo Bowl game, or both. Players also discussed the possibility of holding their own news conference or writing an open letter to media outlets to express their concerns.

When players weren't unanimous on any decisions, the meeting ended abruptly, and players "stormed out of the room amid a flurry of expletives," according to one player, who described the hour-long session as "very, very tense."

Several other players declined comment about the meeting, which took place at South Stadium.

"We met, and we have some concerns that we're just going to keep private right now," freshman linebacker Bo Ruud said.

Nebraska athletic director Steve Pederson fired Frank Solich on Nov. 29 and named Pelini, the team's first-year defensive coordinator, as interim head coach. Many Huskers are growing impatient that Pelini hasn't been named the permanent successor, a player said.

"We feel like we're completely left in the dark," that player said. "There've been so many wounds opened, and everyone wants

Nebraska fans Jordan Stevens (left) and Gary Scott show their preference for the next Husker head coach during NU's Alamo Bowl victory against Michigan State on Dec. 29, 2003. (Eric Gregory)

those wounds to close by hiring Coach Pelini."

Pelini made a brief appearance at the players' meeting, reminding them the importance of being unified, a player said.

Meanwhile, some recruits who officially visited Nebraska over the weekend were impressed with Pelini and seemed hopeful he'd be named head coach.

Joe Manning, one of five recruits from Lincoln High School in Tallahassee, Fla., said he's developed a strong relationship with Pelini.

If Pelini was hired permanently?

"That would increase the chances for all five of us (to commit)," Manning said.

None of the five, however, has done that yet.

"They told us not to commit without a head coach. ... I think that's how it should be done," Manning said. "They're a respectful program, and they're going to do things respectful."

Other players from Tallahassee who visited Lincoln were linebackers Rodney Gallon and Matt

Owens and offensive linemen Danny Muy and Calvin Darity.

Darity, the nation's top-ranked offensive guard according to Rivals.com, said he was impressed with Nebraska's tradition and the overall atmosphere in Lincoln. He has four more visits to take and said he hasn't yet ranked his schools of preference.

"I'm still going to be watching (Nebraska) and see what happens later on, but that's really all I can do," said Darity, noting he had no opinion on the Huskers' coaching situation. "I just don't know much about it."

What advice did the coaching staff give him?

"They were just unsure," he said. "That's all they could tell me."

Scott McPherson, Muy's stepfather, spoke highly of his family's visit to Lincoln, and of Pelini.

"Coach Pelini has been a rock of stability in a sea of craziness in this whole recruiting process," McPherson said. "He's been upfront with us. He's told us the truth. He's never wavered in his belief in Danny.

"Danny and Coach Pelini were close before this weekend, and they got much closer after this weekend."

McPherson wouldn't say whether Muy wanted to commit.

"I'd rather not talk about that right now," he said. "We're waiting for a decision to be made out of Lincoln before we make a decision."

If Pelini were named coach?

"That would be very, very pleasant news if that were to happen," he said.

Chris Owens, a 6-foot-3, 205-pound quarterback from Thousand Oaks, Calif., also visited.

"If Coach Pelini is announced as head coach, that's a place I'd definitely consider," Owens said.

> **He has a mind-set, and he has a plan about where he wants to go with this program, and hopefully he'll get an opportunity to do that.** — NU assistant Marvin Sanders

Dec. 29, 2003

Bo's opening night or swan song?

SAN ANTONIO — Bo Pelini stepped onto a long platform, some 3 feet off the ground, as he addressed the media Sunday afternoon one final time before the Alamo Bowl.

Seemed rather fitting. Pelini, on stage. All eyes and ears on Nebraska's interim head football coach.

Consider it a scaled-down version of the spotlight Pelini will find himself under tonight, when Nebraska faces Michigan State at the Alamodome.

It's his first career game as a head coach, and many wonder if tonight is an audition, of sorts, in Pelini's bid to permanently take over this coveted coaching position.

Well, Coach?

"I don't concern myself with that," said Pelini, the first-year defensive coordinator, who was appointed interim coach one month ago upon the firing of Frank Solich.

"I'm going into the next football game ... to compete. Period. That's why I'm in this business. I like to compete, I like the competitive edge.

"Would that play into me getting this job or not getting this job? I don't think it has anything to do with it. That's more of a question for Steve Pederson than for myself."

Pederson, the Nebraska athletic director, isn't commenting on his personal coaching search until the day he's ready to announce the next head coach.

Until then, speculation continues to swirl. Names of NFL coaches continue to drop like leaves. Pelini, who's made no secret about his desire to become a head coach, is a known candidate, but he says he hasn't interviewed. Same goes for assistant coach Turner Gill.

For all Pelini knows, tonight may be his last game with Nebraska. On the other hand, perhaps this game will serve as a springboard into the Pelini era.

Nobody, besides Pederson, knows for sure.

But amid this swirl of uncertainty, NU players and coaches say Pelini has remained firm as the leader of this team.

"Right now, our coach is Coach Pelini," Nebraska senior Trevor Johnson said. "That's the way we're going about things. For us seniors, he's our coach right now. It might be kind of hard for some of the young guys who don't know what's going on. But for right now, he's our coach, and that's the way we're treating it."

Tyler Watkins, 13, of Omaha holds a sign that expresses what many fans thought of Nebraska interim head coach Bo Pelini. (Eric Gregory)

Nebraska secondary coach Marvin Sanders said he's been impressed with the way Pelini has led the Huskers through a tumultuous period.

Not surprisingly, Sanders spoke as though he was giving Pelini a strong recommendation to a prospective employer.

"When there is a situation that arises, he takes total control, and there is no question that he is leading this team into this bowl game," said Sanders, also in his first year on the Nebraska coaching staff.

"I think he has the characteristics and the making of a great coach. You talk about young, up-and-coming, I think he's a guy that's young and up-and-coming. He has a mind-set, and he has a plan about where he wants to go with this program, and hopefully he'll get an opportunity to do that."

Pelini, who spent nine years in the NFL, says he's ready to become a head coach. Whether that's at Nebraska or somewhere else, he knows his success will hinge largely on recruiting.

"It's pretty obvious out there that the best

teams are the teams with the best players," Pelini said. "You have to recruit, and you have to be passionate about it. And when you get those recruits on campus, and you believe you have the right guys, you have to be teachers. You have to run a disciplined ship — a non-nonsense ship. And at the same time, you have to teach them along the way."

With or without a job at stake, tonight is still Pelini's debut as a head coach, and you'd think the butterflies would be swirling in the pit of his stomach.

Then again, this is **By BRIAN ROSENTHAL** Pelini we're talking about. He'll tell you he's been a part of other bowl games. NFL playoff games. Super Bowls.

His sense of anticipation won't change much tonight.

"None whatsoever," Pelini said. "I've been around a lot of football games in a lot of different situations, in a lot of different environments. I'm going to approach it like any other game I've been a part of. I've prepared the same way, and I have confidence in this staff."

Ah, yes, the staff. The future of the rest of the assistant coaches lingers in doubt, too. If Pelini isn't named the permanent head coach, their chances of remaining at Nebraska would appear slim.

"It hasn't been an easy situation on anybody," Pelini said. "But guys have been pros about it and they've gone about their job, and the players have done a good job of sticking with what we've asked them to do."

First-year Michigan State coach John L. Smith only met Pelini for the first time last week. Although he doesn't know Pelini well, Smith knows enough to understand the stress under which the NU coaches have been operating.

"You have to pat that staff on the back, because that's a very, very tough position to place them in, and they've been very professional and how they've approached it," Smith said. "You have to compliment them."

Indeed, it's been an unusual situation for Pelini. He says he's taking notes, with hopes of growing from his experiences of the past month.

"Every situation is unique," Pelini said. "You just have to approach it within your philosophies and your beliefs and what you believe is right."

Dec. 30, 2003

"I was asked to do a job. I didn't attack it any differently than I have (anything) my whole life. I'm a pro. I'm a football coach.
— Bo Pelini

Bo passes test with flying colors

SAN ANTONIO — Bo Pelini was introduced over the Alamodome public-address system as Nebraska's interim head coach when the Huskers took the field before Monday's Alamo Bowl.

Before the start of the second half, the announcer left off the interim tag.

It could have just been a slip of tongue. Then again, maybe it wasn't? Perhaps the Huskers already have their next leader in place and just don't know it.

By CURT McKEEVER

The common notion is the longer athletic director Steve Pederson's search has gone, the greater a longshot Pelini has become to remain in charge of Big Red. I'd tend to agree, but at this point, we shouldn't discount anything.

After Monday's 17-3 dismantling of Michigan State, the headstrong Pelini deserves nothing less than serious consideration.

For starters, Pederson should grant him an interview — that is, if he hasn't already struck a deal with someone else.

Pelini might not be Nebraska-bred, but he definitely looks good in Husker red. He's a straight shooter, takes no bull from anybody and in one season quickly convinced a group desperately in need of a confidence boost that it could play with anyone.

Pederson recognized it, too, or else he wouldn't have handed Pelini the reins at such a critical juncture. Of course, from the beginning, Pelini played down his added responsibility.

"I was asked to do a job. I didn't attack it any differently than I have (anything) my whole life," he said, not trying to hide the satisfaction of Monday's win. "I'm a pro. I'm a football coach.

"Fortunately, I had a lot of warriors standing there right by me."

If Monday's game was an audition, Pelini mastered all of his lines — including the one he used on an official midway through the fourth quarter that drew an unsportsmanlike-conduct call.

Pelini had taken exception to Michigan State being allowed to maintain possession after a Nebraska player came out of a pile with the ball with 7:06 to play, and when he went off it gave the Spartans their best scoring opportunity of the second half. The Huskers took

Nebraska's Bo Pelini questions a call during the third quarter of the Alamo Bowl game against Michigan State. Later in the game, he was penalized for unsportsmanlike conduct for protesting an official's call. (Ted Kirk)

exception to the flag, and four plays later, cornerback Pat Ricketts intercepted a Jeff Smoker pass to end the threat.

By the end, Michigan State had been held out of the end zone for the first time in 17 games. The Spartans' three points also represented the fewest the Huskers had given up in 42 bowl games.

That didn't happen by accident.

True, bowl games aren't often a true indicator of teams' strengths. Most have a hard time finding the crispness they developed in the regular season. And while Nebraska was far from perfect in the climate-controlled atmosphere of the Alamodome, the Huskers showed

little rust from having been idle since Nov. 28.

That credit goes to Pelini (and his staff), who gave the team a long break before starting its bowl preparations. When they began, practices were shorter, but, according to the players, conducted at a higher intensity.

In return, Pelini also allowed the players plenty of rope during their free time in San Antonio, giving them a 2 a.m. curfew (although after Monday's game I-back Cory Ross said he wouldn't be going to bed).

On the field, Pelini also made sure he stuck with what got him to this point — coaching the defense. He stayed away from offensive coordinator Barney Cotton and his unit.

Nebraska interim head coach Bo Pelini gets his first college coaching win, and his first dousing, after the Huskers defeated Michigan State 17-3 in the Alamo Bowl on Dec. 29, 2003, in San Antonio. (Ted Kirk)

Well, there was that one time in the first half after Nebraska quickly moved 80 yards to go ahead 17-3 that he charged up to offer congratulations to senior center Josh Sewell, junior guard Jake Andersen and sophomore tackle Richie Incognito.

Yeah, Bo was into it. With gusto, he argued what looked like a phantom second-quarter pass-interference call.

He also kept the Huskers from coming unglued under a barrage of dead-ball personal-foul penalties committed by the Spartans.

Bo's a crafty fighter, and if Pederson lets him get away, he'd better produce a great counter puncher who can battle through a mob that is sure to be more incensed than when Frank Solich was let go last month.

Following Monday's game, Nebraska fans chanted in unison, "We want Bo."

Defensive tackle Patrick Kabongo took the podium in the middle of the field and made a similar plea.

And then there was the P.A. announcer, who asked, "What about the coaching job of Bo Pelini?"

What about it, Steve?

Dec. 31, 2003

Regardless of what happens, it was a good decision to come here.

— Bo Pelini

Bo says he's in 'shutdown phase'

SAN ANTONIO — The way Bo Pelini sees it, he finished a job Monday night.

When he was appointed Nebraska interim head football coach a month ago, Pelini understood he would have that title through Monday's Alamo Bowl.

With a 17-3 triumph over Michigan State in the record book, Pelini said that it was time to relax and consider his future.

By STEVEN M. SIPPLE

"To a certain extent, it's a shutdown phase," Pelini said. "I just kind of have to sit back and wait and make some decisions."

NCAA Division I-A teams are in a recruiting "dead" period that lasts through Jan. 7, the end of the American Football Coaches Association convention in Orlando, Fla.

That means coaches won't be on the road recruiting during the next several days.

That means Pelini and his fellow Nebraska staff members will have ample time to consider their futures, which were thrown into doubt Nov. 29 when Husker head coach Frank Solich was fired.

All nine Nebraska full-time assistants and two graduate assistants were retained to prepare the team for the bowl game.

"They're all pretty much unemployed right now," Pelini said. "You have to do what you have to do."

Asked if he will start considering other jobs, Pelini said, "I have to make sure my family's taken care of."

Pelini is considered by many to be a leading candidate for the Nebraska head coaching position. Pelini said he had a time in mind for when he wants to know his future at the school, but declined specifics.

"I will let you know when that

Bo Pelini leaves the Lincoln airport the day after the Huskers won the 2003 Alamo Bowl. (Journal Star archives)

day comes," he said.

Nebraska athletic director Steve Pederson has maintained a no-comment policy since his coaching search began the day after Solich was fired despite the Huskers' 9-3 record.

Rumors have persisted that Pelini has been in negotiations with Pederson, trying to work out a deal that would allow Pelini to succeed Solich.

"That's inaccurate," Pelini said.

If Pelini is indeed hired by Pederson, many will speculate that Pelini was a second or third option.

"I don't think it matters," Pelini said. "No. 1, I don't know why anybody would make that deduction. No. 2, there are a lot of second choices out there who've been pretty successful."

Meanwhile, Pelini's name al-

ready has been linked to defensive coordinator positions at Oklahoma and Ohio State.

Following Monday's win on national television, Pelini's name undoubtedly will crop up for other job openings.

Pederson shook Pelini's hand and said, "Nice job," after Monday's win.

After Nebraska defeated Colorado in the regular-season finale, Pederson was nowhere to be found. The next day, he fired Solich despite NU's improvement over last season's 7-7 record.

In the wake of Nebraska's 2002 struggles, Solich revamped his staff, hiring six new assistants, including Pelini, 36, the former Green Bay Packers linebackers coach. Pelini had spent the last nine seasons with three different NFL teams.

Pelini, however, enjoyed the college game.

"Regardless of what happens, it was a good decision to come here," Pelini said.

Pelini described Monday's win as "a culmination of a lot of hard work. It's an emotional game, and this game was probably even more emotional than usual for a lot of guys, especially the seniors and the other assistants. They were pretty emotionally attached to this program."

Pelini led Nebraska through turbulent waters throughout the past month. For now, the seas still churn, as Pederson's silence about his coach search continues.

Asked what his immediate plans entail, Pelini said, "Relax. I'm not going to do much of anything, to be honest with you. I'll just let things take their course."

Bo Pelini hugs wife Mary Pat after NU's Alamo Bowl win. Less than two weeks later, NU's defensive coordinator and interim head coach was out of a job. (Eric Gregory)

Coach search derailed confidence

**STEVEN M.
SIPPLE**

He arrived in Lincoln in early 2004 with plenty of baggage, and not the kind of baggage in which you tote items like hair gel and slacks.

The player-relations issues Bill Callahan experienced as head coach of the NFL Oakland Raiders are well-documented.

Indeed, Callahan often is portrayed as being cold and unfeeling toward his athletes.

That said, I was somewhat surprised by the general indifference Nebraska players showed in November 2007 after Callahan was fired by Tom Osborne. It's not as if the players were happy with the news, but they didn't seem overly sad or angry, either. They just seemed ready to move on.

Most Nebraska players no doubt anticipated the firing.

But their general indifference was telling, because it reflected their lack of fire in many games during a 2007 season that ended with a 5-7 record (2-6 in the Big 12). Maybe the players had lost confidence in Callahan and his staff. Or perhaps Callahan is simply incapable of consistently connecting with college athletes at a level needed to win championships.

Or maybe Callahan underestimated the unmistakable importance of emotion in the college game. Before coming to Nebraska, he had last coached in college in 1994 as an offensive line coach at Wisconsin. He's still well-regarded throughout football for his ability as a line coach and for being something of a West Coast offense guru.

At any rate, Callahan has returned to life as an assistant

Autograph seekers mob Husker coach Bill Callahan during a Husker Nation tour stop at SouthPointe Pavilions in Lincoln in the summer of 2004. (William Lauer)

coach. In January 2008, he took over as offensive line coach for the NFL New York Jets. He has declined interview requests from Nebraska media, telling friends and family he wants to lay low.

"Players liked Coach Callahan as a guy, but players (on defense) didn't quite trust he'd put them in the right positions to succeed," says one former Nebraska defender, speaking on the condition of anonymity. "He was always so wrapped up in his offense. As the head coach, he should've been involved in the whole team. It was like, 'Coz, the defense is your deal, I'll stay out of it.'"

Alas, Kevin Cosgrove's deficiencies as a defensive coordinator played a huge role in Callahan's demise as Nebraska's head coach, as the Huskers in 2007 allowed more points (455), yards (5,722) and first downs (299) than any team in school history.

As Nebraska scuffled along, Callahan came under intense fire from Nebraska media and fans. He was criticized for many things — probably too many to list. But at least one criticism — that he

wasn't always particularly accessible to his players — was unfounded, according to Ben Eisenhart, a safety and special-teams standout in 2007.

"That's B.S.," Eisenhart says. "He was very accessible. I also hear people say he wasn't personable. That's not true at all."

Nevertheless, Eisenhart understands Osborne's decision to fire Callahan.

"What (Callahan) is, he's an offensive coordinator," Eisenhart says. "He is a great offensive coordinator. He handled the team OK, but he never seemed to give us much input on anything except his offense."

Callahan just wasn't a good fit for Nebraska. In hindsight, perhaps we shouldn't be surprised. For one thing, Steve Pederson's coaching search in late 2003 and early 2004 didn't exactly inspire confidence in the former Husker athletic director. In short, the search became a bungled mess.

This much is certain: Pederson met face-to-face with at least five other coaches — Bo Pelini, Turner Gill, Mike Zimmer, Houston Nutt

and Al Saunders — before officially hiring Callahan.

Pederson's initial target was believed to be Dave Wannstedt, who wasn't interested. Wannstedt suggested Nutt, a close friend.

After a resounding Alamo Bowl triumph on Dec. 29, 2003, Nebraska fans chanted Pelini's name, apparently hopeful he would be named head coach. Little did they know that Pederson, during halftime of the Alamo Bowl, spoke via cell phone to Saunders, then the Kansas City Chiefs' offensive coordinator.

The next day, Pederson and Saunders met at Saunders' home in Kansas City. At that point, Saunders informed Pederson he wasn't interested in the Nebraska job.

If Callahan had not accepted Pederson's offer, what was going to be NU's next move? We might never know, although then-North Carolina State head coach Chuck Amato was mentioned as a potential next target.

What a fun period for Nebraska fans (not really).

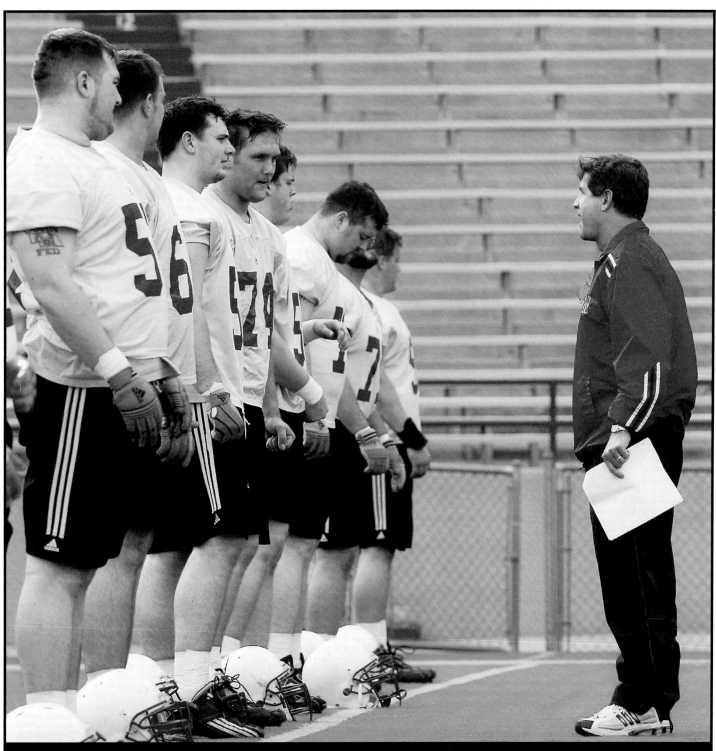

According to some Husker players, Bill Callahan spent most of his time and energy working with players on the offensive side of the ball. (Ted Kirk)

Jan. 9, 2004

Within two or three years, I think Nebraska will be a powerhouse offensively. Anybody who saw the Raiders in 2002, that's Callahan to a T. — Tom Lemming

Sources say Callahan AD's choice

Bill Callahan is about to become the next head football coach at Nebraska.

Callahan, 47, was still in Lincoln on Thursday night, and two sources close to the situation, speaking on the condition of anonymity, told the Journal Star that the former Oakland Raiders coach would be hired to replace Frank Solich, who was fired Nov. 29.

However, there was no indication of when an official announcement might be made.

By STEVEN M. SIPPLE

Callahan's oldest son, Brian, a redshirt freshman quarterback at UCLA, told the Journal Star he expected to get a call when a deal had been finalized, but he had yet to hear from his father.

While leaving Embassy Suites in downtown Lincoln at about 7 p.m. Thursday, Bill Callahan told reporters, "I'll talk to you guys later."

Callahan's agent, Gary O'Hagan, told the Journal Star on Thursday night: "Things are progressing. That's all I can say."

The San Francisco Chronicle cited an unnamed source close to Callahan as saying he had accepted the job. ESPN also reported the hiring.

Details of a potential deal were unavailable, but NU athletic director Steve Pederson has said he is willing to pay about $1.5 million per year.

Nebraska assistants Bo Pelini and Turner Gill interviewed for the job Wednesday and were awaiting official word Thursday night.

"I thought it'd be over today," said Pelini, a 36-year-old defensive coordinator.

"I'm just waiting like everyone else," said Gill, a 41-year-old quarterbacks coach.

Callahan, who was fired by the Raiders on Dec. 31, one season after leading them to the Super Bowl, met with Pederson on Thursday morning at Memorial Stadium before heading back to Embassy Suites.

Pederson picked up Callahan at Embassy Suites about noon and politely declined to disclose details of Callahan's visit.

"I'll let you know when there's something to say," Pederson said.

Callahan's wife, Valerie, briefly visited Lincoln Pius X High School Thursday afternoon, according to school officials.

The Callahans have four children, including a daughter in grade school, a daughter in

Former Oakland Raiders head coach Bill Callahan (right) leaves the Lincoln airport with Marc Boehm, NU associate athletic director, on Jan. 7, 2004. (William Lauer)

junior high and a son in high school.

Tom Lemming, an ESPN recruiting analyst and longtime friend of Callahan, said Nebraska would be getting a "great offensive mind" if Callahan indeed is NU's next head coach. What's more, Lemming said, Callahan has a keen eye for talent, communicates well with young players and is a tireless worker.

"He's relentless," Lemming said. "Within two or three years, I think Nebraska will be a powerhouse offensively. Anybody who saw the Raiders in 2002, that's Callahan to a T."

Jeremy Crabtree, a recruiting analyst for rivals.com, also praised Callahan's recruiting prowess.

"He's a bulldog," Crabtree said. "He gets after it. His reputation in the coaching community is first-rate."

Callahan was reportedly scheduled to fly to New York on Thursday to interview for the offensive coordinator job with the New York Giants. Lemming, however, said Callahan never mentioned a New York trip during their 30-minute phone conversation Wednesday.

Callahan's interview process at NU actually began Wednesday afternoon in Lincoln.

On the same day Gill and Pelini interviewed for the job, Callahan, wearing a black overcoat and carrying a black briefcase, arrived at Lincoln Municipal Airport at about 4:45 p.m.

Pelini, asked Thursday if he'd consider remaining at Nebraska as an assistant, declined comment.

Nebraska secondary coach Marvin Sanders said he had been approached about a coaching position at another school, but was holding off on a decision until the Husker head coaching spot was officially filled.

"I'm trying to delay this thing as long as I can," Sanders said.

Callahan was the latest in a string of NFL coaches linked to the NU position. Miami Dolphins head coach Dave Wannstedt, Kansas City Chiefs assistant Al Saunders, Philadelphia Eagles assistant Brad Childress and Dallas Cowboys assistant Mike Zimmer were all reported to be in the mix.

In addition, Arkansas head coach Houston Nutt last week decided to remain with the Razorbacks after receiving a visit from Pederson.

> **If the defensive coaching staff is broken up, things are going to be a real mess, and it's going to take a long time for Nebraska to come back.** — Benard Thomas

Jan. 9, 2004

Players will give Callahan chance

Bill Callahan isn't Bo Pelini.

But three Nebraska football players, responding to reports that Callahan will be named the Huskers' head coach, say they're willing to give the former Oakland Raiders coach a chance.

"If he's the coach, I'm going to stick behind him and see what's the plan," said sophomore cornerback Fabian Washington, who made an unsolicited call to the Journal Star. "We're not going to write off the coach without getting to know him."

Of course, Washington said he'd rather see Pelini, the team's interim head coach, take over permanently for Frank Solich, who was fired Nov. 29.

At the very least, he'd like to see Pelini remain on staff as defensive coordinator.

"I hope so, but c'mon ... I seriously doubt it," Washington said. "But I really hope so."

Callahan, who was fired by the Raiders on Dec. 31 following a 4-12 season, has been in Lincoln since Wednesday interviewing with athletic director Steve Pederson and chancellor Harvey Perlman. He becomes the 27th head coach in Nebraska history.

"I'd like to get to know him and see how he is," freshman receiver Ronnie Smith said. "It's good for recruiting, bringing a big name in. It just seemed like (recruiting) was going to go down the drain."

Smith, like Washington, said his first choice would've been Pelini, but that he wouldn't object to Callahan's hiring.

"Yeah, I mean, I really have no choice but to give him a chance," said Smith, a receiver from Carson, Calif.

"I think he likes to pass. I've been hearing that. Me being a receiver, I like that part of it, but I really don't know too much about it."

Junior defensive end Benard Thomas — the player who made headlines when he personally questioned Pederson during the news conference that announced Solich's firing — said he had no choice but to give Callahan a chance.

"Let him take care of the offense and let Bo take care of the defense," Thomas said. "If the defensive coaching staff is broken up, things are going to be a real mess, and it's going to take a long time for Nebraska to come back. Nobody really understands this, except for the players who are there right now.

"I guess the scariest thing is going to have to play against Bo if he goes somewhere else. He's going to bring every ounce of fight out of everybody he's coaching."

By BRIAN ROSENTHAL

Thomas, who also called the Journal Star, said players were hearing about Callahan's hiring via Internet and media reports, and not from Pederson, who told players they would be the first to know about their new coach.

"That's just another time we were lied to," Thomas said. "We were told the players would know first before anybody else knows."

Smith said he'd been following the coaching search every day on the Internet.

"It was getting really crazy," he said. "I got a call saying Houston Nutt was the coach. I was like, 'Oh, my God.' I was hearing so many names, I was like, 'Just forget it, just name someone, whoever they name.'"

Washington questioned how seriously Pelini and quarterbacks coach Turner Gill, both of whom interviewed for the head coaching position Wednesday, were considered.

"Why didn't Coach Gill or Coach Pelini get a chance?" he said. "(Pederson) gave them an interview just to make things look right, just to make it look like he gave them a chance. How far along the line were they? Were they going to be a last resort?"

In Callahan, the Huskers have a coach who led the Raiders to the Super Bowl a year ago, when Oakland boasted the NFL's top offensive unit.

"I know he's a good offensive mind," Washington said. "He knows a lot about offense. I guess that would be good for our team, him knowing a lot about offense."

Heisman Trophy winner Johnny Rodgers introduces his daughter Jewel, 7, to Husker head coach Bill Callahan in September of 2004. (Ted Kirk).

Jan. 10, 2004

> To take a team and lead it to the national champ-
> ionship is my main objective for myself and the
> staff.
> — Bill Callahan

Pederson: Callahan is a rare find

Saying he embraces his boss's lofty expectations, Bill Callahan was introduced Friday as the 27th head coach in the 114-year history of Nebraska football.

"The expectations are high at any level, professionally or collegiately," said Callahan, who plans to scrap Nebraska's vaunted ground-based offense. "I want to add to the dimension of success they've had here in the past. To take a team and lead it to the national championship is my main objective for myself and the staff."

By STEVEN M. SIPPLE

In firing Frank Solich on Nov. 29, Nebraska athletic director Steve Pederson announced that he wants his football program competing for, or gaining on, the national championship on a consistent basis. No longer does he want the Huskers to take a back seat to Oklahoma and Texas.

Pederson evidently thinks Callahan, the former Oakland Raiders head coach, can lead Nebraska to consistent top-five finishes. The 47-year-old Chicago native agreed to a six-year contract worth $1.5 million annually.

"Coach Bill Callahan is a rare find," Pederson said.

In hiring Callahan, Pederson bypassed two internal candidates, defensive coordinator Bo Pelini and quarterbacks coach Turner Gill. It was suggested Friday that perhaps Pelini and Gill received only token interviews.

Pederson disagreed, saying he spent three hours informally discussing football with Pelini and Gill in separate sessions early in the hiring process.

"I was around them through bowl time and spent another couple of hours with them (Wednesday)," Pederson said, referring to the coaches' official interviews. "I

Bill Callahan and his wife, Valerie, after Callahan was announced as NU's new head football coach by athletic director Steve Pederson on Jan. 9, 2004. (William Lauer)

don't know what's left."

Pederson also denied having a personality conflict with Pelini, the fiery 36-year-old former NFL assistant who pumped life into a Nebraska defense that spearheaded the Huskers' 10-3 season.

A few hours before Callahan was announced as head coach, Pelini met with Pederson at South Stadium. Pederson informed Pelini of the decision to hire Callahan, Pelini said, although word of Callahan's hiring had started to spread Thursday afternoon.

Asked whether he'd consider remaining at Nebraska as defensive coordinator, Pelini declined to comment. Pelini has had discussions with Oklahoma head coach Bob Stoops about a job on the Sooner staff.

"We'll see what happens," Pelini said. "I'll comment more at an appropriate time."

Callahan, fired Dec. 31 as head coach of the Raiders, said he planned to meet with Nebraska recruiting coordinator Scott

Downing later Friday to evaluate recruiting. Callahan said he plans to meet Monday with all of the Husker assistants individually and collectively.

"It'll be quick as we move forward with hiring a staff," Callahan said.

Callahan acknowledged Nebraska's tradition of winning while saying he wants to try to improve the program. He'll do so with a West Coast offense instead of the ground-based, option-heavy attack the Huskers have used for the last 20-plus years.

"It's a system that's flexible and can be tailor-made to suit the players' talents," Callahan said of his offensive approach.

Pederson and Callahan called former Nebraska head coach Tom Osborne and left messages about the hiring. Osborne, now a U.S. representative from Nebraska's 3rd District, said he returned Pederson's message and wished Pederson and Callahan well.

Regarding Nebraska's impend-

ing switch to the West Coast offense, Osborne said, "You always have to coach what you understand."

Osborne said he used to use some three-step-drop plays that resembled the West Coast style.

"Fans for years have wanted to see the ball in the air more," Osborne said.

Solich, 58-19 in six seasons as Nebraska head coach, declined to comment about Callahan's hiring.

Pederson said he had face-to-face discussions with six candidates. Based on previous reports, those six coaches were Callahan, Pelini, Gill, Dallas Cowboys defensive coordinator Mike Zimmer, Arkansas head coach Houston Nutt and Kansas City Chiefs assistant Al Saunders.

Callahan was available because Al Davis dismissed him following Oakland's 4-12 finish this season. In 2002, Callahan led the Raiders to an 11-5 regular-season record. The Raiders lost to Tampa Bay in Super Bowl XXXVII. He became just the fourth NFL rookie head coach to lead his team to a Super Bowl.

Under Callahan, the Raiders featured a multiple offense. Indeed, the 2002 Raiders became the first team to win games in the same season while rushing at least 60 times (in beating Kansas City 24-0) and passing 60 times (in beating Pittsburgh 30-17).

Callahan last coached in college in 1994, completing a five-year stint as Wisconsin's offensive-line coach. Callahan is regarded as one of football's foremost offensive-line coaches.

"I went to the NFL hoping someday I could come back into the college environment," Callahan said.

"We got ourselves a difference-maker," Pederson declared with a smile.

Open heart, open mind
Woman goes through bypass surgery wide awake — on purpose. Local/1B

40 16
Details: 8B

LINCOLN JOURNAL STAR

www.journalstar.com

SATURDAY, JANUARY 10, 2004
LINCOLN, NEBRASKA

★★

Committee, senator present options to save the fair

Nebraska State Fair Board endorses a report listing ways to fix the fair's financial problems.

BY ART HOVEY
Lincoln Journal Star

The Nebraska State Fair Board endorsed a list of wide-ranging ideas Friday for saving State Fair Park that seemed to leave room for just about everything except a second Great Platte River Road Archway and Monument.

Among the selling points for the strategies offered by attorney Kent Seacrest and other committee members is the need for speed during the 2004 legislative session.

And state Sen. David Landis of Lincoln became a symbol of that urgency when he came to the board's meeting to announce he had just introduced legislation that calls for Nebraska voters to consider a constitutional amendment that would give the fair 10 percent of the state's lottery proceeds.

Landis called that approach "an ongoing, reliable source of revenue that doesn't rise or fall with the budgetary process."

Seacrest, also at the board's meeting to present the draft of the committee report, due on Gov. Mike Johanns' desk by Thursday, said a lottery revenue source worth an estimated $2 million per year was among the recommendations in the draft by the "partnering committee."

The committee grew out of concern about losing the fair and its annual $27.8 million contribution to the area economy. It also grew out of

See STATE FAIR, Page 2A

A fair future

Some options offered Friday to the Nebraska State Fair Board for resolving financial problems:

■ Create a bigger and better fair that might require as much as $3 million more a year for added entertainment and other costs.

■ Create a smaller, better fair that might involve bringing the county fair back to the state fairgrounds or moving the State Fair to the Mahoney State Park interchange along Interstate 80 or another, more accessible site.

■ Mix and match alternatives — for example, moving agricultural parts of the fair to Grand Island and keeping urban parts in Lincoln.

■ End the fair altogether.

Mission to Mars would be tricky for NASA

Space experts say the trip's effects on the human body — and mind — may be the biggest hurdle.

BY SETH BORENSTEIN
Knight Ridder Newspapers

WASHINGTON — Returning astronauts to the moon and sending them on to Mars can be done, but doing it — as President Bush will propose next week — won't be easy and it certainly won't be cheap.

Getting there involves leaping technological hurdles, including designing new spaceships, creating a permanent lunar base and perhaps turning lunar ice and the Martian atmosphere into rocket fuel.

Space experts say those challenges can be overcome. But they're less sure about the human challenges: Can the human body stand long periods of low gravity in an environment prone to deadly solar radiation? Can the human mind withstand extreme isolation for at least 18 months at a time? Can an ossified and graying NASA do the job?

And — most important — are Congress and the country willing to invest $130 billion to $240 billion in the project? Last year's tax cuts, by comparison, are expected to reduce federal reserves by some $135 billion this year.

"The technology is here; it's not a matter of new technology," said Hans Mark, a former NASA deputy administrator and aerospace engineering professor at the University of Texas at Austin. "Money is the biggest obstacle. You can buy this now."

In 1992, Mark and his students figured it would cost about $157 billion in today's dollars to send astronauts to the moon and another $76 billion to go on to Mars.

Humboldt Mandell, NASA's former Mars/moon exploration program manager and an expert on government cost estimates, said to go to Mars directly would cost NASA about $80 billion. Going to the moon would cost another $50 billion to $70 billion, he said. Mandell now is a research fellow at the Center for Space Research at the University of Texas.

When the first President Bush, the current president's father, proposed the same expeditions, Mandell said, the estimated cost was $400 billion over 20 years, half for the moon and half for Mars.

Christopher Kraft, the famed NASA mission control director who oversaw NASA's heyday of manned Mercury, Gemini and Apollo launches, said the biggest challenge "is Congress, it's the country. The biggest challenge is getting the na-

See SPACE, Page 2A

HUSKERS WELCOME THEIR NEW HEAD COACH

He plays to win

WILLIAM LAUER/Lincoln Journal Star

Bill Callahan (right), the Huskers' new head football coach, is introduced Friday by University of Nebraska athletic director Steve Pederson.

Callahan sets his sights on returning NU to No. 1

BY STEVEN M. SIPPLE
Lincoln Journal Star

Saying he embraces his boss's lofty expectations, Bill Callahan was introduced Friday as the 27th head coach in the 114-year history of Nebraska football.

"The expectations are high at any level, professionally or collegiately," said Callahan, who plans to scrap Nebraska's vaunted ground-based offense. "I want to add to the dimension of success they've had here in the past. To take a team and lead it to the national championship is my main objective for myself and the staff."

In firing Frank Solich on Nov. 29, Nebraska athletic director Steve Pederson announced that he wants his football program competing for, or gaining on, the

national championship on a consistent basis. No longer does he want the Huskers to take a back seat to Oklahoma and Texas.

Pederson evidently thinks Callahan, the former Oakland Raiders head coach, can lead Nebraska to consistent top-five finishes. The 47-year-old Chicago native agreed to a six-year contract worth $1.5 million annually.

"Coach Bill Callahan is a rare

See CALLAHAN, Page 6A

Bill Callahan's deal

■ Athletic director Steve Pederson estimated Callahan's total package at $1.5 million a year, or around $100,000 more than former coach Frank Solich's deal. Included in the total package is income from "outside sources" — the NU Foundation, the Big Red Football School, radio and television appearances and apparel deals.

■ The former Oakland Raiders coach is guaranteed $1.95 million, or a minimum annual base salary of $325,000, paid through athletic department revenues for the six-year term of the contract.

■ There are no buyout clauses written into the agreement. "It's a very straightforward contract," Pederson said.

Perlman relieved the hunt is over

BY MATTHEW HANSEN
Lincoln Journal Star

Harvey Perlman is tired of football.

It was right there in the University of Nebraska-Lincoln chancellor's weary eyes and his weary jokes at Friday's news conference announcing Bill Callahan as Nebraska's next football coach.

"I hope that teaching and research are still going on at the university," Perlman cracked at the formal end of a hiring process marked by

PERLMAN

its length and public heat.

A 41-day coaching search and 40 stormy Husker nights began with a longtime coach fired and ended with a Super Bowl coach hired.

In between, fans screamed. Boosters threatened to pull their financial support. Players threatened to boycott the Alamo Bowl. The University of Nebraska Board of Regents fretted.

And, fittingly, this search ended, as it began, with a controversy: whispers that Perlman and Athletic Director Steve Pederson disagreed about who should be the next football coach.

The chancellor tried to clarify his role in Callahan's hiring Friday. He also fended off rumors that he

See PERLMAN, Page 6A

Inside: More Callahan coverage

Fans offer a wary reception: 6A ■ A look at Pederson's highly scrutinized search: 1C ■ Curt McKeever column:

Jan. 18, 2004

This is one of the top programs in the country. We know we have our work cut out for us to keep it that way.
— NU defensive coordinator Kevin Cosgrove

Coz understands expectations

Kevin Cosgrove coached for 14 years at Wisconsin under Barry Alvarez, a former Nebraska football player and longtime friend of ex-Husker head coach Frank Solich.

Consequently, Cosgrove understands Nebraska football tradition.

"When you say Nebraska football, people listen," said

By STEVEN M. SIPPLE

Cosgrove, one of five assistants hired so far by new Husker head coach Bill Callahan. "This is one of the top programs in the country. We know we have our work cut out for us to keep it that way."

Cosgrove, 48, has been in Lincoln since Monday night. He said he's left the office for only a few hours to drive around town, as Callahan and his underlings scramble to make sure Nebraska ends recruiting season on a high note.

It wasn't until Thursday that Cosgrove, Wisconsin's defensive coordinator for the past 10 years, phoned Alvarez and told him he was officially taking the same job at Nebraska. Eventually, Cosgrove wants to become a head coach, and he said this move could help him toward that goal.

What's more, Cosgrove couldn't turn down the 47-year-old Callahan, whose friendship with Cosgrove dates to their teenage years on Chicago's south side. They were roommates at Illinois Benedictine in Lisle, Ill., and served as assistants under Mike White at Illinois (seven years) and Alvarez at Wisconsin (five).

In other words, their bind is tight, their respect mutual.

"Billy's the most detailed guy I've ever been around," Cosgrove said Saturday, noting Callahan's penchant for writing down virtually everything he learns. "He

Kevin Cosgrove (left) joined longtime buddy Bill Callahan (right) on the Nebraska coaching staff in January 2004. Callahan named Cosgrove the Huskers' defensive coordinator, while Jay Norvell (center) was offensive coordinator. (Ted Kirk)

makes sure he's on top of everything."

Callahan succeeds Frank Solich, who was fired Nov. 29, a day after Nebraska finished the regular season with a 9-3 record. Callahan led the Oakland Raiders to the Super Bowl in 2002, but the Raiders this season finished 4-12, and Callahan was dismissed.

As soon as Callahan accepted the Nebraska job on Jan. 8, Cosgrove knew he would be getting a call from his friend.

"Our expectations here are to compete for the Big 12 championship every year," Cosgrove said. "That's Nebraska football. We're just going to try to take it to the next step."

Solich went 58-19 in six seasons as Nebraska head coach, but the Huskers won only one Big 12 title under his watch.

"There are high expectations

here," Cosgrove said. "But the opportunity is there because of all the tradition."

Nebraska's storied tradition will make it easier for him to recruit players than it was at Wisconsin, Cosgrove said. He noted that when people think of Big Ten football, Michigan and Ohio State typically are the first teams that come to mind.

"It's still a challenge every year at Wisconsin to get in on the top players," Cosgrove said.

Cosgrove brings to Lincoln his multiple defense with a 4-3 base alignment.

"I have a lot of energy, and I'm very experienced," said Cosgrove, who helped lead Wisconsin to three Rose Bowl triumphs. "We're going to play aggressive defense, and we're going to be fundamentally sound.

"I wouldn't say we'll be a big

blitz team, but we'll pick our spots."

Callahan, meanwhile, will call the plays on offense.

Cosgrove noted he and Callahan always have worked on different sides of the ball. As graduate assistants at Illinois, they used to tease each other about who would eventually become a head coach.

It turns out Callahan won that battle. Now, once again, they'll go to battle together.

Cosgrove accepted the Nebraska job after getting the OK from his family, including wife Shelly, daughter Shannon, a high school junior, and son Connor, a seventh-grader.

"The timing was right, the family was supportive, and I'm back with my buddy," Cosgrove said.

Jan. 18, 2004

Pelini says Oklahoma a good fit

Bo Pelini ultimately aspires to become a head coach.

"But that's not what drives me," the former Nebraska assistant said Saturday. "What drives me is winning. When you're around winning programs, good things happen."

The 36-year-old Pelini joined a winning program Saturday, taking over as co-defensive coordinator and secondary coach at perennial power Oklahoma, a longtime Husker rival.

This season at Nebraska, Pelini served as defensive coordinator for a unit that led the nation in pass-efficiency defense and turnover margin while ranking second in scoring defense.

After Husker head coach Frank Solich was fired Nov. 29, Pelini was named interim head coach and led the team to a 17-3 victory against Michigan State in the Dec. 29 Alamo Bowl.

Pelini interviewed for Nebraska's head coaching position, but Husker athletic director Steve Pederson ultimately hired former Oakland Raiders head coach Bill Callahan.

"I think Pederson was determined to bring in somebody from the outside," Pelini said. "I don't think I got much consideration, though I was led to believe I would."

Which perhaps explains why Pelini already has Nov. 13 imbedded in his consciousness. That's when Nebraska plays Oklahoma in Norman.

"All of our games are on my mind, but the Nov. 13 game will be ... a little bit special to me," Pelini said.

In taking the Oklahoma job, Pelini joins a staff headed by lifelong friend Bob Stoops. Like Stoops, Pelini hails from Youngstown, Ohio, where Pelini played for Stoops' father, Ron Sr.,

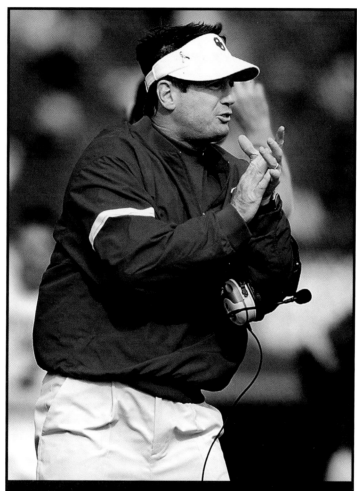

Oklahoma head coach Bob Stoops welcomed Bo Pelini to his staff after Pelini was let go along with most of the Husker staff when Bill Callahan was hired. (William Lauer)

at Cardinal Mooney High School and was one year behind Bob's younger brother, Mark.

"Cardinal Mooney is different from a lot of high schools," Pelini said. "Once you're in the family, you're in the family."

Pelini on Wednesday interviewed for the defensive coordinator job with the NFL New York Jets. He also drew interest from the Pittsburgh Steelers and Atlanta Falcons for defensive coaching positions.

However, Pelini said, Oklahoma had been atop his list of

destinations ever since Callahan on Monday dismissed all but two of Nebraska's 2003 assistants.

Stoops chose Pelini after reportedly talking with Houston Texans assistant Jon Hoke and Marvin Sanders, the former Nebraska secondary coach who on Friday took over as co-defensive coordinator at North Carolina.

"I want to win, that's the No. 1 thing," Pelini said Saturday. "And I want to be around quality people, people I can trust. I also wanted to be in the best situation for my family."

Pelini will share the co-defensive coordinator's title at Oklahoma with Brent Venables, though Venables will retain the final word on defensive decisions.

That's fine with Pelini, he said.

"What I've found, even this year at Nebraska, is that you have to work together," said Pelini, who completed his first season as a co-ordinator.

"It wasn't just me. You work

By STEVEN M. SIPPLE

as a team. That's how I operate. It's about winning. That's all that matters. As for who gets the credit, who cares?"

Nebraska's defense this season used an aggressive zone-blitz package, which helped the Huskers force 47 turnovers to tie a school record established during the school's 1971 national championship run.

Bob Stoops took notice.

"Everyone understands we've been longtime personal and family friends," Stoops told reporters Saturday in Norman. "That relationship's been built for a lot of years. But more than that, Bo comes in with great credentials and he'll help continue our tradition of being a great football team."

Oklahoma loses only four seniors from a 2003 defense that ranked third nationally in yards allowed (259.6), spearheading the Sooners' 12-2 season.

"The talent's very good," Pelini said.

More importantly, Pelini said, he feels comfortable working with Stoops.

"That weighed a lot in my decision," Pelini said. "He's a person I trust and respect both as a person and a coach. Personally and professionally, this job is just a good fit."

Feb. 4, 2004

> *It's an extraordinarily difficult situation for any head coach to come in and in a month try and go land big-time players.* — Recruiting analyst Jamie Newberg

Approach puts NU on fast track

Nebraska's penchant in the past for recruiting to the needs of its system as opposed to going after four- or five-star players at most positions has always made me careful not to put much stock into how its classes are judged.

Let's face it, the national analysts have tended to view the Huskers as antiquated, which translates into low ratings.

By CURT McKEEVER

With Bill Callahan bringing a new approach, those days may be over. Still, the fact that NU's class of 2004, which will be announced by Callahan this afternoon, has climbed into some top-25 lists must make fellow Big 12 Conference coaches a bit nervous.

Callahan's been on the job for a little more than three weeks and the Huskers are already taking shots at some heavyweights? They dare think they can steal coveted quarterback Rocky Hinds from national champ Southern California? Come on!

"It's an extraordinarily difficult situation for any head coach to come in and in a month try and go land big-time players. I thought what they did was smart," said Jamie Newberg, national recruiting analyst for theinsiders.com. "They swung and missed with a lot of those guys, but they also came up big on Lydon Murtha and Cortney Grixby."

Murtha, an offensive tackle from Minnesota, and the Omaha Central cornerback Grixby are ranked among the nation's best at their positions. The marquee players in this class stand out as examples of Callahan and his staff taking a quick inventory of what key ingredients need to be added.

By the way, Nebraska also landed running back Brandon Jackson, considered the best player in Mississippi, and Santino Panico from

Lincoln Southwest High School lineman Ty Steinkuhler was part of Bill Callahan's first NU recruiting class. (Eric Gregory)

suburban Chicago, a versatile athlete who was named the Illinois Gatorade Player of the Year.

"It's a remarkable recovery," Tom Lemming said of Nebraska.

Like Newberg, Lemming, ESPN.com's recruiting analyst and publisher of Prep Football Report, has the Huskers hovering around his top 25.

Like Callahan, he's from Chicago, and he has known Nebraska's new coach since 1980. Their history doesn't sit well with Colorado's Gary Barnett.

"He's calling kids and telling them to visit Nebraska," Barnett said in the Denver Post. "The coaches' association has tried to get him once. I'll guarantee you, Tom has been involved in that. He says, 'Why don't you at least take a visit?' It's illegal and unethical."

Lemming denied that claim, saying he merely sent Callahan a list of questionnaires from players who had yet to commit to a school.

"I sent that same list to Colorado six months ago," Lemming said Tuesday.

Jeremy Crabtree of rivals.com had Nebraska's class ranked No. 23. Oklahoma, Texas, Texas A&M, Kansas State and Texas Tech all were ahead of the Huskers, while Missouri came in at No. 25.

On one hand, Crabtree said he's not surprised at the Huskers' late run because Callahan, a proven recruiter from his days at Wisconsin and Illinois, hired Kevin Cosgrove and John Blake, also regarded as crafty pitchmen. But he still marvels over what they've done in their short time together.

"I think it's a very good class, a

foundation class," Crabtree said. "Next year is when we'll start to find out."

Lemming also buys into that line of thinking but notes that what matters most in recruiting is whether there's an air about a place. What he sees in Nebraska is "that something special is going to happen."

In this case, a nationally ranked Husker recruiting class is indeed something that should generate a lot of excitement — because Callahan and company are just getting warmed up.

"Our recruiting will take off next year when our players here know the coaches," offered Nebraska's new associate athletic director for football Tim Cassidy, "because they're your best sales people."

I didn't want to have our names stay on the building and have people assume that what happened did so with our approval or with our consent. — Tom Osborne

Feb. 7, 2004

Building will carry Osborne name

Tom Osborne won't pull his name from the University of Nebraska athletic department's planned $50 million training and office complex.

Osborne made the announcement Friday, soothing the fears of project supporters who worried that a withdrawal by the legendary former football coach and U.S. congressman could doom the project.

But at the same time, Osborne spoke passionately about the sorrow he feels over seeing a 42-year foundation of loyalty, trust, continuity and caring within the Husker football program end with the firing of head coach Frank Solich.

"I didn't want to have our names stay on the building and have people assume that what happened did so with our approval or with our consent," Osborne said, speaking for his wife, Nancy. "It wasn't something that we would have agreed to, and it wasn't the way we'd like to see it happen.

"But we made a commitment, and we'll stay with it."

Osborne, however, offered to give up naming rights to any individual or corporation that steps up with a significant-enough contribution.

NU needs $40 million in donations to fund the project, which calls for a 5,000-seat addition to Memorial Stadium beginning in 2005.

The new facility will house a locker room for the football team, training facilities and a weight room, as well as office space for the football staff and athletic department administration.

Athletic director Steve Pederson unveiled plans to build the Tom and Nancy Osborne Athletic Complex in November, just weeks before firing Solich.

Solich was Osborne's hand-picked successor in 1997, and his dismissal came as a shock.

"I had absolutely no knowledge or inkling that that was going to happen," Osborne said.

When seven of Solich's nine assistants were let go last month, Osborne's frustration peaked. It was still evident to those who crowded into a meeting room at The Cornhusker hotel to hear Osborne.

"I don't like to see him like that," said Matt Davison, an Osborne recruit who played at Nebraska from 1997 through 2000. "I think you can tell by the tone of his voice and the look in his eyes that a lot of this has hurt him.

"This program is, and has been for a long time, built around him. So it is weird to me that he has not been consulted."

Osborne said he sent letters outlining many of his concerns to Pederson and UNL Chancellor Harvey Perlman last month and followed up with hour-long, face-to-face meetings.

"It's not my job to intervene, but I've listened to everybody and heard all sides of the story, and I just don't see anything that maybe we couldn't have sat down in one room and in 45 minutes to an hour hashed out and maybe had it back on track," Osborne said. "But that's not my job anymore.

The only reason we're here today is the darned naming of the building."

By TODD HENRICHS

Neither Pederson nor Perlman attended the news conference, held several blocks from campus.

In a written statement issued Friday evening, Pederson repeated his November pledge to name the new facility for "the greatest college football coach of all time."

"Change is not easy for anyone, particularly those directly impacted," Pederson said. "These have not been easy times for any of us. I appreciate Tom's advice that we should now try to put this behind us and move forward."

In a separate statement, Perlman said: "I really appreciate the fact that he will continue to support the football program. Like him, my hope is that fans will put the decisions behind them and rally behind the new coaches and student-athletes."

Osborne described his relationship with Pederson as OK and said he'd like to remain friends with the man who was his former recruiting coordinator.

Osborne holds no animosity toward the new head coach, Bill Callahan, and hopes to meet with Callahan's coaching staff in the next few weeks.

Osborne said he's taking his lead from Jimmy Williams, one of the fired assistant coaches, who played under Osborne from 1979 through 1981.

The two met for lunch recently, and Williams, a husband and father of six, said he has no regrets.

"A guy like that would probably be bitter," Osborne said, but "having said everything I've said, Jimmy's attitude is the only constructive attitude to have at this time.

"This has happened," Osborne said. "It's behind us. And whether it's right or wrong, it's done."

Nebraska officials, including former coach Tom Osborne and current coach Bill Callahan, broke ground for the new Tom and Nancy Osborne Athletic Complex on Aug. 10, 2004. (Journal Star archives)

Friendship with 'Coz' cost Callahan

STEVEN M. SIPPLE

"Get me out of this hotel," Kevin Cosgrove told a Nebraska football staff member soon after arriving in Lincoln in January of 2004.

Seems the hotel in the heart of Lincoln didn't live up to the new Husker defensive coordinator's standards. So NU officials moved the former Wisconsin assistant to a much newer and nicer place downtown.

Of course, living accommodations eventually would become the least of Cosgrove's concerns at Nebraska. After leading decent Husker defenses in 2005 and 2006, the roof caved in on Cosgrove and company in 2007, as Big Red allowed more points, yards and first downs than any team in school history.

You can point to Bill Callahan's throat-slash gesture, hillbillies comment, complicated-yet-productive offenses, or apparent disregard for Nebraska's football traditions as defining elements of his four-season run at NU. What's more, the numerous blowout losses obviously are painful memories for Husker fans. It all adds up. But one could argue that the biggest factor in Callahan's demise as Big Red's head coach was a defense that at times faltered in stunning fashion.

Of course, many factors contributed to the defense's problems. For one thing, too many players didn't trust the system. What's more, Callahan has admitted to friends the staff might have relied too heavily on junior college players on defense (five juco defenders started at least three games apiece in 2007). It didn't help matters that the coaching staff missed out on a few key defensive recruits, while a few players didn't pan out as expected. At any rate, as the leader of the unit, Cosgrove received the brunt of the criticism.

Those close to Callahan say loyalty was a huge factor in 2004 in Callahan's decision to hire Cosgrove. Callahan liked the idea of having a close friend he could trust as his right-hand man. Their friendship dates to their teenage years on Chicago's south side. They became roommates at Illinois Benedictine and worked together as assistants at Illinois and Wisconsin.

Did Callahan even consider retaining Bo Pelini as Nebraska defensive coordinator in 2004 after Pelini worked magic with Nebraska's defense in 2003? It's hard to say for sure,

Kevin Cosgrove was a childhood friend of Bill Callahan and knew when Callahan was hired by Nebraska AD Steve Pederson in January of 2004 that his friend would give him a call. In hindsight, it appears that Cosgrove's hiring as Husker defensive coordinator played a role in Callahan's downfall at NU. (Ted Kirk)

Bill Callahan (right) and Kevin Cosgrove (left) coached together at Nebraska for the last time on Nov. 23, 2007. It wasn't a happy time, as the Huskers lost to Colorado 65-51 in Boulder, Colo. (William Lauer)

but probably not. Hiring Pelini obviously would've been awkward for Callahan since much of the Husker fan base had clamored for Pelini to be the head coach.

After taking over as the Huskers' head coach, Callahan had the obligatory one-on-one meetings with each of the 2003 NU assistants. Callahan's meeting with Pelini was extensive — it lasted about an hour — which was much longer than the other assistants' meetings, according to a former Big Red staff member. However, Callahan still seemed set on Cosgrove. Indeed, Cosgrove told the Journal Star in January of 2004 that he knew he would get the call from Callahan after Callahan was hired by Nebraska.

"I'm back with my buddy," Cosgrove said then.

They almost parted ways after the 2005 season when Cosgrove strongly considered an offer to become the Minnesota Vikings' linebackers coach. In fact, Cosgrove at one point

told friends, including former Wisconsin head coach Barry Alvarez, he planned to take the Vikings job.

Cosgrove instead stayed in Lincoln and helped lead Nebraska to a 9-5 record in 2006, including 6-2 in the Big 12 North Division. The Husker defense played particularly well in the final two games of 2006, though Big Red lost both contests — to Oklahoma (21-7) in the Big 12 title game and to Auburn (17-14) in the Cotton Bowl.

Then the wheels fell off in 2007.

In hindsight, Callahan's loyalty to his childhood buddy became costly from a career standpoint. However, many questioned Callahan's hiring of Cosgrove from the start. After all, in 2003 — Cosgrove's final season at Wisconsin — the Badgers lost five of their last six games and were 43rd nationally in scoring defense. They were 63rd, 58th and 73rd in total defense the previous three seasons.

Alvarez, Cosgrove's boss at Wisconsin, did-

n't exactly beg Cosgrove to stay after Callahan came calling. According to people who follow Badger football closely, there was talk the game had passed by "Coz."

For instance, some say he was clearly more comfortable defending conventional offenses than the spread attacks that were starting to become prevalent.

"Coz" disliked defending spread attacks, said former Wisconsin linebacker Jeff Mack, who started for Cosgrove from 2000-03.

"He's able to relate well with players and get them to be gap-sound and fundamentally correct," Mack said. "But I think sometimes we were too reactionary. Something would happen in a game, and we'd react after the fact. I sometimes felt we were on our heels."

After leaving NU, Cosgrove turned down at least one offer from a Division I school and eventually decided to work as a volunteer coach at a Wisconsin high school. He also plans to consult with college programs.

We need to, obviously, get a lot better. We are certainly capable of being a better club. — Bill Callahan

No spin can erase the ugliness

LUBBOCK, Texas — The process of bringing Nebraska back to the top of the college football world now involves recovering from the worst loss in school history.

How ridiculous is that?

The Huskers might have proven in 2003 that they weren't ready to take Austin, Texas, by storm. But things hadn't eroded near to the point that, one year later, they should leave Lubbock looking like shocked victims of a lightning strike.

By CURT McKEEVER

It remains to be seen whether the 70-10 bolt they received from Texas Tech on Saturday will wind up being like a fluke of Mother Nature or cold, hard proof that Nebraska no longer qualifies as a heavyweight contender.

What it definitely will do is challenge the faith people have in NU's leaders.

"We need to, obviously, get a lot better," first-year coach Bill Callahan offered. "We are certainly capable of being a better club."

Perhaps the best news for NU is the Red Raiders probably won't win the Big 12, so they can't highlight Saturday's ugly score on their championship rings like Colorado did in 2001.

It's also probably a good thing for Callahan there are no Tim Browns on this team, because he was no match for the cancerous attitude that reportedly was spread through the Oakland Raiders' locker room last year.

Even without bad seeds, Callahan will have a tough time trying to put a positive spin on Saturday's four-plus hours of entertainment. In fact, if he's smart, he won't even attempt to, because Nebraskans aren't easily fooled.

As for defensive coordinator Kevin Cosgrove? My guess is he'll need to call on all his psychiatry skills to fix the damaged ego of his defense.

While cutting up the nation's fifth-ranked defense, Texas Tech's fifth-year senior quarterback Sonny Cumbie looked like the second coming of Sonny Jurgensen. Before Mike Leach called off his top dog late in the game, Cumbie added to his nation-best passing average by completing 44 of 56 attempts for 436 yards and five touchdowns.

Cumbie rarely touched the Jones Stadium turf while roasting the Husker linebackers and secondary with a mixture of shallow crossing routes and pick plays that Bobby Knight should teach the Tech men's basketball team.

Husker Nation stunned by loss

At Misty's less than half an hour after Nebraska's loss to Texas Tech, Husker fans watching the TV newscast about the pummeling couldn't take it anymore.

So they turned on cartoons.

"This is what you need after a good beating: 'Futurama,'" said Rosie Demma, an off-duty waitress at the downtown Lincoln restaurant.

And, really, what else is there to do when a college football juggernaut, a cultural and economic cornerstone of your city, a team you have seen win three national championships in the past 11 years, gets its helmet handed to it by a team it has never lost to before?

The 70-10 shellacking by the Red Raiders on Saturday night left football fans in some downtown bars stunned, but vowing to weather the hard times with their team.

"What my heart wants to say is give (Bill) Callahan two to three years," said Joyce Tienken, who watched the game at the bar of Embassy Suites. "He'll use his recruits and build the program up."

The Huskers lost, said Tienken, 43, of Scribner, because they are mostly made up of players recruited by former coach Frank Solich, who played a different style of game than Callahan.

"They're like high school freshmen in college, learning a college offense," she said.

Her husband, Gary, 46, agreed. "It's a learning process," he said. "They just showed they are trying to learn the offense. They're not going to overwhelm anyone yet."

Down the street at BW-3, Brody Bowman, 22, of Lincoln also blamed an inexperienced offense.

"We don't have the personnel to carry out the West Coast offense," he said. "I think it'll be better in a few years. Right now we're just going off Solich's recruits."

Back at Misty's, Jason Sandblom, 23, was simply stunned.

"I'm a huge Husker fan," Sandblom said as he stared at the TV screen. "But about halfway through the third quarter, I couldn't do much but laugh."

But a defeat, even a crushing one, won't change everything. Everybody interviewed said they would remain loyal to Big Red.

And even a loss couldn't keep football off the TVs at Misty's. Minutes after changing to "Futurama," the channel had been changed back to the Missouri-Baylor game.

— Andrew Nelson

"We just have to come back next week and continue to get better," said NU free safety Daniel Bullocks, who got the Huskers' lone interception on what seemed to be the only play Cumbie had a communication breakdown with his receivers.

I'd just like to know what area Bullocks thought the Huskers got better in since last week's 14-8 nail-biter against Kansas. Could it be in the area of denial?

Let me offer another: Joe Dailey only threw one interception. Go ahead, laugh, but those are the kind of baby steps Nebraska has to take before it can even think about getting pedal-to-the-metal results like Tech.

Though his 14-of-34 passing line will make you think he struggled mightily, most of Dailey's throws were strong and on target. What he fought more than making proper reads was Nebraska being forced into playing catch-up against a team that had an extra defensive back on the field every play of the second half. When Dailey couldn't produce against that, Callahan yanked him for freshman Beau Davis.

Davis committed four turnovers on his first four possessions, so there's obviously not going to be any quarterback controversy. But what Callahan has now might be worse — a starter whose confidence has been shaken to its core.

Maybe Callahan can check out the arm of Nebraska's newest highly touted recruit — Motley Crue drummer Tommy Lee — sometime during practice next week. Yeah, I realize that's ridiculous. But after Saturday's debacle, the Huskers should leave no stone unturned.

It was a long night for Nebraska head coach Bill Callahan (left) and defensive coordinator Kevin Cosgrove when the Huskers visited Lubbock, Texas, on Oct. 9, 2004. Texas Tech handed NU its worst loss in school history, 70-10.
(Ted Kirk)

Nov. 14, 2004

Pelini praises his former charges

NORMAN, Okla. — Barrett Ruud was escaping, leaving flying oranges and a depressing Gaylord Family-Oklahoma Memorial Stadium scoreboard in his rear-view mirror.

Then, he suddenly stopped. A familiar voice was calling.

The Nebraska senior linebacker reversed field like there was one more ballcarrier to tackle. He ran to meet the voice at the 5-yard line.

By BRIAN CHRISTOPHERSON

It wasn't right to leave without hugging Bo Pelini, the man he had given so much to a year ago.

Pelini — who coached the Husker defense last season and even served as NU's interim coach for the Alamo Bowl — patted Ruud's shoulder pads and whispered something into his ear.

The Oklahoma co-defensive coordinator did the same to many other Huskers after the No. 2 Sooners' 30-3 win Saturday night, even sharing a consoling moment with NU quarterback Joe Dailey.

"Obviously, I have a lot of strong feelings toward those men over on that other side," Pelini said. "But what was said? That's pretty personal."

Pretty personal is what Pelini could have made this game. He was, after all, the popular choice among many Nebraskans to take over as NU's head coach after Frank Solich was let go last year.

Instead, Nebraska athletic director Steve Pederson hired Bill Callahan, who then told Pelini he was going to go another route and hire another defensive coordinator — Kevin Cosgrove.

Under the new regime, the Huskers are 5-5, which sure would be an easy record for Pelini to take shots at.

NU was 10-3 last year, and certainly never gave up 70 points in a single game — as this team did to Texas Tech — with many of the same cast of characters on defense.

When asked if this Nebraska team is underachieving at 5-5, Pelini said: "That's not for me to say. I don't know. I have a lot of respect for the guys over there as football players and as men. That's for the powers-to-be to make the decision, not me."

He was pressed again. C'mon, Bo. Has Nebraska's talent fallen so far in just one year?

"You know," said Pelini, taking a very long pause to choose his words with care, "you deal with the cards you're dealt. There's a lot of good football players over on that football team. For me to stand here and say that they're not talented football players, that'd be lying.

"They played tremendous for me. And the things that they did … they fought. I'm not going to sit here and say they're not talented football players. I'd be lying to you."

To say Nebraska players didn't fight Saturday would also be a lie. But the Husker offense simply had no answer for Pelini's defense. And Nebraska's Blackshirts found out why Oklahoma quarterback Jason White won the Heisman Trophy a year ago.

White carved up the Nebraska defense, completing 16 of 19 passes for 203 yards and two touchdowns to lead OU to a 23-0 halftime lead. At one point in the second half, the senior broke his own school record by connecting on 18 straight throws. By game's end, he missed on just 6 of 35 passes.

"As far as taking care of the ball and making good decisions, this is the best stretch that I've had," said White, who seemed to gain an advantage in this year's Heisman race over teammate Adrian Peterson.

The true-freshman running back played with a dinged shoulder and managed 67 yards on 15 carries, which may not read shiny enough in the box score today for many Heisman voters.

But OU hardly needed Peterson. White, and Pelini's boys, made sure this thing was never in doubt.

The Huskers managed 274 yards, but didn't get on the scoreboard until a 39-yard field goal by David Dyches at the final gun. The kick was met with a chorus of boos and a field full of oranges thrown by angry Oklahoma fans with sights on the Orange Bowl.

How upset was Pelini about losing the shutout?

"Not one bit. We played well. We shut them out until the last second of the game. We dominated," Pelini said.

OU head coach Bob Stoops also didn't have a problem with Nebraska's three points.

Stoops had his team throwing the football even with a 30-point lead late in the game. He said he reluctantly did it for style points, since the Sooners are in a mad chase with Auburn to be second in the BCS rankings and earn a slot in the national title game.

"In hindsight, I probably shouldn't have done that," Stoops said.

But in hindsight, hiring that Pelini guy was a pretty good idea. Stoops praised his new defensive coach for his game plan against the Huskers.

After the win, Pelini refused to succumb to reporters who wanted him to say it was tough coaching against his former players. Instead, he said preparing for Nebraska was just like preparing for everyone else.

"I have a job to do and I did it. I moved on from (Nebraska)," Pelini said. "You know, you can't just eliminate the feelings you have for the players, but at the same time, I'm here. I feel fortunate to be here. I'm having a great experience here at Oklahoma.

"It's another time, another place."

One year after helping Nebraska to a 10-3 record, Bo Pelini was on the Oklahoma sideline as the Sooners' co-defensive coordinator. (Ted Kirk)

> **I am distressed when people are shooting off guns and throwing fruit at our players. I just have a hard time with that.**
> — Bill Callahan

Nov. 16, 2004

Callahan sticking to his principles

You've got to hand it to that fiery son-of-a——— Bill Callahan.

Asked Monday to address a newspaper report that he uttered an expletive and a derogatory comment while leaving Owen Field on Saturday night, Nebraska's football coach came out shooting like an Oklahoma Ruf/Nek.

"I probably could've used a better choice of words," he said.

But it is what it is — and he wasn't taking it back.

How do you like them oranges, you "———ing hillbillies?"

Those words — "———ing hillbillies" — and a pre-game incident involving Husker offensive tackle Darren DeLone were the two topics that dominated Callahan's 10-minute slot on the Big 12 coaches teleconference.

Unlike Kansas' waffling Mark Mangino — who rescinded a biting comment he made about the officiating in his team's last-minute loss to Texas — I'm glad Callahan stuck to his guns.

Check that. There's probably a better choice of words for what Callahan did — given his affection for the 12-gauge shotgun salutes fired off by members of the Oklahoma spirit group prior to Saturday's game.

Apparently, that "continual" act sat about as well with him as did the Sooners' decision to throw a fourth-down pass deep into Nebraska territory with less than a minute left in a game they led 30-0.

And then you get to the sticky matter of the "barrage" of oranges that hit all around the Huskers.

"I don't think any team should be subjected to the type of treatment we were subjected to. ... I am distressed when people are shooting off guns and throwing fruit at our players," Callahan said. "I just have a hard time with that."

That scene landed one Ruf/Nek, Adam Merritt, in a Norman hospital with cuts to his face and some missing teeth. Witnesses say that was an act of assault by DeLone, but also that he was being provoked by the Ruf/Neks.

If that's the case, and Merritt was one of the hecklers, I have a hard time having much empathy. Goading a 315-pounder in battle gear, on his turf, is akin to stepping inside a lion's cage and letting out a roar. Who do you think gets torn limb by limb?

"To have these students, with these guns, and they continually blow them off. ... It's astounding to me that these kids can be right in the midst of a warmup between these 300-pound-plus linemen," Callahan said. "To have them do that is unsafe. You know, those warmups are very explosive. You get down to that wall area in that end zone, and there are so many people down there that it seems inevitable that something is going to happen."

Callahan said he spoke to Oklahoma athletic director Joe Castiglione following Saturday's game and was told of the Ruf/Neks' long tradition of appearing at home games and at the annual showdown with Texas in Dallas.

Callahan noted that two of his assistants saw the incident near the end zone where the Huskers were warming up, but that he wouldn't comment until receiving more information from a police investigation expected to be completed later this week.

Meanwhile, Castiglione declined comment, but Oklahoma released a strongly worded statement that expressed disappointment in Callahan's statements, "especially since the incident re-

sulted in serious injury to a student who was standing off the field within the sideline boundaries."

As for Callahan's take on the crowd? Who's to say his words of choice were intended solely for OU fans? Heck, maybe he was thinking about the Nebraska media when those words popped out. Or he spied some lost group of Razorbacks from Arkansas, where it's common, and I'm not making this up, for loyalists to stand in unison and squeal out a hog-call chant?

Granted, we could've done without the potty mouth. But what concerns me more than Callahan's choice of adjectives is his obvious bias against oranges.

"We were involved in a Monday night game in Denver one year where we were coming off of the field and the entire (Oakland)

Raider team was pelted by snowballs, which created an incident," he said. "But I've never seen anything like this."

Had Callahan been around when oranges were the preferred object to launch at Memorial Stadium, he'd have a different opinion. I just cross my fingers if Nebraska beats Colorado the day after Thanksgiving that his comments **By CURT McKEEVER** denouncing the citrus fruit don't jeopardize NU's chances of playing in the Champs Sports Bowl. That game in Orlando was previously known as the Tangerine Bowl.

I'm guessing if Callahan can get the Huskers there, they won't have to deal with any more fruit-flingers or popgun-firing, ———ing hillbillies.

An Oklahoma cheerleader picks up oranges thrown on the field by fans during the Sooners' 30-3 victory against Nebraska on Nov. 13, 2004. (William Lauer)

Gesture-gate or out of proportion?

Nebraska football coach Bill Callahan said his infamous throat-slash gesture stemmed from frustration, wasn't directed at game officials and has been blown out of proportion.

"It's Gesture-gate or something," Callahan said Tuesday, drawing laughter at his weekly news conference.

"I don't know where this is all coming from. I was frustrated at the time, and I did make a gesture out of frustration, which I normally have done with my own children, when I've had it up to here with a certain aspect.

By BRIAN ROSENTHAL

"I'm 49 years old, and I don't go around (with) throat-slashing signs and symbols. I don't use that type of demeanor. I never have."

Callahan's gesture occurred after he argued with an official in the fourth quarter of Saturday's 31-24 loss to Oklahoma. Callahan, with his right index finger extended, made a motion from his left shoulder to his right shoulder, crossing his throat.

The Big 12 Conference is reviewing video, and Nebraska officials have until today to respond to the league office with a written review of the situation and any actions they may take. The Big 12 can accept those actions or request further punishment.

"I don't think they're going to send me to Alcatraz or anything," Callahan said.

"I was really frustrated, and I'm going to fight for our team. I'm going to fight for our players. That's my prerogative as a head

Referee Steve Usechek and Nebraska head coach Bill Callahan don't see eye-to-eye on the officiating after an Oklahoma touchdown in the fourth quarter of the Oct. 29, 2005, game at Memorial Stadium. (Ted Kirk)

coach."

Callahan said he spoke Monday night with Tim Millis, coordinator of football officials for the Big 12, and assured Millis he meant no malicious intent with the gesture.

Millis' response?

"He said, 'Bill, we don't know anything that you're talking about. There was no flag, there

was no report.'"

Callahan took the same "what are you talking about?" approach Tuesday when initially asked about the gesture. He then elaborated, at times humorously.

Players seemed unfazed by the gesture hoopla.

"I didn't even realize it until this morning," defensive end Jay Moore said. "Some of the guys

didn't even realize it happened. No one's really talked about it. There is no distraction whatsoever."

Quarterback Zac Taylor, who said he hasn't seen video of the gesture, said the situation has been blown out of proportion.

"I know Coach Callahan, and when he says he's not doing that," Taylor said, "I believe him."

Quarterback Zac Taylor led Nebraska to an 8-4 record in 2005. The Oklahoma native helped the Huskers nearly beat the Sooners that season, falling 31-24. (Eric Gregory)

It was priceless win for Nebraska

SAN ANTONIO — The 2005 MasterCard Alamo Bowl really did live up to the game sponsor's slogan.

You would have been tickled to pay face value for a ticket if you knew Nebraska would give a gritty performance against a more-talented Michigan team in the Alamodome here Wednesday night.

But a 32-28 win, coming from 11 points down in the fourth quarter? Now that's what you call priceless.

By CURT McKEEVER

It's almost unbelievable. We're only two years into the Bill Callahan era and the Huskers are just as the head coach claims, right on schedule to being a reborn, once-again proud nation. Actually, they might be arriving early.

The attitude Nebraska displayed here Wednesday, one that shined brightest through junior quarterback Zac Taylor, senior I-back Cory Ross and junior cornerback Zackary Bowman, is above and beyond the kind of table setter Callahan could hope for his 2006 charges.

"I can't be any prouder of the way we fought back," he said after the Huskers improved to 5-0 in this building.

If you saw the ease with which Michigan's mammoth defensive front and athletic linebacker corps toyed with the NU O-line and left Taylor mangled in the pocket, you would have known why the Wolverines were picked to win the Big Ten.

But even though he was given little chance of having a big statistical evening, the Husker quarterback delivered in the clutch and ended up with a trio of touchdown tosses. There should be no question now that Taylor, undoubtedly the sorest Husker late Wednesday night, is the key to Nebraska's hopes next season.

Thrown off rhythm early by Michigan's smothering up-the-middle pressure, the junior kept his cool, endured like most of his teammates and delivered a performance that would leave you thinking the Harrison Beck show won't be set for release until 2007.

Taylor's ability to hang in for the long haul allowed him to one-up Michigan sophomore quarterback Chad Henne, who's done nearly all he could to position himself as the next Joe Montana — the guy who you know will get it done in the playoffs or, for now, the bowl season.

Bill Callahan got a celebratory bath in the Alamodome in San Antonio before the 2005 Alamo Bowl was even over. The Huskers rallied from an 11-point deficit to take a 32-28 lead against Michigan, but the Wolverines had one final trick up their sleeves. (William Lauer)

The play of Nebraska cornerback Zackary Bowman (1), including this interception of a pass intended for Michigan's Mario Manningham in the third quarter, helped the Huskers defeat the Wolverines in the 2005 Alamo Bowl.
(Eric Gregory)

Except that unlike Montana, Henne now is winless in the postseason, and for that he can blame the Big 12 Conference. Last year it was Texas' Vince Young who got the best of him in the Rose Bowl. Now Taylor.

Henne looked like he had delivered the final nail in the Huskers' coffin when he scrambled for a TD that made it 28-17 with 11:40 to play.

At that point, I never would have imagined that after another 5:40 had ticked off the clock, a colleague would be uttering: "Wow, this is a good game. Nebraska's going to have a chance."

NU was down 28-25 then, and on the next play, blitzing free safety Blake Tiedtke knocked the ball from Henne and Ola Dagunduro picked it up and the Huskers were in business at the Wolverine 17-yard line.

Taylor came through again with a 13-yard touchdown strike to Terrence Nunn to put Big Red up with 4:29 to go.

Back comes Michigan, driving with machine-like efficiency to a first down at the NU 20. But the nation's least-penalized team committed an illegal-procedure infraction and after Jason Avant made his fourth catch of the drive, the Blackshirts forced three straight incompletions, the final coming on a fourth-and-9 play in which Bowman reached in front of Mario Manningham to deflect Henne's second-to-last attempt.

After the Wolverines forced a punt to get the ball back with seven seconds left, defensive end Adam Carriker hurried Henne into another misfire before a wild final play in which the ball exchanged hands eight times. It ended when Bowman and Titus Brothers pushed tight end Tyler Ecker out of bounds at the NU 13. It occurred amid a mass of Husker hysteria that had flowed onto the field and left one recalling the famed Stanford-Cal band-incident finish.

This one was the kind that left you hoping it'd be cool if these teams met again next year in a more significant venue.

That, of course, can wait. For now, the Huskers should have no thoughts other than the ones they have from a remarkable 8-4 season that included three straight wins at the end for the first time since the 12-1 campaign of 1999.

That one was completed by a dominating Fiesta Bowl win against Tennessee. By the way, the Fiesta Bowl is the site of next year's BCS championship — but let's not get too carried away.

Nebraska fans walking around this city proudly wearing their "Restore The Order" T-shirts that emerged following the regular-season finale at Colorado are smart enough to know the Huskers still have a long way to go before that's truly the case.

But are they on their way? You'd better believe it.

How priceless is that?

> You can't jump over all of the hurdles at once. You have to go through the process of getting to where you want to go.
> — Steve Pederson

Nebraska finally closes the deal

COLLEGE STATION, Texas — One could almost hear the angry cries of Husker Nation as Texas A&M made its second-half charge.

Once again, Nebraska wasn't putting away an opponent, wasn't landing the knockout blow. Husker fans were no doubt steaming on their sofas, as they had been two weeks ago, for instance, as NU failed to put away Oklahoma State.

By STEVEN M. SIPPLE

Turns out, Nebraska can finish off an opponent after all. The Huskers can in fact close a deal. They did so Saturday as a long afternoon of momentum swings faded into darkness. Yes, indeed, they finally put away a foe.

Never mind that Nebraska waited until the final play to close out 24th-ranked Texas A&M, with Husker defensive end Adam Carriker wrapping quarterback Stephen McGee in a massive bear hug and flinging him to the Kyle Field grass to cap NU's wild 28-27 victory.

"It's a great win for our program, for our state," said Nebraska coach Bill Callahan, whose Huskers clinched the program's first Big 12 North championship since 1999 and a berth in the Dec. 2 conference title game.

Nebraska athletic director Steve Pederson called winning the North Division "a step we needed to take."

"We hoped it'd be this year," he said. "But you can't jump over all of the hurdles at once. You have to go through the process of getting to where you want to go."

If you're a Nebraska fan, that process involves a roller coaster of emotions and ample patience. At least that was the case Saturday, as the Huskers somehow es-

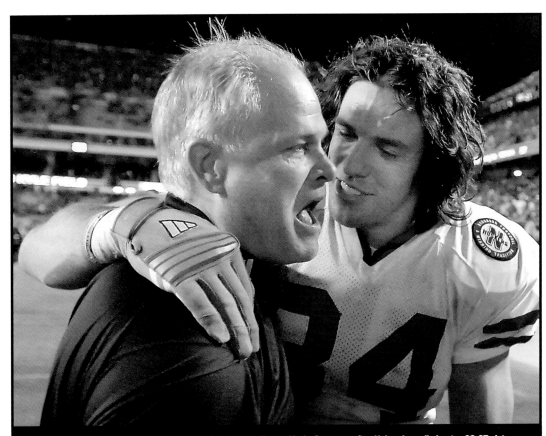

Husker linebacker Stewart Bradley embraces defensive coordinator Kevin Cosgrove after Nebraska pulled out a 28-27 victory against Texas A&M in College Station, Texas, on Nov. 11, 2006. (Journal Star archives)

caped Kyle Field with a record of 8-3 overall and 5-2 in the league.

Nebraska led 21-10 at halftime and seemed to be in control. Slowly, however, Texas A&M regained momentum. More than anything, the Aggies punished the Huskers with big gains on third-down plays.

Nebraska coaches — all coaches — preach the importance of "finishing." And here was NU, failing repeatedly to finish off Texas A&M on key third-down situations. Indeed, here was Big Red failing to complete its stated goal of winning the North. Or so it seemed.

"It's been our whole goal since the day after the Alamo Bowl,"

said Nebraska defensive lineman Barry Cryer, referring to the Huskers' 32-28 win against Michigan last December.

Nebraska would've gotten another opportunity to clinch the North on Nov. 24 when it played Colorado in Lincoln. And it appeared the Huskers would have to wait until then to do it, especially after linebacker Mark Dodge picked off Zac Taylor's pass with 2:50 remaining Saturday.

At that point, Texas A&M led 27-21. The Aggies seemed ready to put away the Huskers with 1:57 remaining as Layne Neumann lined up for a 42-yard field-goal try. But Barry Turner blocked the kick, and NU suddenly had life.

"Boy, special teams is a big part of the game," Callahan said. "That block meant everything."

Yes, Turner's block meant Nebraska still had life. Perhaps more important, the Huskers had Taylor, the steady senior who so often seems to hold things together when all seems lost.

"When it's all on the line, in who else's hands would you want the ball?," Callahan asked.

After Nebraska took over at its 25-yard line, Taylor led the decisive touchdown drive, completing 5 of 11 passes for 67 yards. A few completions went to a couple rather unlikely players — Todd Peterson and Dan Erickson, who had one career reception before his 16-yard catch on the big drive.

After Marques Thornton's roughing-the-passer penalty handed Nebraska first-and-goal at the A&M 9, Taylor addressed his favorite target, Maurice Purify, in the huddle. The ball's coming your way on a fade route, the quarterback told the 6-foot-4, 210-pound wideout.

Taylor lofted a pass into the end zone, where Purify was isolated in one-on-one coverage with 5-10, 185-pound freshman cornerback Jordan Peterson.

No contest. Purify leaped and pulled down the ball as if he were pulling down a rebound.

"Big play Mo! Big play Mo!" Nebraska I-back Cody Glenn chanted as he walked off the field. Purify, meanwhile, was being interviewed by television reporters as a pocket of Big Red fans celebrated in a corner of the massive stadium.

"Well, that was exciting, wasn't it?," Callahan asked reporters.

He said such last-moment comebacks were what championship teams were all about.

Yes, finally, Nebraska had closed the deal. Had finished off an opponent. And just in the nick of time.

"I wish you could see the faces in the locker room," Callahan said.

Nebraska wide receiver Maurice Purify (16) goes high in the air to snag a pass in front of Texas A&M's Jordan Peterson with 21 seconds left as the Huskers rallied for a 28-27 victory. The win gave NU its first Big 12 Conference North Division crown since 1999. (Journal Star archives)

Oct. 14, 2007

I'm not worried about my job. I'm just going to do the best I can. Whatever happens, happens.

-- Bill Callahan

It can't get much worse than this

By BRIAN CHRISTOPHERSON

As he left the field and came upon the angry voices, Bill Callahan's eyes focused straight ahead.

Despite the 45-14 embarrassing loss to Oklahoma State, Husker fans clapped for players as they trudged toward the locker room.

"Keep your head up Cortney," a man shouted at Husker senior Cortney Grixby, who flipped his sweat bands to a young boy.

But as the Husker coach came off the field, clapping gave way to shouting, lots and lots of shouting.

"You suck!" one fan shouted, and another repeated it.

An older woman leaned over the balcony rail and yelled in a shrill tone: "Fire Callahan! You're a loser, Callahan!"

You'd be hard-pressed to find a much lower day in Husker history than Saturday at Memorial Stadium, where an average Oklahoma State team simply beat the bejabbers out of Nebraska.

Mediocrity would look pretty good right about now.

The voices were no more easy on Callahan in the postgame news conference, where he was asked if he was now worried about his job being in jeopardy, in this, his fourth year at NU.

"I'm not worried about that," said Callahan, composed. "I'm just coaching for these kids, and that's why I got into this. I just feel terrible for these players. It just hurts to watch these kids hurt.

"I'm not worried about my job. I'm just going to do the best I can. Whatever happens, happens. I don't think you can coach in fear or coach like you're scared of something. I've never coached like that in my life. I've been in this business for 30 years, and I

sure as hell ain't going to start (coaching scared) now, that's for sure."

He was asked if he'd consider making midseason staff changes.

"No. No, I would not," he said.

He was asked how he'd explain Nebraska's last two performances to chancellor Harvey Perlman and athletic director Steve Pederson.

"More or less, we've tried hard putting a package together where our players can be prepared and perform, and it didn't happen. It's very disappointing," he answered.

He was asked if he's lost this team.

"I don't think so," he said, citing the way his team competed in the second half despite trailing big.

It's the first half Husker fans

won't soon forget.

Go to the thesaurus. Find the word ugly and all the words that befriend it and there you have it.

The whole scene was absolutely bizarre.

There were a few fans with bags over their heads, a "SURRENDER STEVE PEDERSON" banner and sarcastic cheers when the Huskers finally got a first down, almost 12 minutes into the game.

It was 38-0 at halftime and there were pockets of empty seats in Memorial Stadium when the Homecoming royalty was announced.

Several thousand fans had decided their time could be better spent elsewhere, a few reaching for their car keys just five minutes into the second quarter.

"It was the worst half I can

Nebraska's loss to Oklahoma State at Memorial Stadium on Oct. 13, 2007, was hard to take by Husker fans, who streamed to the exits long before the game was over. The Cowboys led 38-0 at halftime and went on to a 45-14 victory. (William Lauer, Gwyneth Roberts)

This sign held up by a fan during the Oklahoma State game in 2007 speaks for itself. (Ted Kirk)

ever remember playing, especially in a first half," Husker senior linebacker Bo Ruud said. "That was just terrible. There's no excuse for that. It was just poor."

The 38 points were the most a Nebraska defense has given up at home in a first half.

Oklahoma State had lost 20 straight in Lincoln, dating to 1960. But on this day, OSU piled up 551 total yards, gashing the Huskers for 317 yards on the ground.

Dantrell Savage had 212 of those yards, averaging 8.5 yards a carry.

The Huskers have now given up at least 40 points in four of the past five games. No Nebraska defense before this one gave up at least 40 points four times in a season.

Husker quarterback Sam Keller said players are angry, confused.

"It's not that easy when you're hurting inside so bad," Keller said. "I know some guys are just searching for what's going wrong. Some guys are confused or angry, but a lot of guys, myself included, don't really know how to deal with this kind of situation and the weight of this situation."

Not impressed with the football, fans did the wave to entertain themselves with 11 minutes left and the Huskers down 31 points.

When Oklahoma State made it 45-7 with 5:25 left on a 30-yard run by Savage, the stadium was only half full.

Don't look now, but the schedule only gets

tougher for the 4-3 Huskers.

Coaches and players talked about fixing things. But at this point, what reason is there to believe there's any chance of that being accomplished?

"There's always hope," Callahan said. "That's a part of life, is believing. You just have to believe. As a coach and coaching young men, you have to keep hope alive for those young kids. You can't walk away from them and point fingers and blame and do anything like that.

"They're hurt more than anybody. They're embarrassed. They really hurt. Those kids in that room I just left, they're gutted. They're mentally, emotionally, physically gutted. They are sick."

> **Whether it was during my time as a student, staff member or athletic director, I have always been proud to call myself a Cornhusker.** — Steve Pederson

Leader's discordant reign ends

By BRIAN ROSENTHAL

A big, red Nebraska flag hung in the rain from the porch of Steve Pederson's home in Lincoln on Monday evening.

A watery-eyed man came to the door. It wasn't Steve Pederson.

"It's been a long day," responded the man, who said he was a family friend.

He said Pederson wasn't available for comment and wouldn't say whether Pederson was home.

We know where Pederson wasn't: Hosting his weekly radio call-in show at Memorial Stadium.

Pederson was fired Monday as Nebraska's athletic director, ending a tumultuous, controversial tenure that began nearly five years ago.

It featured the firing of a 9-3 football coach, a cloaked 41-day search to replace him, the much-needed upgrade of football facilities and the divide of a fan base that had previously taken pride in its unity over a tradition-rich football program.

Through it all, Pederson enjoyed his position.

"Being Nebraska's athletic director was not merely a job for me," Pederson said Monday in a statement released by university officials. "I viewed it as an honor and important duty to serve the Nebraska tradition of academic and athletic excellence.

"During the last five years we have enjoyed many successes and also faced a number of difficult challenges. In the midst of both, we always made our decisions based on what was in the very best interests of our university and its outstanding student-athletes."

For every fan or booster who lauded Pederson's vision and passion for Nebraska, there was a fan or former athlete blasting Pederson's leadership style that caused division within and around the athletic department and the state.

Two key members of the athletic department resigned this year — Paul Meyers, associate athletic director for major gifts, and Paul Miles, associate athletic director for marketing.

Many fans were critical of Pederson's evasiveness, particularly during troublesome times. Fans and media were uninformed during Pederson's one-man search for a football coach until a Jan. 3 news conference — 34 days after Frank Solich was fired.

That same evasiveness recently stirred more discontent. Pederson, during the football team's recent struggles that have left fans upset, has not taken calls on his weekly show.

Pederson, who signed a five-year contract extension in July, was fired two days after the football team suffered its worst home loss since 1958, and its second lopsided loss in two weeks. Pederson declined media interview requests after Saturday's game against Oklahoma State in Lincoln. He didn't answer repeated calls Monday to his cell phone or return messages.

Pederson, a North Platte native and University of Nebraska graduate, was hired on Dec. 20, 2002. He'd served the previous six years as athletic director at Pittsburgh, where he helped rebuild that program's facilities.

He initially arrived in Lincoln with great fanfare, lauded by many as a Nebraska native with Midwest values who understood the culture and would fit perfectly in his new position.

Those thoughts changed a year later, when Pederson fired Solich on Nov. 29, 2003, saying the following day, "I refuse to let this program gravitate to mediocrity," and that he wouldn't surrender the Big 12 Conference to Oklahoma and Texas.

Those are comments critics have used against Pederson after each of Nebraska's troubling defeats under Bill Callahan's watch. Callahan, in his fourth season, is 26-18 overall and 14-13 in Big 12 Conference games. Pederson signed Callahan to a five-year contract extension on Sept. 4.

Pederson also helped revamp Nebraska's football facilities, leading the $50 million expansion of North Stadium — a project that increased Memorial Stadium's capacity to 81,067 and boosted Nebraska's recruiting edge with a new locker room, weight room, indoor practice building and training facilities. His hire of basketball coach Doc Sadler has been popular, and the athletic department has remained financially sound.

"On and off the field, we worked passionately and tirelessly to not just win, but win the right way," Pederson said in the statement. "We can take great pride in the fact that Nebraska still sets the national standard when it comes to producing Academic All-Americans. We have been able to build state-of-the-art facilities like the North Stadium project, but in a financially responsible way. And we have hired new coaches and staff members who are dedicated to success on the field, in the classroom and in the lives of our student-athletes well after their last game has been played."

Pederson's first job in college athletics was as a Nebraska sports information assistant in 1980. He was Nebraska's football recruiting coordinator from 1982-86 and also served as recruiting coordinator at Tennessee and Ohio State. He returned to Lincoln as an associate athletic director for football operations from 1994-96 before leaving for Pittsburgh.

Pederson, in his statement, thanked friends and supporters of Nebraska who've remained loyal. He also thanked student-athletes, coaches and staff.

"The University of Nebraska has been an incredibly special place to my family and me for more than three decades," Pederson said. "Whether it was during my time as a Nebraska student, staff member or athletic director, I have always been tremendously proud to call myself a Cornhusker."

Walking distance
Find out if your neighborhood has the goods, The (402)/1C

AG opposes new trial
Bruning says Lotter sentence should be upheld in 1993 slayings, Local/1B

62 47
Details, 6B

TUESDAY, OCTOBER 16, 2007
LINCOLN, NEBRASKA

LINCOLN JOURNAL STAR

www.journalstar.com

★★

SACKED

With Husker losses mounting and complaints against Athletic Director Steve Pederson rising, the university decided it was time for a change.

BY BRIAN CHRISTOPHERSON
Lincoln Journal Star

The sign on the door seemed written by a cheery person.

"Welcome to the Visitors Center! Press Conference at 4:00 P.M. Today.

Please join us . . . "

It was as though you were walking into a church potluck.

Turns out it was a guy's firing.

University of Nebraska-Lincoln Chancellor Harvey Perlman dismissed Athletic Director Steve Pederson on Monday afternoon.

About 200 people crowded around to hear the news that kept the state's work productivity at a minimum on this day.

Perlman said there was "no real joy in his heart" in making the announcement.

"I want to be clear on some things. I know that every one of you thinks this was because of a foot-ball game that was played last Saturday," Perlman said.

"Let me tell you that this decision was made prior to this weekend. I have become aware since July or August of a number of concerns from people in the athletic department about Steve's management style, about his connection with his staff, with donors, with fans, with former athletes."

Perlman said the decision was actually made "in my mind" on Thursday, but was not made public then due to the lateness in the week, with a football game looming.

He said Pederson's credibility had been lost to a point where he was no longer positioned to move the athletic department forward.

It certainly did not help Pederson's cause that the football team is going through one of the worst seasons in modern Husker history.

See **PEDERSON**, Page 6A

> *"For one reason or another, he lost the respect of the people he worked with."*
> — Harvey Perlman, University of Nebraska-Lincoln chancellor

> *"I hope they find a new donor. They're going to need to find a new donor. I'm off the roster."*
> — Dan Cook, longtime NU booster

One way or another, Osborne will play role in Huskers' future

BY BRIAN CHRISTOPHERSON
Lincoln Journal Star

Tom Osborne watched the spectacle from his home, taking no delight in the firing of a man who once worked for him.

OSBORNE

The former Husker coach liked Steve Pederson enough to endorse him for the Nebraska athletic director job five years ago.

Pederson seemed the perfect hire to so many then — a North Platte native, a Husker grad, the guy down the street.

It was Pederson's dream job, one he learned Monday he'd have to give up.

"I feel bad about it," Osborne said. "I thought Steve would do really well."

With the athletic director job now open — in the middle of a football season, no less — the 70-year-old Osborne is now being proclaimed as the perfect hire by some.

His name is being tossed about as the guy to be inter-im athletic director, maybe even full-term AD.

OK, OK. Is Osborne even interested?

"Well, I'd rather not even talk about that right now because I don't know what that means, or what those duties would be," Osborne said. "I've had no serious conversations about it."

University of Nebraska-Lincoln Chancellor Harvey Perlman, who will make the hire, said Monday that Osborne would "be one of many people I would consult."

Perlman said he has often consulted Osborne on matters, sometimes on things not dealing with athletics.

"I'm not turning the program over to him, but he's knowledgeable, he has experience," Perlman said. "He knows people in the

See **WHAT'S NEXT**, Page 6A

HUSKER ECONOMICS
■ Some local businesses are feeling the effects/**Page 6A**

PARTING WORDS
■ Being Nebraska's athletic director was more than a job to Steve Pederson/**Page 1D**

UNDER THE INFLUENCE
■ Steven M. Sipple: Steve Pederson uprooted Nebraska's football culture/**Page 1D**

IN THE HUDDLE
■ Uncertain times for NU's football coaching staff amid adversity/**Page 1D**

@ JournalStar.com
■ **Audio/video:** Listen to the entire news conference and video highlights.
■ **Video:** Husker fans react to Steve Pederson's dismissal.

Journal Star file photo

WEDNESDAY, OCTOBER 17, 2007
LINCOLN, NEBRASKA

LINCOLN JOURNAL STAR

★★

www.journalstar.com

OSBORNE IS INTERIM ATHLETIC DIRECTOR

NU turns to Tom

UNL chancellor brings back legendary coach to restore unity to Husker fans.

BY CURT McKEEVER
Lincoln Journal Star

Blue skies

For the first time in three days — since Nebraska lost 45-14 to Oklahoma State at Memorial Stadium — weather conditions in Lincoln were reported as "fair" at 3 p.m. Tuesday, when former football coach Tom Osborne was named the Huskers' interim athletic director.

Viewpoints

"To give an analogy: Hiring Tom Osborne is like giving everyone who cares a warm hug. It's needed."
— Mitch Krenk, former Husker and president of the NU lettermen's club

■ ■ ■

"I've always tried to maintain a relationship with Coach Osborne. I touch that statue every day I walk in."
— John Cook, NU volleyball coach

COOK

■ ■ ■

"If I were Callahan or one of his assistant coaches, I would take his comments to mean that these next five games are (the) most important in my coaching life."
— From the "Life in the red" blog at HuskerExtra.com

JournalStar.com

■ **Video:** The news conference announcing Tom Osborne as interim athletic director

■ **Audio:** Coach Bill Callahan's Tuesday morning news conference

■ **Photo gallery:** Osborne's athletic and political career

■ **HuskerExtra vidcast:** Steven M. Sipple examines the positive aspects of ousted Athletic Director Steve Pederson's tenure

Look out, Bill Straub: Tom Osborne's watching.

Oops, wrong Bill.

But just in case he was thinking otherwise, the University of Nebraska-Lincoln women's bowling coach was put on alert that his new boss is coming back to NU to do more than help keep the struggling football program from throwing too many gutter balls.

"I will certainly serve all sports equally," Osborne said before a packed crowd in the Van Brunt Visitors Center late Tuesday afternoon after being announced by UNL Chancellor Harvey Perlman as Nebraska's interim athletic director.

And you thought the Huskers' legendary former coach — who agreed to an open-ended deal that pretty much means he can be in the position for as long as he wants — had gotten out of politics.

Oh, well. At least he didn't have to think of something nice in case someone asked him about his initial thoughts of Lincoln.

For 31 years before he was elected to represent Nebraska's 3rd Congressional District and then failed in a gubernatorial bid, the 70-year-old Osborne was at the center of the Nebraska football program, serving six seasons as a full-time assistant under Bob Devaney before succeeding him in 1973.

Osborne led the Huskers to 12 Big Eight Conference titles, one Big 12 crown and three national championships that continued to unify the state from border to border, an effect brought on by his predecessor, Devaney.

Essentially, that is why Perlman came to him Friday and then again on Sunday, after he had determined Steve Pederson had lost the credibility to move the athletic department and, particularly, the football program forward.

Pederson, who twice had served under Osborne and came to Nebraska as athletic director in January 2003, was fired on Monday, and Perlman moved swiftly to entice Osborne into returning.

See NU, Page 2A

Sports/1C

■ Steven M. Sipple: Bringing in Osborne is a good start.

■ Callahan gives his take on the situation.

Local/1B

It looks like our suffering may be over/Cindy Lange-Kubick column

Opinion/7B

■ What's needed next? The restoration of order.

■ Readers weigh in with Letters to the Editor.

TED KIRK/Lincoln Journal Star file photo

Former Nebraska coach Tom Osborne jogs into Memorial Stadium during pregame activities Saturday honoring the 1997 national championship team.

Lotter denied new trial

Judge rejects recanted testimony from former friend as reason to reopen murder case for man on death row.

BY JOE DUGGAN
Lincoln Journal Star

FALLS CITY — It seems infamous killers from Nebraska are out to get John Lotter.

Marvin Thomas Nissen helped put the 36-year-old Falls City man on death row in 1996. On Tuesday, Charles Raymond Starkweather helped keep him there.

In the same courtroom where a jury convicted Lotter of first-degree murder 12 years ago, Lotter lost his motion for a new trial for the 1993 killings of three people in a Humboldt farmhouse.

District Judge Daniel Bryan denied Lotter's motion Tuesday in Richardson County District Court. The judge made the decision after hearing about 20 minutes of, at times, spirited arguments from attorneys in the case, including references to a decision on recanted testimony in the Starkweather case.

A sworn statement from Nissen, which says he lied when he told a jury that Lotter shot all of the victims, failed to convince the judge that a new trial was necessary.

Afterward, the relatives of one of the murder victims embraced and expressed relief that they won't have to endure another trial.

"I was glad he (the judge) denied it," said JoAnn Brandon, whose daughter Teena Brandon was among the three people who died of gunshot wounds in the rented farmhouse.

While the judge's ruling was a blow to Lotter's efforts to escape execution, he still has other legal avenues to pursue. Lincoln attorney Paula Hutchinson, who is representing Lotter, said she will appeal Bryan's decision to the Nebraska Supreme Court.

Before Tuesday, the motion seemed to offer a reasonable chance for Lotter, who always had maintained his innocence. Lotter pinned his hopes on the affidavit from his former friend Nissen, who is serving a sentence of life in prison for the killings. Nissen's statement, given this summer, says he's the one

LOTTER

NISSEN

BRANDON

See TRIAL, Page 2A

Oct. 17, 2007

Old friend will give Huskers hope

He didn't exactly descend from a mountaintop. He came down a short hallway. But you get the idea.

He once again stood before the media Tuesday, as he has countless times, understated as ever. He was like a friend from an old neighborhood you haven't seen in years. You just pick up the conversation where it left off and walk away somehow feeling better.

He's like the grandfather a family leans on in tough times (or when you need a buck or two). The Nebraska football program has endured its share of tough times of late. Never mind that he shares blame in creating some of those tough times. Right now, that's not important.

At this moment, the Big Red family needs a steady hand, someone who has seen it all, done it all and won it all a few times.

Enter Tom Osborne, the most powerful interim athletic director in the history of college sports. Show me an interim athletic director who's being counted on to unify and energize an entire state, perhaps raise millions of dollars, not to mention rescue a tradition-rich football program from sinking to irrelevancy.

Show me an interim athletic director who next month probably will have to fire a football coaching staff and hire another.

Well, we knew the guy enjoys challenges.

This one will be a bear. That became clear watching Nebraska coach Bill Callahan during his weekly media luncheon earlier Tuesday. "These are tough times," Callahan admitted.

Indeed, Nebraska athletic director Steve Pederson's firing Monday created a "huge, huge distraction" for the Huskers, Callahan said. As if this team needed any more issues.

Pederson's dismissal likely rep-

UNL chancellor Harvey Perlman (left) chose former football coach Tom Osborne to take over the Husker athletic program from Steve Pederson. (Journal Star archives)

resented step one toward the end of Callahan's four-year run as head coach. It feels inevitable.

The 70-year-old Osborne would have to take care of step two — the firing of Callahan and his staff — barring a miraculous turnaround in the final five games by a woebegone team that has seemed rudderless for almost the entire season.

Osborne said he wouldn't evaluate the football program in a serious manner until the season ends. So, no staff changes for now.

However, Osborne clearly has made some observations about Callahan's crew. For instance, "Naturally, we'd like to see the intensity level pick up," he said.

No, it wasn't all shiny and happy. Osborne said he has only met with Callahan and his staff a cou-

ple times in Callahan's four years. There's really no relationship there, Osborne said. He wasn't complaining or trying to make it an issue. It was just a fact.

Four years and no relationship? That didn't feel right. Nor did it feel quite right Tuesday when Callahan was asked how he felt about the possibility of Osborne becoming athletic director.

"I would welcome anyone who's going to be in that leadership position," Callahan said coolly. "I have tremendous respect for whoever is at the helm."

So, why not mention Osborne's name? Why avoid it?

Maybe I'm reading into things, but probably not. This much is certain: Callahan looks tired. He sounded like a man who sees the writing on the wall. His program

looks tired. Fans are sick and tired. Pederson, love him or hate him, is a native son. His ouster was difficult to watch if you have any heart at all.

Yes, it's all very tiring and distressing.

Which is why Nebraska needs Osborne right now more than ever. Yes, the situation's become that dire. The Huskers have degenerated to levels nobody could've anticipated. There exists nobody more capable than Osborne of pumping life into the program and healing the fractures in Husker Nation.

Nebraska needs to get that "feeling" back. The sellout streak suddenly seemed in jeopardy. Not anymore. NU needs to continue filling the big stadium, or all else crumbles in the athletic department. Osborne to the rescue; indeed, there was no other choice for Harvey Perlman.

In a sense, Osborne returns to lead the cleanup of a mess he helped create. He did Frank Solich no favors by strongly suggesting Solich retain assistant coaches when new blood was needed. But this is no time to reopen those wounds.

NU needs to look forward. Perlman deserves kudos for acting swiftly. The thing is, this could get interesting. Behind the scenes, influential people already are building cases for the next Husker head coach. Bo Pelini and Turner Gill are the ones being mentioned most. It's all very speculative at this point, yet all very possible.

As of shortly after 5 p.m. Tuesday, when Osborne was introduced as the nation's most powerful interim AD, Nebraska fans once again found reason to believe. Reason to dream.

"There are no miracles, no quick fixes," Osborne cautioned.

His hire was a good start.

Oct. 25, 2007

'I think it's really a mistake to try to meddle. Where you see that being done, I don't think it usually works very well.

— Tom Osborne'

AD learning about department

Tom Osborne sat and chatted with embattled Nebraska football coach Bill Callahan on Wednesday morning.

It was nothing earth-shattering.

"We just talked in general," Osborne said late Wednesday afternoon. "It's not appropriate for me to try to intercede in anything."

Osborne has been Nebraska's interim athletic director for exactly one week. He's basically in an orientation period, he said, and trying to do more listening than talking.

By STEVEN M. SIPPLE

This much is certain: He wants to model his management style after that of former Nebraska athletic director Bob Devaney. The late Devaney was a Hall of Fame coach for the Huskers (1962-72) before working full-time as athletic director from 1967-93, serving as Osborne's boss while Osborne strolled the sideline.

"Bob just hired people and let them do their thing," Osborne said. "I think it's really a mistake to try to meddle. Where you see that being done, I don't think it usually works very well."

Osborne chose his words carefully. The Nebraska football team (4-4, 1-3 Big 12) has lost three straight games by wide margins, and many fans assume Callahan won't be back next season. Osborne reiterated that the fourth-year coach and his staff would be evaluated at the end of the season.

"With anything I say, I don't want to have people assume I'm necessarily out looking for other coaches, because I'm not," Osborne said. "I just hope we can finish strong these next four games."

For the most part, Osborne said, he has been trying to respond to correspondence, numbering in the hundreds, if not thousands.

"I'm being inundated with a lot of mail and phone calls," he said. "They're mostly well-wishers. Not much negative."

Osborne received about 50 letters Tuesday, said Randy York, Nebraska associate athletic director for communications. Osborne's e-mail bin, of course, overflows, as did the briefcase he carried out of the Tom and Nancy Osborne Athletic Complex around 5:30 p.m. Wednesday.

He was headed home to watch Nebraska play Texas in volleyball on television. He also

Consultant changed culture

Several Nebraska athletic department employees this week cited Steve Pederson's hiring of a consultant from the East Coast as a source for the troublesome culture that began to permeate the department this past summer.

William J. DeLeo, a retired executive for Light Holdings Inc. of Duquesne, Pa., was hired by Pederson "to come and help me evaluate the future growth of this department," Pederson said in August.

DeLeo, described by Pederson at the time as "a longtime friend and colleague," arrived in Lincoln for the first time in January to meet with top-level Nebraska athletic administrators. DeLeo began full-time duty in August, hired to help streamline operations and increase productivity within the department.

The consultant's hire ended up being counterproductive, according to four Nebraska athletic department employees and a university employee, who all spoke this week on the condition of anonymity.

When Pederson was fired on Monday, his management style and the resulting negative culture in the athletic department were cited as the primary reasons behind NU chancellor Harvey Perlman's decision.

Said one Nebraska athletic department employee: "(DeLeo) was big business, definitely corporate in nature. He attached a ton of formality to everything he did, which made it less efficient instead of more efficient. In my mind, he was the main contributor as to why Steve lost his job."

Before DeLeo came on board, Pederson essentially had an open-door policy for

staff members, according to the athletic department employees interviewed by the Journal Star. After DeLeo's arrival in January, Pederson became much less accessible, and DeLeo became a "protector" of sorts for Pederson, the employees said.

Pederson's dismissal effectively ended DeLeo's association with the university as well. DeLeo was paid a total of $30,000, plus expenses, for August and September and will receive approximately $7,500 for his work this month, according to Randy York, NU associate athletic director for communications.

Asked Friday about DeLeo's contributions at Nebraska, Husker executive assistant athletic director Marc Boehm said, "I'd rather not go into it." He declined to comment further.

Before this week's events, DeLeo had recently announced there would be quarterly performance evaluations for all employees. Under DeLeo's plan, employees' standard cost-of-living raises would have become merit-based increases, a plan that turned up the pressure throughout the department and created an extremely competitive and uncomfortable environment.

The plan won't go into effect now that Pederson has been fired.

"You're trying to focus on the student-athletes, and then all of a sudden we were going to be competing with our neighbors for money," one employee said.

Morale declined in the department as a "culture of fear-based leadership" developed, an employee said.

— Steven M. Sipple

planned to answer some of those letters.

"You don't want to have people feel you're not appreciative and that you don't care, so I'm trying to answer as many as I can," Osborne said. "That's taking a lot of time."

He had a meeting with the entire athletic department — about 230 people — Tuesday morning.

"My main priority is to get around and see

all of the personnel," Osborne said. "I want to get around and see them all personally. See where they work and talk to them a little bit. I want to find out a little bit more about what they do and what kind of things they think are priorities."

He has met individually with a few coaches and eventually wants to meet with them all.

"I think the thing I have to do right now

Nebraska interim athletic director Tom Osborne and Texas A&M athletic director Bill Byrne, a former Husker AD, were in the media spotlight before the Aggies took on the Huskers Oct. 20, 2007. (Ted Kirk)

more than anything is to listen to all of our coaches — not to tell, but to listen as carefully as I can," he said.

Osborne was hired as interim athletic director after Steve Pederson's firing last week. Pederson's management style was cited as a key reason for his dismissal.

Asked how he would describe morale in the athletic department before his hiring, Osborne said, "I know there were some people struggling. I don't know that I was around enough previously to have a real good sense of it.

"They tell me it's better now, that things are going well. It seems like the meeting (Tuesday) generally was well-received. I tried to express an appreciation for what they do and encourage them to express appreciation to other people who work with them.

"Hopefully, we can get that turned around."

Oct. 27, 2007

Promising picture was an illusion

AUSTIN, Texas — Nebraska football coach Bill Callahan frequently uses catch phrases. We've heard "Pound the rock," "Third down is the money down," and "Games in November are the games to remember," and so on.

And who can forget, "We're flipping the culture here."

It's more like he flushed the culture here.

No use piling on Callahan at this point. It's an unfair fight. His reign as Husker coach nears finality. Four games to go, and it figures to be a brutal march. Husker fans probably will wince several times today as Texas rolls up big yardage. Yes, the score could get ugly, as it has the previous three weeks.

By STEVEN M. SIPPLE

Nebraska has an 0-16 record under Callahan in games it has trailed at halftime. Any reason to believe the Huskers are going to suddenly rally behind the coaching staff at this stage?

I picture a casual college football fan from, say, New Mexico turning on the television today. I can imagine the guy turning to a buddy and saying, "So, there's Nebraska. It's wearing the same uniforms it always has worn. But, man, it just doesn't seem like Nebraska. Doesn't feel right. Something's missing. Where's the punishing ground attack, the attacking defense? Something must have happened."

A culture flip/flush — it stands as perhaps the most telling occurrence during Callahan's four-year tenure at NU. It's arguably played the lead role in the Huskers' startling demise.

Blame Steve Pederson more than Callahan. No need to pile on Pederson, either. He has been pilloried enough already. But let's face it, Pederson turned his back on many of the traits that made Nebraska unique when, in December of 2003 and early the following January, he doggedly pursued NFL coaches in the wake of Frank Solich's firing.

You know the story. Pederson became desperate in his search. Callahan was unemployed. You could almost hear Callahan saying, "Sure, I'm interested in the job, Steve, but you have to know what you're getting. I'm an NFL guy at heart, and I specialize in a West Coast offense that bears little resemblance to Big Red's previous systems."

And thus the spin began. Pederson would sell to Nebraska fans the notion that the

Assertions by athletic director Steve Pederson and football coach Bill Callahan that they could change the culture of Nebraska football turned out to be an illusion. (Robert Becker)

Huskers would upgrade talent because, after all, the West Coast system is NFL-friendly, and Callahan and his staff could lure talent in part by dangling NFL dreams in front of young prospects' cherubic faces.

Nebraska's culture — developed and nurtured over four-plus decades — has been missing ever since.

Suddenly, too many Huskers were playing at dear old NU and not for dear old NU, an important distinction.

Suddenly, the program lacked a significant amount of walk-on players willing to run through a wall if only to earn a spot on the kickoff-coverage unit.

Suddenly, the Huskers weren't doing much hitting in practice.

Nebraska, to a large degree, lost its identity. It says here that Nebraska needs an identity and culture more than most traditional powerhouse programs. Texas, Oklahoma and Southern California endured extended dry spells before returning to prominence without distinct identities. But unlike Nebraska, those schools are located in or near hotbeds of talent.

The Husker program needs something extra. It faces built-in limitations. It needs a strong and identifiable culture and a certain modus operandi that specializes in drawing the most out of players that don't necessarily come to campus with five-star ratings and NFL aspirations.

"It's about matching your scheme with the personnel and the situation you're in," said ESPN and ABC college football analyst Bob Davie, the former Notre Dame coach (1997-2001). "It's who can match the place they're at and the uniqueness it possesses (with) the personnel you can get on a consistent basis."

Notre Dame, for instance, traditionally has needed a physical ground game to win, Davie said. Ohio State, same thing. Florida, on the other hand, has plenty of speedy athletes at its disposal in a talent-rich state, so the Gators will spread the field with those burners and throw the ball to them.

"You may change that style initially," Davie said. "But there's a reason that over a period of years and years, schools have taken on certain identities. I think that's a huge part — figuring out a specific fit."

During his tenure at Nebraska, Bill Callahan found out that in college football, a team needs to have chemistry and an identity. The Huskers appeared to have neither in 2007. (William Lauer)

Callahan's system evidently isn't the right fit at Nebraska. What's more, this particular Husker team clearly lacks chemistry, synergy, and an identity — all those crucial intangibles that become especially important these days because talent is more evenly distributed nationally than ever before.

Some will say it's a lot of hyperbole, a lot of hocus-pocus, this discussion about culture and identity and chemistry. I respectfully disagree. And I broach this topic mostly because the Huskers' deficiencies in these areas — not to mention their substandard front seven on defense — probably preclude any chance of them pulling off a stunning upset today, thus sparking a late-season rally that would leave Huskerville more confused than ever.

Which is saying a mouthful, considering the unsettled feeling in the program since a 62-36 loss to Colorado in November 2001.

"It's easy to get the chemistry out of whack," said Nebraska interim athletic director Tom Osborne. "It's a lot more fragile than people think. It can be brought back, but sometimes it isn't going to be a one-year fix. It might not even be a two-year fix. Those are things I think people have to realize."

At season's end, Osborne, the laconic legendary former Husker coach, will sit down with Callahan and say something like, "Bill, it's just not working," and Callahan probably will retreat into a dark room to watch film as an NFL assistant coach or offensive coordinator. Not a bad fall-back plan.

His final Nebraska team will have no All-Big 12 players and no great leaders despite all those lofty recruiting rankings. The 2005 recruiting class that was ranked No. 5 nationally by Rivals.com? Well, it appears it ultimately will produce exactly one all-conference player — quarterback Zac Taylor last year.

In defending his program this week, Callahan cited Nebraska's current 11th-ranked recruiting class, as if fans will forget the Huskers' defense ranks 105th nationally.

Still, I feel for Callahan. He fell short at Nebraska not for lack of effort. He's a grinder and a passionate student of the game. He sells himself well. He sells his program well. Sells his methods well. He seemed to be making progress last season. He painted a promising picture of the future, but it turned out to be an illusion.

Sports/3C: Husker recruits top Super-State football teams

LINCOLN JOURNAL STAR

SUNDAY, NOVEMBER 25, 2007
LINCOLN, NEBRASKA

47 20
Details, 8B

★★

www.journalstar.com

'You have to remember that we never had a losing season over 40 seasons,
and now in the last four seasons we've had two. So the issue becomes, at what point are you still viable?'
— Nebraska's interim athletic director Tom Osborne

SEARCH IS ON

Osborne says 5-7 finish sealed the fate of Callahan and his assistants. The process of finding a new coach is under way.

Who's next?

Former Husker defensive coordinator Bo Pelini, defensive coordinator at LSU, is the name that keeps coming up as a possible candidate for the head coaching job at NU.

PELINI

Pelini has been contacted by an Atlanta search firm about the Husker position. Former NU star Turner Gill, now head coach at Buffalo, also is a possibility. Interim athletic director Tom Osborne has said he would like to talk to four or five potential candidates in the next few days.

GILL

A costly dismissal

With Saturday's firing of Bill Callahan, the University of Nebraska's athletic department is obligated to pay more than $5 million to 10 football staff members over the next 19 months.

Under terms of a five-year contract agreed to in September, Callahan is due $3.125

COSGROVE

million in a lump-sum payment within 60 days. Another $1.9 million is due NU's nine assistants, though such obligations would be reduced by whatever compensation those coaches would earn if they were hired elsewhere. The assistants were under contract through Jan. 31, 2009, except for defensive coordinator Kevin Cosgrove, whose contract extended to June 30, 2009. Cosgrove, the highest-paid of NU's assistants, would be due $372,000 over that period.

Beginning with the $2.2 million paid Oct. 31 to former athletic director Steve Pederson, the athletic department's total obligation to fired staff is close to $7.25 million. Funds are available through athletic department reserves held by the NU Foundation, officials have said.

ERIC GREGORY/Journal Star file photo
Bill Callahan leaves the field after Colorado's 65-51 victory over Nebraska on Friday, the day before the firing of the Nebraska head coach was announced.

READ MORE · SEE MORE · HEAR MORE

JournalStar.com

At Huskerextra.com

■ **Audio:** Hear interim athletic director Tom Osborne discuss the firing of Bill Callahan.

■ **Video:** Watch highlights of Osborne's news conference and see a retrospective on the 2007 season.

■ **Gallery:** Check out the photos that defined the Bill Callahan era.

■ **Weblog:** Have an opinion? Chime in at Life In The Red.

More in Sports

■ Tom Osborne said he expects to talk to "four or five" coaches about the job in upcoming days, **Page 1C**

■ Steven M. Sipple: Nebraska football forever will be about "More Than Winning," **Page 1C**

■ Joe Ganz and other Huskers react to Callahan's exit, **Page 2C**

Lincoln Journal Star

Bill Callahan's stay at Nebraska was awkward from the start.

Shortly after accepting the job in January 2004, Callahan gave a fiery speech to Husker fans during halftime of an NU basketball game at the Devaney Sports Center.

Callahan talked about how he needed the fans' "juice." At one point, the new coach said in an excited tone, "There is no place..."

Then he paused, glanced at his notes and finished with a loud" ... like Nebraska!"

Awkward indeed.

Callahan's uncomfortable four-year run as the head of the Husker football program came to an end Saturday.

Interim athletic director Tom Osborne terminated the contracts of Callahan and all of his assistant coaches, although some coaches have agreed to stay on and help with recruiting while Osborne looks for a new coach.

Osborne expressed regrets about the fact that a search was necessary. He had hoped Callahan and his staff would make it work.

After the team dropped to 4-4 with a loss to Texas A&M, Osborne met with the coaches.

"If you can win the next four games and go 8-4," he said, "there's no question that things are going to be fine."

He also said, "If we have a losing season, I don't think there's any way that this will work."

The team finished 5-7 after losing to Colorado 65-51 on Friday in Boulder.

Like every coach, Callahan had his critics, and he had his supporters.

He'll be missed at The Clipper, Callahan's barber shop on 12th Street.

Your eyes need to drift all the way down the corkboard, past the "CLIPPER CLIENTS in the NEWS" sign, past Herb and Ruth Henry's 60th anniversary announcement, past best wishes to Jerry L. Sellentin, past weddings and retirements and joy.

To the right of Roger Fred strom, holding high a 9-by-7-point buck across a full

See CALLAHAN, Page 2A

> *Where you start (recruiting) is in Nebraska. That's got to be your base. Then you get the best players you can from other places.* — Tom Osborne

Nov. 25, 2007

At NU, you win, doing it right way

Turns out, this Tom Osborne guy is a demanding boss, albeit one with compassion.

He says he dislikes sitting in judgment of anyone. He never envisioned firing anyone. He has never been fired himself.

But he came close.

We interrupt Nebraska's second national search for a football coach in the past four years to relive a thought-provoking bit of Osborne lore. It was 1976, four years into his exalted tenure as Husker head coach. His first four teams went 9-2-1, 9-3, 10-2 and 9-3-1.

The 1976 team ended the season with a 27-24 victory against Texas Tech in the Astro-Bluebonnet Bowl. It seemed a rather mundane triumph at the time.

Hindsight shows it was gigantic.

"That evening, one of the regents got me aside and said, 'I'm glad you won tonight because if you hadn't, you would've been fired,'" Osborne recalled Saturday.

Yes, fired despite a 76 percent winning percentage.

"Yet that was the nature of the deal here," he said.

Still is.

Always will be.

Nebraska football forever will be about "More Than Winning." You do things the right way, the Nebraska way. But you'd better win consistently along the way.

Osborne, Nebraska's interim athletic director, made that clear in announcing the firing of Bill Callahan and his staff. The second week into his new job, with the Huskers sporting a 4-4 record, Osborne laid out some ultra-challenging parameters for Callahan and company:

Run the table for the rest of the season, and you'll be welcomed back.

Win three of the last four games, and maybe things will work out for you.

Split the last four, and prepare for discouraging news.

So, Nebraska's 1-3 record down the stretch basically left Osborne with no choice.

In the end, the coaches knew exactly where they stood.

"It isn't all about winning and believe me, I understand that," Osborne said. "But if you lose a fairly large number of games by a significant margin, and you have reasonably good players — which I think we have — that means there may be some systemic issues, some underlying issues."

Here's the issue in a nutshell: Not only did Callahan's teams lose too often, the Huskers too often lost in embarrassing fashion.

By essentially telling Callahan he had to run the table to ensure his employment at Nebraska into 2008, Osborne applied intense pressure, especially considering the Huskers were underdogs in each of the final four contests.

Interestingly, Steve Pederson and Osborne sent the same message; they just expressed themselves differently. Pederson, in announcing Frank Solich's firing following the 2003 season, addressed the media in a manner that sounded like he was prepared by a PR firm. He was slick. Unlike Pederson's announcement of Solich's dismissal, Osborne said nothing about the program "gravitating toward mediocrity," but those parameters he outlined spoke volumes.

Osborne spoke from the heart. He doesn't need a PR firm. A search firm? Yeah, maybe.

Osborne spoke from experience — not as an athletic director, but as a former coach who understands the inherent pain and pressure of the coaching profession.

Osborne obviously has a big heart. But he also retains high expectations for the program. Parity? That's an excuse for other schools. At least that was the impression Osborne left Saturday.

Hear that Bo? Turner?

You knew Bo Pelini would be contacted. You have to figure Turner Gill eventually will be contacted. After that, well, stay tuned.

Nebraska ties would be nice for the next head coach, Osborne said, but aren't a prerequisite.

This much is certain: The next Husker head coach had better be prepared to make in-state recruiting a focus. Callahan came up short in that area.

"We're going to look hard in the state

By STEVEN M. SIPPLE

and find out every player we think can play," Osborne said. "I think these guys (Callahan's staff) did a pretty good job recruiting, but a lot of the focus was national. If we have lost some of the state's high school coaches along the way, we'll try to get them back. Because where you start is in Nebraska. That's got to be your base. Then you get the best players you can from other places."

Osborne speaks of a return to the Nebraska way — with walk-ons as a foundation. And without the baloney of national recruiting rankings.

He would like a quarterback who can run for first downs, if necessary, and a coach who understands Nebraska's football identity — an identity that has temporarily disappeared.

Osborne obviously longs for the days when teams used to despise playing Nebraska, "because they felt it for two or three weeks afterward. And I'm not saying we go back to running the wishbone or running 30 options a game. I'm just talking about how you play. You have to play with intensity."

It remains a fundamental expectation for Nebraska football.

Still is.

Always will be.

In announcing the firing of Bill Callahan, NU interim athletic director Tom Osborne spoke from experience. As a former coach, he understood the inherent pain and pressure of the coaching profession. (Ted Kirk)

Chapter 5: Bo is a go

Pelini made quick impression

The whole state watched as Nebraska interim athletic director Tom Osborne announced the firing of Bill Callahan on Nov. 24, 2007. Less than 10 days later, the media were again in attendance as Bo Pelini was named NU head coach. (Gwyneth Roberts)

STEVEN M. SIPPLE

The interview took place early on a Sunday afternoon on Nov. 25, 2007, in a small building at the Baton Rouge, La., airport.

"It was raining awfully hard, as I recall," Tom Osborne said months later.

Osborne, then Nebraska's interim athletic director, had fired Husker head coach Bill Callahan on Nov. 24 and was now just beginning to interview candidates for the vacancy. Bo Pelini was first up. No surprise there. As Callahan's program faltered late in the 2007 season, Pelini's name became prominent in speculation about

who would take over if Callahan were indeed fired. Heck, the Journal Star ran a four-column photo of Pelini on the day after Callahan was fired — the day Osborne and UNL chancellor Harvey Perlman traveled to Louisiana.

Before that rainy Sunday, Osborne and Pelini had never formally met. After their interview, Osborne strongly suspected he would ultimately hire Pelini.

"I think Bo struck me as being authentic," Osborne said. "So often when people do a job interview, you have a sense that you're not necessarily talking to the real person. They're trying to put their best foot forward, but maybe you're not seeing the whole person. I think Bo is fairly unpreten-

tious. What you see is pretty much the way Bo is. I like that part of it."

Osborne said he talked to four other coaches about the job (he declined to name them). But he said that one of the other four candidates specialized mostly in offense, another mostly defense and "two of them had been head coaches long enough that I don't know that you would distinguish offense or defense. They were head coaches."

Former Nebraska quarterback and assistant coach Turner Gill, the head coach at the University of Buffalo, was known to have interviewed for the position (Gill calls the offensive plays for the Bulls). It was widely believed that veteran

Wake Forest head coach Jim Grobe also interviewed for the NU job.

"Each of the guys I talked to had excellent qualities," Osborne said. "I think the value of that process is it gave me an opportunity to compare and contrast those individuals with what Bo brought to the table."

The process moved quickly. After interviewing Pelini in Baton Rouge, Osborne and Perlman traveled to Atlanta, site of Parker Executive Search, to interview the other four candidates all the same day. Schools hire search firms in part to protect the confidentiality of candidates.

"I met with them (the four other candidates) for an hour each, or an hour and a half," Os-

Tom Osborne had a special bond with running back Mike Rozier (30) and Turner Gill (12). Along with wideout Irving Fryar (27), Gill and Rozier had Osborne on the verge of his first national championship before a heartbreaking loss to Miami in the 1984 Orange Bowl. This photo was taken in 1983 at Memorial Stadium as Osborne and Steve Pederson (far right) waited with the Huskers to go onto the field. Pederson was Osborne's recruiting coordinator from 1982-86. (Journal Star archives)

borne recalled. "It was pretty well organized. I told Harvey I thought Bo would be the best, and he didn't disagree."

Osborne liked the fact Pelini specialized in defense because Nebraska faltered badly in that area in 2007 and the Big 12 features a slew of pinpoint passers and savvy offensive coaches. What's more, Osborne liked what he heard about Pelini as a leader — to be sure, players speak passionately about how hard Pelini gets them to play. Plus, having been defensive coordinator at Nebraska in 2003, Pelini was familiar with Husker tradition and the nuances of the program.

Gill, though, also offered some intriguing qualities. He not only was a sentimental choice among many Nebraska fans, he truly has proven to be a strong head coach at Buffalo. In 2007 — his second year at the school — Gill guided the Bulls to a 5-7 record. In the previous seven years, Buffalo had won a total of 10 games.

Of course, Gill also had played for Osborne, going 28-2 as Nebraska's starting quarterback (including 20-0 in the Big Eight) from 1981-83. Osborne was a groomsman in Gill's wedding.

"Coach Osborne, to be honest with you, was like a father to all of us," said former Husker I-back Mike Rozier, the Heisman Trophy winner who played with Gill. "We all re-

spected him. We wanted to play hard for him. He was a good leader. You know what I mean?

"But with those two? It was like father and son. I could say the same thing about me and Coach Osborne. But they were more that way. Coach Osborne was in charge of the team, and Turner was second in command, because he was the quarterback. And we all knew that. They were very close. Forever close."

So, yes, Gill's involvement in Osborne's hiring process tugged at a lot of fans' heartstrings.

But hiring Pelini, in this particular case, simply made more sense.

Dec. 1, 2007

"He (Pelini) really wasn't a big yeller and screamer. But when he did yell, it served a purpose. -- Barrett Ruud

Pelini brimming with confidence

In his only game as a head coach, albeit interim, Bo Pelini led the Huskers to a 17-3 victory against Michigan State in the 2003 Alamo Bowl. (Ted Kirk)

He doesn't remember all of the details. But he recalls that it was a home game. The sun was shining. The opposing team was driving down the field. The ball was snapped, the quarterback was just starting his five-step drop into the pocket, and ...

By STEVEN M. SIPPLE

"I hear Coach (Bo) Pelini say, 'Ah, crap, that's going to be a touchdown' — literally before the quarterback even finished his drop, long before he started his throwing motion," former Nebraska linebacker Steve Safranek said this week. "And Bo just turns around and walks away. He doesn't even watch the play. Three seconds later, the ball is thrown down the middle of the field. Touchdown."

Safranek, a backup Nebraska linebacker from 2001 to 2003, signaled in plays from the sideline for Pelini in 2003 when Pelini served as the Huskers' defensive coordinator. On this particular play, standout middle linebacker Barrett Ruud was assigned the deep middle part of the field. It was tough duty, but Ruud was especially fast and athletic.

However, Ruud took that one false step forward. Bad news. The slot receiver bolted toward — you guessed it — the deep middle part of the field. Pelini right away noticed Ruud's errant step, and that was all the coach needed to see. Indeed, touchdown.

Would Nebraska score a touchdown by hiring Pelini as its next head coach? The hiring appears to be on the verge of occurring.

A lot of people feel Pelini is a strong fit for the Nebraska job, although Turner Gill has garnered ample support. Both men are relatively young coaches excelling in their current roles — Pelini, 39, as LSU's third-year defensive coordinator, and Gill, 45, as Buffalo's second-year head coach. Both have bright futures in the business. Players obviously play hard for both guys.

Pelini, however, possesses some intangible qualities that might make him particularly well-suited for the Nebraska job. For instance, Pelini's relatively rugged and cocksure persona probably would hold up well under the withering pressure that often permeates the Husker head coaching position.

Pelini is ultraconfident in both his defensive approach and his overall coaching ability. He said recently there's "absolutely no question" he's ready to be a head coach.

Bill Callahan struggled with the expectations and scrutiny at Nebraska. You could see pressure taking a toll on him. Any Husker head coach had better have thick skin. He had better be ultraconfident and unwavering in his assuredness with his system. I'm not suggesting Gill wouldn't handle the heat at NU, I'm just saying I think it might come more easily for Pelini. It's just a thought.

Pelini's confidence in large part stems from his wisdom, his players say. The Youngstown, Ohio, native has worked for a long list of the game's top minds in the NFL and college, men such as George Seifert, Pete Carroll and Bob Stoops.

Pelini's intelligence, confidence and hard edge tend to rub off on his players. In 2003, as Nebraska's interim head coach for the Alamo Bowl, Pelini's personality obviously rubbed off on both sides of the ball. The Huskers emerged from the pregame locker room snorting fire and defeated Michigan State 17-3. Big Red was razor-sharp that night.

Ruud, now a starter for the NFL Tampa Bay Buccaneers, is a strong backer of Pelini. Like Safranek, Ruud speaks of Pelini's ability to foresee occurrences on the field and anticipate how offenses will respond in certain situations.

Huskers who played under Bo Pelini in 2003 say they appreciated the way he related life's events to football. One of his most frequent messages was: "The time is now." (Journal Star archives)

Ruud remembers Pelini installing a new blitz early in the week of the Texas A&M game in 2003. Pelini guaranteed the blitz would work well and, in fact, told Ruud he would pick off a pass as a result. Sure enough, Nebraska employed the blitz, a Texas A&M receiver ran a slant route, and Ruud jumped in front of the receiver, snared the ball and sprinted for a touchdown.

Maybe this Pelini guy really would be a touchdown for Nebraska.

One coach has told me that he always appreciated Pelini's will-

ingness to try to learn why a player makes mistakes. Pelini tells fellow coaches that players aren't trying to make mistakes. He tells coaches to take time to ask players what was going through their minds on a certain play.

"He really wasn't a big yeller and screamer," Ruud said of Pelini. "But when he did yell, it served a purpose. You knew something was wrong. Sometimes when a coach yells all of the time, it goes in one ear and out the other."

Safranek and Ruud appreciated the way Pelini related life occurrences to football. He often

wowed Nebraska players with his messages on Friday nights, when the defense met as a group in the team hotel. Special-teams players eventually began showing up for the Friday night sessions.

One of Pelini's most frequent messages: "The time is now," he would say. Seize the moment.

All signs indicate the time is now for Pelini to lead Nebraska.

He'll be the first to tell you that he's ready for the challenge, and the Huskers could use a big dose of unwavering confidence right now.

Dec. 1, 2007

"He always had a way of motivating the defense. It was something I've never seen before or heard. He was just so intense. -- Ex-Husker punter Sam Koch"

Sources say Pelini has the job

While the men whose voices mean everything in this deal won't confirm it, others are saying the search for Nebraska's next football coach is over.

According to multiple sources, Nebraska will hire Louisiana State defensive coordinator Bo Pelini some time early next week.

By BRIAN CHRISTOPHERSON

Two sources told the Journal Star that a news conference could come as early as Sunday. ESPN reported the deal, "barring any last-minute snags."

Contacted by the Journal Star by phone on Friday night, Pelini denied the report, and then said:"I honestly don't know where they're getting their information."

When reached, Nebraska interim athletic director Tom Osborne was asked if the report was true.

"I'm not going to comment," Osborne said. "There are so many reports with the Internet and the radio and all of that. When the time comes, there will be an announcement, and it will be final."

He said such an announcement is still "a couple two or three days away. ... We've interviewed several people. I don't know if we'll interview anybody else. We're just going to let things take their course."

The Journal Star first reported on Nov. 24, the day that Bill Callahan was fired, that Pelini had been contacted by a private search firm working with NU officials.

The next day, Pelini was the first of three known candidates to interview with Osborne, the others being Buffalo head coach Turner Gill and Wake Forest head coach Jim Grobe.

Though never a head coach, Pelini has been mentioned often in connection with various job openings around the country. Syracuse and Pittsburgh are

Turner Gill and Bo Pelini were both assistants under Frank Solich in 2003. And in 2007, they were both candidates to succeed Bill Callahan as Nebraska's head football coach. (William Lauer)

among schools that have shown great interest in Pelini.

Pelini has been something of a cult hero in Nebraska ever since his one year as the Huskers' defensive coordinator in 2003. NU ranked 11th in total defense and led the country in turnover margin that season.

The year before Pelini arrived, Nebraska ranked 55th in total defense. The year after he left, the Huskers were 56th.

Since coming to the college game in 2003, teams Pelini helped coach have won 10 or more games every season.

It's true some have wondered if Pelini's temperament is suitable to be a head coach. Often cited is the day Pelini raced across the field after a 38-9 Husker loss and unleashed a verbal barrage on then-Kansas State coach Bill Snyder.

Then there was the time Pelini was assessed a 15-yard penalty for yelling at officials about a questionable call in the 2003 Alamo Bowl.

But Pelini's fire seemed only to endear him more to NU fans.

When he left the field after the 17-3 win against Michigan State in the Alamo Bowl, fans chanted: "We want Bo! We want Bo!"

As former Husker punter Sam Koch recently told the Journal Star, Pelini just had a way about motivating players.

"I loved the day before a game, going into defensive meetings just to hear his words," Koch said. "He always had a way of motivating the defense. It was something I've never seen before or heard. He was just so intense."

Many have predicted that Osborne will choose either Pelini or Gill for the job.

Buffalo athletic director Warde Manuel told the Buffalo News that Gill told him he hadn't heard anything from Nebraska regarding the job.

As for Pelini, some thought he should have been picked as the Husker head coach four years ago when he interviewed with Steve Pederson.

Instead, it was Callahan. Was Pelini ready then to be a head coach?

"Oh, yeah, I was ready," Pelini recently told Yahoo! Sports. "But I'm even more ready now."

> **We wanted to come out and win it for (Pelini). ... We wanted to send him out with a bang if he wants to leave.**
> -- LSU defensive end Kirston Pittman

Leaving LSU for his dream job

ATLANTA — He laughed as two players dumped a cooler of water on him. He literally jumped into the arms of 6-foot-5 senior linebacker Luke Sanders.

And then Bo Pelini did a curious thing.

As Louisiana State football players celebrated their Southeastern Conference championship in one end zone, Pelini jogged off toward the opposite end of the Georgia Dome alone and through a tunnel leading to the locker room, perhaps leaving a field for the final time as the Tigers' defensive coordinator.

Before Saturday's game — a 21-14 triumph against Tennessee — Pelini told his defenders he's leaning toward taking over as Nebraska's head coach, said senior defensive end Kirston Pittman.

Pelini didn't say he was leaving LSU for sure, Pittman said.

"He didn't say it in those exact words," Pittman said. "But he did tell us that (Nebraska) was his dream job and the opportunity of a lifetime. We respect him as a coach for coming out and telling us that he was leaning toward it."

Pittman said Pelini told his players he would inform them of his situation either after the game or today. Turns out, Pelini didn't discuss the matter with players right after the game, according to several of them, and the coach was tight-lipped with reporters in the postmortem. He declined to say if he's taken the NU job.

Friday night, multiple sources told the Journal Star that a news conference could occur as early as today formally announcing Pelini's hiring as Nebraska head coach. The 39-year-old Pelini has spent the last three seasons as Louisiana State's defensive coordinator. He had the same job at NU in 2003.

He said after Saturday's game he was "totally consumed" this past week with beating Tennessee.

"We'll see what happens over the next couple of days," Pelini said of the Nebraska job. "I'm just enjoying this championship. We worked long and hard and went through a lot together. There are a lot of teams that would've folded after that Arkansas loss (last week). There were a lot of disappointed young men. They showed their heart. They showed their character and what it takes to be champions."

After allowing Arkansas to gain 513 yards — including 385 on the ground — in last week's 50-48 triple-overtime loss in Baton Rouge, La., Louisiana State held Tennessee to 343 yards, and the Tigers came up with two critical interceptions, including one that produced the winning touchdown.

"A lot of teams were doubting whether we could come back," Pelini said. "I heard it all week long. But there was no question in our mind."

Said Pittman: "We wanted to come out and win it for (Pelini). ... We wanted to send him out with a bang if he wants to leave."

Louisiana State cornerback Chevis Jackson said he was surprised before the game when Pelini told his players he was leaning toward leaving for Nebraska.

Said Tigers linebacker Derry Beckwith, whose late interception helped preserve the victory: "Coach Pelini's meant a lot to us. He's a players' coach, and he's always there for you when you need a helping hand."

Nebraska's defense — which ranks 112th nationally in yards allowed and points allowed — obviously could use a boost.

"I'll tell you what, he would deserve a head coaching job," Louisiana State athletic director Skip Bertman said of Pelini. "He's an excellent, excellent coach. And he's the kind of guy who's been in this business long enough to know enough people to fill a coaching staff."

Good programs should expect their assistant coaches to be hired by other teams as head coaches, Bertman said.

"Now, I'm not saying that's happened in this case," the AD said.

At any rate, signs point toward Pelini succeeding Bill Callahan, who had a record of 27-22 in four seasons at Nebraska.

"It's a hard business," Pelini said. "Winning championships doesn't come around every year. We put a lot work in. We went through a lot together. We wanted to finish this season off the right way and win the SEC. That's really all I was concerned with. Speculation, that was for other people to concern themselves with.

"I'm just looking to go relax and get some sleep on that (team) plane. We'll see what happens over the next couple of days."

By STEVEN M. SIPPLE

Bo Pelini spent three years as the defensive coordinator at Louisiana State. Before that, he was co-defensive coordinator at Oklahoma and led the Blackshirts for one year. But when the Nebraska head coaching position opened, he said it was his dream job. (Journal Star archives)

Dec. 3, 2007

From the get-go, I always thought Bo Pelini was a good guy. He's gonna get people excited.

— NU fan Dan Hoien of Lincoln

Pelini: It's time to go to work

We hardly recognized the man.

Why, Bo Pelini looked like about 1.7 million bucks as he strolled before the people Sunday afternoon wearing a sharp suit and a fancy new title — Nebraska's head football coach.

No gray sweat shirt. No wad of gum.

Four years ago, after serving as Nebraska's interim coach for one game, he left a football field to chants of "We want Bo!"

By BRIAN CHRISTOPHERSON

The people got Bill then. They have Bo now.

"We were only here for nine months or a year, whatever it was; it seemed like three years," Pelini said, his wife and three kids sitting close by. "But you recognize something special. Everything associated with Nebraska football and the University of Nebraska is something special."

Pelini said all of the proper things, thanking Tom Osborne, praising Frank Solich, speaking of the importance of the walk-on program.

On Saturday, before his LSU defense took the field to play in the SEC title game, he told his players he could be leaving for Nebraska.

He told them it was his dream job.

"I think that's what makes the University of Nebraska unique over any place I've been coaching — how much it means to the state," Pelini said. "It's like one big family, and that's what I want it to be."

His words were heard by many across the state who listened on radio or watched on television.

At 3:57 p.m., TV screens at Brewsky's downtown went to a

Nebraska interim athletic director Tom Osborne thrilled Husker Nation when he announced on Dec. 2, 2007, that Bo Pelini was the new Husker football coach. (Ted Kirk)

live shot at Memorial Stadium.

A buzz filled the room of red-clad diners.

At 4:02, Osborne appeared at the podium.

Suddenly, quiet. When The Wizard speaks, you put down the club sandwich and listen.

Osborne cracked a few jokes, drawing laughter, and then he introduced the man Husker fans hope is the saving grace of Nebraska football.

Applause. Hope. Bo.

"There he is! There he is!" someone shouted.

"You can't do much worse, Bo!" someone else said.

Yes, Pelini's arrival seems sweet relief for fans, sore after a 5-7 season that led to Bill Callahan's firing Nov. 24, eager for a new

leader to fire up a team that has produced some of the worst statistics in Husker history.

Their verdict: Give Bo a little time. The Huskers will be back.

"From the get-go, I always thought Bo Pelini was a good guy," said Dan Hoien, 30, of Lincoln. "He's gonna get people excited."

Echoed Jordan Henthorne, a University of Nebraska-Lincoln freshman from Papillion: "He's going to be a good fit. He seems to be really fired up."

Fans spoke almost unanimously about the need for a new-and-improved defense — a specialty for Pelini, who for the past three years has been Louisiana State's defensive coordinator.

In fact, they wouldn't mind a

bit if Pelini calls a few defensive plays himself.

"We need to get the Black-shirts back," said Luke Kruse, 25, of Norfolk.

They also spoke of the importance of recruiting, which had slipped a bit as Callahan's firing drew near.

Oh, and if Pelini happens to go on a rant or two against a referee next year?

Seems safe to say fans are going to give him a pass.

Well, at least 25-year-old Brandon Fisher will cut him some slack.

"I'm glad we got him," Fisher said. "We need some intensity, someone that has some fire."

LINCOLN JOURNAL STAR ■ MONDAY, DECEMBER 3, 2007 ■ SECTION D

HUSKER EXTRA

SEARCH COMPLETE

BACK TO THE BAYOU?: LSU coach Miles says Pelini will coach in BCS title game; Pelini wants to talk to Osborne about it, **PAGE 5D**

ASSISTANT COACHES: Former Husker Alberts says Nebraska will have one of the best coaching staffs in the country, **PAGE 5D**

PLAYERS REACT: Huskers have brief meeting with new coach and already like his energy, **Page 5D**

CURT McKEEVER: Osborne approached this search the right way, **Page 6D**

Bo's show

PELINI BECOMES NEBRASKA'S 28TH HEAD FOOTBALL COACH

ABOVE: Bo Pelini walks the sideline during the 2003 Alamo Bowl — his last game at Nebraska prior to his hiring. BELOW: Pelini addresses the media during Sunday's news conference while Tom Osborne listens.

LINCOLN JOURNAL STAR file photo

A long, busy journey brings Pelini to Lincoln

BY BRIAN CHRISTOPHERSON
Lincoln Journal Star

Let the speculation cease. The stories of who you just saw at Duncan Aviation are no longer important to the masses.

Nebraska has a head football coach, and after the Sunday he had, you couldn't blame Bo Pelini when he laughed and said: "I'm just looking forward to taking a nap."

Sunday morning started simply enough for the Pelinis. Dressed the kids. Went to 9 o'clock Mass.

Ordinary stuff. Then things got a little nuts. A flight on a charter airplane. A handshake with a new boss. A news conference viewed by about everyone in Nebraska.

"I'm more prepared today than I was four years ago to be a head football coach," Pelini said.

Four years ago, after just a year as a defensive coordinator at Nebraska, Pelini was the people's choice to coach the Huskers after Frank Solich was fired.

He wasn't Steve Pederson's. Pelini left for other adventures. Nebraska football turned south.

But the story of four years ago is an old one, one Pelini wasn't about to get into on a day as joyous as Sunday was for him.

At age 39, he's a head football coach for the first time.

"You never know in this life," Pelini said. "Things come back around."

In introducing Pelini as the replacement for Bill Callahan, Nebraska interim athletic director Tom Osborne said the LSU defensive coordinator "fit the bill in all respects."

"Of greatest concern to me was defense, the ability to stop people," Osborne said. "As you know, occasionally you'll win a game if you give up 50 points, but you're not going to win very many.

See PELINI, Page 5D

MICHAEL MANNAMARA/Lincoln Journal Star

READ MORE • SEE MORE • HEAR MORE

JournalStar.com

AUDIO: Listen to Sunday's news conference.
VIDEO: Watch Sunday's news conference.
VIDEO: Listen to what Tom Ganz, Trev Alberts and Tom Osborne have to say.
VIDCAST: Steven M. Sipple's take.

☑ OSBORNE'S CHECKLIST

A look at the three things interim athletic director Tom Osborne wanted in a Nebraska football coach:

Emphasis on defense

Nebraska ranked near the bottom of the NCAA in total defense this past season. Since Bo Pelini left Nebraska after the 2003 season, the Black shirts haven't been the same. Pelini's defenses at Oklahoma and LSU ranked no lower than 13th.

Leadership

Pelini hasn't been a head coach at any level. He put together a strong game plan for the 2003 Alamo Bowl as interim coach — and the result was a 17-3 win against Michigan State. He's been mentored by the likes of George Seifert, Pete Carroll and Bob Stoops.

Knows NU's tradition

Pelini got a taste of Husker Nation in 2003.

" ... that's what makes the University of Nebraska unique over any place I've been coaching — how much it means to the state. It's like one big family, and that's what I want it to be."

Pelini, Osborne form an intriguing team

STEVEN M. SIPPLE
Journal Star Staff Writer

Bo Pelini isn't real big on small talk.

"I don't always say a whole lot," he told me recently. "But I notice everything."

As he climbed the coaching ladder, Pelini presumably noticed the strongest traits of George Seifert, Ray Rhodes, Pete Carroll, Mike Sherman, Les Miles, Bob Stoops and Frank Solich — men Pelini mentioned Sunday as being mentors.

Now comes the chance to learn from another mentor. This will be fascinating to watch — Pelini and Tom Osborne. The brash and at times only emotional former Ohio State free safety learning from the famously calm and understated former congressman and legendary coach. Together they will try to pull Nebraska from the depths of a startling football depression that sometimes seems surreal.

Pelini will notice everything about Osborne, if the 39-year-old Pelini is as wise as he seems.

Some will say it's an odd couple. Well, Bob Devaney and Osborne were disparate personalities who seemed to mesh OK.

People often forget Osborne was a fiery coach in his younger days. However, few have forgotten Pelini's angry con-

See SIPPLE, Page 5D

Dec. 3, 2007

> **I'm going to be who I am. I'm not going to change. Bo Pelini's not going to change.** — Bo Pelini

An odd couple? Not necessarily

Bo Pelini isn't real big on small talk.

"I don't always say a whole lot," he told me recently. "But I notice everything."

As he climbed the coaching ladder, Pelini presumably noticed the strongest traits of George Seifert, Ray Rhodes, Pete Carroll, Mike Sherman, Les Miles, Bob Stoops and Frank Solich — men Pelini mentioned Sunday as being mentors.

Now comes the chance to learn from another mentor. This will be fascinating to watch — Pelini and Tom Osborne. The brash and admittedly emotional former Ohio State free safety learning from the famously calm and understated legendary coach and former congressman. Together they will try to pull Nebraska from the depths of a startling football depression that sometimes seems surreal.

By STEVEN M. SIPPLE

Pelini will notice everything about Osborne, if the 39-year-old Pelini is as wise as he seems.

Some will say it's an odd couple. Well, Bob Devaney and Osborne were disparate personalities who seemed to mesh OK.

People often forget Osborne was a fiery coach in his younger days. However, few have forgotten Pelini angrily confronting Bill Snyder in 2003. People remind Pelini of the incident at seemingly every turn. In fact, he was reminded just before dinnertime Sunday, as he was announced as Nebraska's 28th head football coach.

Surely the Snyder situation was the impetus behind the reporter's question: Your emotions and passions, will you have to temper them now? After all, goes the line of thinking, Pelini's now a head coach for the first time.

Pelini paused. He chuckled. It was a nervous chuckle. He started to answer, then paused. It was sort of uncomfortable for a few seconds.

No problem. Pelini's newest mentor was sitting right behind him. Pelini turned and looked at Osborne, as if seeking guidance. Osborne shrugged his shoulders, as if to say, "You're on your own on this one, young fella."

Everyone laughed and comfort returned.

Let the Pelini era begin.

"I'm going to be who I am," Pelini said. "I'm not going to change."

He repeated it for emphasis.

Back in 1973, Tom Osborne faced the media after being named NU football coach amid high expectations. So he knew what Bo Pelini was going through when he took over the NU program. (Journal Star archives)

"Bo Pelini's not going to change."

The native of Youngstown, Ohio, is a boxing fan and a devoted family man. He enjoys Bruce Springsteen and coaching defense. Baby, he was born to lead (my apologies to The Boss). At least that's what virtually every one of his former players will tell you. They'll tell you he has a natural way of inspiring them. Maybe it's his glare, or his tough-guy persona, or his ultraconfident demeanor, or his sheer intelligence. He's whip-smart.

Whatever the case, he gets players to play hard.

"If you don't play hard, you don't have much of a chance," said Osborne, the most powerful interim athletic director in the history of college sport.

Consider this particular hire. Consider the ramifications. How much farther can Nebraska football sink before it permanently becomes a mere shadow of its former power, prestige and utter brilliance? There's plenty of pressure here, folks.

It's interesting that Osborne is entrusting his beloved program to a first-time head coach. He said he hired Pelini after considering "a lot of well-qualified people," including Turner Gill, the beloved former Husker quarterback who Osborne adores like a family member. Gill, 45, is showing signs of becoming a top-shelf major-college coach.

However, Osborne analyzed the program and determined defense, or lack thereof, topped the list of concerns

"As you know, occasionally you'll win a game if you give up 50 points, but you're not going to win many," Osborne said.

In coming days, Pelini will turn on film of Nebraska's games this season and the new Husker coach will be repulsed. He will see a team that struggled to adjust on the fly. Worse, he will see a defense that too often lacked energy. That too often played with little-to-no passion. Its ineptitude was stunning at times.

Pelini may not be as smooth with the media as Bill Callahan. Callahan sounds like a corporate CEO at times. Pelini is more of a salt-of-the-earth type. Yes, it sounds trite, but Pelini is a people person. He's a notorious prankster. He likes being around players. He means it when he says he'll have an open-door policy. His players seem to trust him and

enjoy playing for him, which probably explains why they swarm to the ball and force turnovers — Pelini trademarks.

Never will a Pelini defense (or team) play without emotion.

Pelini is only half-joking when he tells friends with a straight face that he's the only one who can handle this mission. He has a way of expressing confidence that's much more endearing than it is a turnoff. Nebraska needs his confidence badly right now.

Some will say Nebraska needed a veteran head coach right now, someone who's been there, done that in a power conference. But given the Huskers' immediate needs, Pelini fits well — right man, right time.

Hard decisions loom. What type of offense will he employ? For now, he says only that Nebraska will be "very multiple." Reading between lines, it appears Pelini may favor an offense that resembles the one in place, meaning Shawn Watson may well be in line for offensive coordinator. Stay tuned.

Will Pelini continue to coach Louisiana State's defense as it prepares for the national title game? That's a tough call, he says. Again, stay tuned.

Pelini's first day as Nebraska head coach seemed to go well. He passed the news conference test with flying colors. It was especially nice to hear Pelini acknowledge Solich, who hired Pelini in 2003 to revive the Huskers' defense.

"I think people along the way have forgotten how important he was to Nebraska and what he did over a long period of time," said Pelini, who now begins the challenging task of trying to restore and invigorate an entire program.

Indeed, it's no time for small talk.

Bo Pelini's fiery demeanor endeared him to Husker fans in 2003. They hope that passion for the game carries over to the team in 2008. (Ted Kirk)

No time for birthday parties

Bo Pelini hit the ground running when he took over the Nebraska football program, recruiting and finalizing his coaching staff. (Michael Paulsen)

A Bo Pelini name plate already has a home on the desk. A basketball owns space on the floor behind it.

By BRIAN CHRISTOPHERSON

Nebraska's new football coach picked it up, bounced it a few times, before offering an imitation of the left-handed jump shot that helped him score more than 1,000 points back in his high school days.

If he wasn't busy with this coaching football, Pelini joked he'd be playing for the Knicks.

Maybe he wasn't joking. The Knicks might need him.

On his 40th birthday, Pelini was in good spirits as he spoke Thursday about his first 11 days on the job, the national title game, and his relationship with Nebraska interim athletic director Tom Osborne.

Life's a blur right about now for Pelini, who will leave early next week to help coach LSU in one more game, a national championship showdown against Ohio State on Jan. 7.

"I can't wait to do it," Pelini

Bo Pelini introduced his staff, many of whom worked with him on Frank Solich's staff in 2003, at halftime of the Husker men's basketball team's game against Kansas on Jan. 13, 2008. (Gwyneth Roberts)

said. "And I expect to be there (someday) as a head coach. That's the next thing. The more times you get in that situation, the more prepared you are when it happens to you."

Pelini said it was easy deciding if he should go back and coach LSU in the BCS title game. He was the Tigers' defensive coordinator for the past three years. You don't walk out on a team when it gets one step from winning it all.

"I could never live with myself. I couldn't walk out on those kids. I like to finish what I start," he said. "They want me to do it. They asked me to do it. I want to do it. Coach Osborne wants me to do it. I think our kids here want me to do it. When I met with them I asked a couple of them how they feel about it. They said, 'Sheesh, you should be (coaching that game).'"

Since taking the Nebraska job Dec. 2, Pelini's been flying around — literally — trying to recruit and finalize his coaching staff.

The staff is now pretty much in place. An official announcement will come in a day or two, he said.

"I feel real good about where we are and what we've accomplished up until now," he said.

And given that Dec. 17 is the start of a re-cruiting dead period that runs through the bowl season, Pelini doesn't think it will be a big deal that he's helping the Tigers.

"It's not like you practice and go all the way through the game. There's time in there around Christmas and the holidays," Pelini said. "If there's something I'm needed to do, to come back and take care of, obviously I will do that."

Pelini is also of the mind that coaching in the national title game could be a great recruiting tool for Nebraska.

"I think that's a fact, but that wasn't my motivation for doing it," Pelini said. "I did it because it's the right thing to do."

It's assumed the national television audience will see plenty of close-ups of Pelini, mentioning his new job at Nebraska along the way.

Yeah, life is good — a new office, a giant Bo birthday cookie on the front counter, and a national title game to get ready for.

And, yes, he'll be ready for it, he assured.

"It's not that big of a deal to me. I'm a multi-task person anyway. You just say, 'OK, this is what you have to do. These are things you have to get done," Pelini said.

"I've had time to get ready. ... I've just had a lot of other things on my plate to do, but I've done a little bit at a time. I'm about ready. I know what Ohio State does."

In this time of transition, Pelini said Osborne has been someone he's turned often to for advice.

"Some things that you may think are very small and trivial, I ask him, 'What do you think here?' Just day-to-day things," Pelini said. "If anything, I probably drive him crazy sometimes."

Pelini made clear that Osborne is not the type of guy who tries to interfere.

"At no point has he ever said, 'I want you to do this, I want you to do that.' He says, 'You need to do what you see as best,'" Pelini said.

Did Osborne suggest that Pelini hire certain guys on the staff?

"No. He just gave me information. And I asked him for information. I said, 'How do you see it? What is your evaluation?' There's not one person he told me to hire. I'm sure he wouldn't have hired some of the guys I did.

"What he does is provide you with information. And, obviously, he has good information."

Dec. 16, 2007

> He had overwhelming confidence, and it sort of rubbed off on the whole team.
> -- Don Bucci, Bo Pelini's high school coach

Coach's Ohio roots remain solid

By BRIAN CHRISTOPHERSON

Mark Pelini grew up in Youngstown, Ohio. It's where he was a star high school athlete. It's not too far from where he attended Ohio State. It's where, his peers say, he became a leader. It's where Mark Pelini became Bo.

This is before the San Francisco 49ers called and before he met Pete Carroll, before there were T-shirt slogans built around his name.

This is before he sat in a room, a 26-year-old missing his fiancee, passing the hours with a guy named Ray Rhodes, watching film, talking football, taking notes.

Scribble down enough lessons, learn enough things, and one day, other people are writing down your wisdom.

This is before the "We Want Bo!" chants, a token interview and a moving van aimed toward Oklahoma, before the "BEAUX TIGERS" signs in Louisiana.

This is a story that goes back to Youngstown, Ohio.

"Hard-working people, that's home," Bo Pelini says. "Yeah, that's home for me. That's where I grew up. That's where I learned everything."

He may seem like he is Nebraska's now, the people's new hope, their football coach, but everything he brings here goes back to that town 900 miles away.

Youngstown is where Mark became Bo, where Bo met Mary Pat, he the quarterback, she the cheerleader. "Started dating senior year of high school," he says. Twenty-some years and three kids later, he calls her his "best friend."

It is where Pelini scored more than 1,000 points at Cardinal Mooney High School with a left-handed jump shot, and it is the place where his football skills caught the recruiting attention of an Ohio State coach named Earle Bruce.

Youngstown is where he goes back to every year, because once a Mooney kid, always a Mooney kid.

"I can give you one story about Bo," says the old high school coach on the other end of the phone.

Don Bucci coached football at Mooney for 34 seasons, won four state titles. He coached four Stoops boys and five Pelini boys, tough kids from the south side of town.

They gave him plenty of stories, stories that still make their way around the hallways today. Many kids play high school football. A few still get talked about 20 years after they walk out the door.

"We were playing a team," Bucci continues. "Bo was at quarterback and we were running what we called a stacked-I offense. So Bo pointed to one of the linebackers and told them we're going to be running the ball right here, off the right tackle. The fullback was yelling at Bo to shut up, stop telling them the play. But Bo told the guy, 'We're going to run the ball here and it's up to you to stop it.' Well, we ran the ball right there. Got about 10 to 15 yards, too. That's the whole story of Bo Pelini. That's Bo."

■■■

Anthony and Mary Catherine Pelini had eight kids, five boys and three girls, and every one of them earned a college degree.

Nancy was the oldest child and Mark was the youngest, though rarely did anyone call him Mark.

The Pelinis lived in a five-bedroom house. Actually, it was more like a three-bedroom house, but ingenuity applied here. A walk-in closet could become a bedroom for two.

Much of Youngstown was made up of families who had been in the United States for less than two generations.

It was a town for a long time dominated by steel mills until they went under in the '70s, not a place for pretty boys, better suited for Springsteen lyrics: "Well my daddy worked the furnaces / Kept 'em hotter than hell ..."

Mostly, the parents of Youngstown hoped that their children would have it better than they did.

Anthony Pelini fought in World War II and went to Ohio State on the GI bill. He was not an athlete like his sons, but still, he never missed one of their games.

"They sacrificed everything for us," Bo says of his mother and father. "He didn't push us into anything. We played when we wanted to play, but if we were out there, we better conduct ourselves the right way. We better act a certain way. If we didn't, that's when we heard it, and he'd get that fixed in a hurry."

Before finishing school at Ohio State, Anthony Pelini was hired as a pharmaceutical salesman, a profession he'd hold for more

than 30 years.

He settled his family in a house with a square driveway on a corner lot. Since it was on the corner, it had a slightly bigger yard than many houses in the neighborhood, a space that was well-utilized.

If a game was too big for the yard, the street soon was filled with a collection of sneakers — a football game breaking out between the mail boxes.

"We competed against each other on a daily basis, whether it was basketball, football, baseball, board games, it didn't matter," Carl Pelini says. "But we were also very supportive. At the end of the day, everyone was pulling for each other. You'd be playing a Little League baseball game, look up in the stands and all your brothers were there."

Sometimes they'd play a game in the front yard in which Carl would get on a knee and try to lead block against his brothers or neighbors. The youngest Pelini played the part of running back and he'd try to dive over the bodies for an imaginary six points.

Though his mom and dad kept calling him Mark, most everyone else took to calling him Bo.

It was a tag derived from a Cleveland Browns running back of the day named Bo Scott — tough guy, cool name.

Bo. Bo Pelini. It just sort of stuck.

■■■

Well, of course, this happened.

That's what they all say now. Of course, Bo Pelini became a head football coach.

People saw the leadership in high school.

"He had overwhelming confidence, and it sort of rubbed off on the whole team," Bucci says.

They saw the signs at Ohio State, where Pelini played as a defensive back from 1987-90.

"You could just tell he was kind of a born leader, a Youngstown, Ohio, guy. If you see who's been successful from Youngstown, there's quite a few," says Greg Frey, a former Buckeye quarterback who was a captain alongside Pelini. "Bo is the type who wears his emotion on his sleeve."

John Cooper had faster and more talented players at Ohio State, but the former coach says you could always count on Pelini for toughness, for playing football the right way.

"He never made any mental mistakes."

His confidence is what seems to strike people the most. Bucci thinks of a conversation he had with Pelini four years ago, shortly after he was passed up for the Nebraska job in favor of Bill Callahan.

Bucci remembers Pelini saying, "I'm not going to let it bother me. I'll be a head coach somewhere in a few years."

Being a coach wasn't necessarily in the plans back in 1992, when Pelini had just completed a master's degree in sports administration from Ohio University.

He worked as an assistant coach at Mooney in 1993, but admittedly things were "kind of at a lull." He was sending out coaching resumes, pondering taking a sales job with Nike.

Then came a call from Dwight Clark of the 49ers. "Want to be a scout?"

Pelini didn't really have ambitions to be a scout, but the 49ers don't call every day, and so he made the trip to San Francisco.

It possibly didn't hurt Pelini that Eddie DeBartolo Jr., then the 49ers owner, and Carmen Policy, then the chief executive officer of the team, were both Youngstown guys, too — Mooney grads even.

"Only guy in America that went from an assistant high school coach to the 49ers," Bucci says with a laugh.

It didn't take very long for Pelini to impress, going quickly from 49ers scout to assistant coach. Just weeks after his arrival, he was being recommended by assistant coach Rhodes as a strong candidate for an assistant defensive backs coach position in the organization.

Those nights of watching film and football chatter had provided more than just entertainment. It was the jump-start to a career.

Pelini was with the 49ers when they won the Super Bowl in 1995. He soon moved to New England to coach with Carroll, then to Green Bay to coach with Mike Sherman, then came a call from Frank Solich.

Pelini came to Nebraska an unfamiliar face. He left several months later as the people's choice, having transformed a Husker defense from mediocre to something that evoked pride again. They cheered his name as he left the field as NU's interim coach after a 17-3 Alamo Bowl win against Michigan State.

He was just 36. Tom Osborne was 35 when Bob Devaney handed him the keys.

Pelini interviewed with Steve Pederson to be Nebraska's permanent head coach. The interview didn't last long. A 41-day coaching search ended with Pelini nowhere in sight.

His career continued to roll anyway, with Pelini showing up in Oklahoma, assisting a Youngstown friend and Mooney grad, Bob Stoops.

Bob's dad coached Pelini in high school. "They're like brothers to us," Pelini says of the Stoopses.

After a year at Oklahoma, Pelini moved again, this time taking over as defensive coordinator at LSU, his job for the last three years.

"The unique thing about Bo, and I give him credit for this — because a lot of guys hang around a school as a grad assistant or maybe stay local — but when Bo left (Ohio State), it's almost like he disappeared," Cooper says. "To his credit, he went out on his own. He got into coaching and moved up the chain quickly."

Now, in a story that would sound ridiculous if it weren't true, Pelini has the job he wasn't given four years ago.

They're selling "Bo Big Red" shirts to prove it.

A couple weeks ago, with speculation swirling about him coming back to Nebraska, Pelini told his LSU players it was his dream job to coach the Huskers.

"When he said he got his dream job, he wasn't just talking," Carl Pelini says. "He did, and it's not just because it's a great BCS school. It's because it's Nebraska, and I know how much he wanted to coach there the first time."

Not surprisingly, Bo asked his brother, the same one who used to block for him in the front yard, to join him on his coaching staff.

It's no easy job, but a couple of guys from Youngstown probably wouldn't want it any other way.

"I can't even express the excitement," Carl Pelini says. "As you go through your career, you want to reach the pinnacle. You want to work for one of the great tradition-rich programs.

"And you always want to work with someone you trust and that has the same values you do, the same philosophies you do. It's even better when it turns out that person is your brother."

Dec. 21, 2007

I care about my players and my players know it. They know I have their back, and I believe they've got mine.

— Bo Pelini

Pelini provided calm, focus in '03

It was quite the deal — a one-month gig to push the buttons for the Nebraska football program.

And, oh, the buttons some people would have liked to have pushed back in December of 2003.

Tempers in the Husker camp were flaring enough two weeks into Bo Pelini's reign as in-

By CURT McKEEVER

terim head coach that players held a private meeting to discuss what could be done to sway athletic director Steve Pederson into giving Pelini a permanent promotion.

There was even a suggestion to boycott the Alamo Bowl game against Michigan State.

Leave it to Pelini, reputed by many to be the feistiest of the bunch, to break into that heated session and deliver a calm, passionate plea for reason.

He reminded the players that regardless of what might happen in his immediate future — left clouded by Pederson's firing of Frank Solich — he'd be fine. And, so, now all they needed to do was finish strong, with their heads up.

"We were out to win a football game, but we're going to do it the right way," Pelini said recently about his first, brief stint leading the Huskers. "That was a bit of a challenge, because there were a lot of guys, at that point, that their emotions were flying high — both within the staff and on the team.

"Part of my job was to draw them in, make sure they stayed together, that they believed in each other and believed in what we were going to do, and not get distracted," Pelini said. "I believe that's one of my strengths, what I've always been able to do.

"Things are going to happen. People are going to drift and there are going to be distractions out there, but you need to find a way

Bo Pelini earned his players' respect with the way he handled the team as interim coach in 2003. (Ted Kirk)

to get a common theme and get a guy to believe that we're going to keep this headed in the right direction no matter what."

Pelini not only stamped out brush fires and got a team that was bitter and confused over Solich's firing following a 9-3 regular season to refocus. He commanded the kind of attention that led to the Huskers' 17-3 victory.

Nebraska limited Michigan State to 174 total yards (209 less

than than its season average). Spartans senior quarterback Jeff Smoker, who averaged 269.9 yards passing, managed just 156, with three interceptions, and was sacked five times.

Offensively, the Huskers produced 389 yards (48 more than their season average), as Cory Ross rushed for 138 and Jammal Lord threw for a career-high 160.

And, yes, in the aftermath, there were even more calls for

Pederson to name Pelini as Solich's successor.

"Believe me, it wasn't just me. It was the whole staff," Pelini said of pulling Nebraska through a trying time. "It was the leadership on that football team. The seniors. There were a lot of people that had a big hand in what happened there, and it was a special group."

A few days later, Pelini interviewed with Pederson about the Nebraska opening, though he came away wondering about the sincerity of it. Eventually, he took the job as co-defensive coordinator at Oklahoma, then left after a year to become defensive coordinator at LSU.

It would be natural for people to think that the end of Pelini's one season with the Huskers intensified his desire to be a head coach. But the 40-year-old Youngstown, Ohio, native — though gratified to finally get a real shot as NU head coach following 14 years as an assistant — sees things differently.

"I try and stay focused, the same way I preach to my players, on the task at hand, the job that I'm in at that point," Pelini said. "I figure if I do that job right and I approach things the right way, that people are going to recognize that (and) maybe opportunities come down the road and things work out. If not, I was perfectly happy.

"I like coaching. I like interacting with the players. My relationships with the players and with the staff and the guys I work with — it's something that I cherish and that'll never change. At the end of the day, I care about my players and my players know it. They know I have their back, and I believe they've got mine. It's about a family, creating a family atmosphere. That's how you have success."

Pelini will tell you the lessons he learned in his month steering the Huskers were no different than others he's learned. Sure, he was in charge of a larger group, but the same principles that helped him connect with his defensive players applied across the board.

He built attitude and expectation, then motivated.

Jay Moore, a redshirt freshman defensive end in 2003, remembers how Pelini paid attention to little things that added up to success in the bowl game. Even something as minute as cutting practice times back because he wasn't worried about the players' conditioning had an impact.

"You felt like he was taking care of you," said Moore, who's now with the San Francisco 49ers.

Fabian Washington was a sophomore defensive back at Nebraska in 2003 and said players appreciated Pelini speaking his mind — good or bad.

"We had a guy that everybody would run through a brick wall for," said Washington, now with the Oakland Raiders.

Washington promises his cousin Latravis will soon feel that way, too.

The younger Washington, who redshirted

Defensive back Fabian Washington said players appreciated Bo Pelini speaking his mind when he was interim coach in 2003. "We had a guy that everybody would run through a brick wall for," Washington said. The Huskers showed that loyalty in the 2003 Alamo Bowl, with a 17-3 win against Michigan State. (Journal Star archives)

this season with the Huskers, was a bit unnerved by the Nov. 24 firing of Bill Callahan. But eight days later, after athletic director Tom Osborne had introduced Pelini as the Huskers' next coach, the cousins chatted again.

"I told Latravis, 'Just calm down, chill out,'" Fabian Washington said. "'Bo will get everything back rolling.'"

That belief comes from the way Pelini pushed the buttons in December of 2003.

Dec. 25, 2007

" I want opposing teams, when they're watching film of us, to say, "Wow, how do they get those guys to play so hard?"

— Bo Pelini "

Core philosophies guide NU coach

At all of his coaching stops, Bo Pelini has held true to his core philosophies about football. (William Lauer)

Bo Pelini's three-year tenure as Louisiana State's defensive coordinator began rather inauspiciously.

In the Tigers' 2005 season opener, Sam Keller — yes, that Sam Keller — torched Pelini's defense for 461 passing yards as Arizona State accumulated 560 total yards in a 35-31 loss to LSU. In LSU's next game, the Tigers fell 30-27 in overtime to Tennessee.

By STEVEN M. SIPPLE

"Believe me, everybody in the state of Louisiana was ready to hang Bo Pelini," says Bo Pelini.

At that point, it might have been tempting for Pelini to make significant changes to his defense. But he declined to deviate from his core philosophies. The result: Louisiana State ended the 2005 season with an 11-2 record and ranked No. 3 nationally in total defense — the ranking it also holds this week as it prepares to play Ohio State in the BCS national title game Jan. 7 in New Orleans.

Pelini's core philosophies?

Well, the new Nebraska head coach (he was hired Dec. 2, but is coaching Louisiana State's defense in the championship game) addressed them last spring in a presentation to Louisiana high school coaches. A kind reader e-mailed me the presentation in the form of an audio link from fastandfuriousfootball.com, which provides a variety of learning resources for coaches.

It's informative listening material, another chance to get to know Bo, and a nice Christmas surprise for sure. Some highlights

from the 60-minute presentation:

■ Pelini tells the coaches his goal always is to field "the best-effort defense" in the nation.

"Our philosophy is to create a culture of swarming to the football — that's the first thing we do," he says. "I want opposing teams, when they're watching film of us, to say, 'Wow, how do they get those guys to play so hard?'"

To that end, Pelini grades defenders' effort on every play in practice, always looking for "11 guys playing in one continuous motion from the time the ball is snapped to the time the ballcarrier is on the ground."

■ Pelini avoids "beating guys down" with negative tones and harsh language.

"I take this philosophy: There hasn't been a player ever that has tried to make a mistake out on the field," Pelini says. "If he made a mistake, he made it for a reason. Well, as a coach, you need to search for that reason — search for a way to get through to that kid. Ultimately, when you coach that way, the players are going to believe in you. And at the end of the day, they're going to want to run through a wall for you."

Pelini tells a story from 2003 when he served as Nebraska's defensive coordinator. A defender made a mistake in practice, and one of the Husker assistant coaches castigated the player. The assistant ranted and raved and even ran from the sideline into the defensive huddle to get in the player's face.

"I called the assistant coach over to me and said, 'All that stuff you just did: Was that for you or for the player? Because I heard you yelling at that kid and not one time did you tell him what he did wrong,'" Pelini says. "I told the coach, 'So, the next time, it's on you.'"

The key, Pelini says, is "getting kids to understand what they're doing so they can do it fast."

"If I get after a kid, (later) I'll walk up and put my arm around him and say, 'You're better than that, right? You know you're better than that, right?'"

■ Pelini says a lot of coaches get too caught up in X's and O's and fail to get to know players on a personal level. He says it's important to spend time with players away from the football setting, "so you know what makes them click." He says he wants players to have fun. "Don't make it doom and gloom for them," he says.

■ One of his main objectives is to take the opposing offense out of its comfort zone and disrupt the quarterback's play-calling rhythm. To that end, Pelini says, he's somewhat rare among defensive coordinators in that he scripts his calls early in games. In scripting his calls, he says, he tries to gives the offense "multiple, multiple looks" early on. He uses this tactic "to get in the heads" of offensive coordinators while simultaneously trying to dissuade the offense from using certain plays later in the game.

"If an offense has a couple of plays I know I don't want to see, I'm going to run some blitzes and pressures and things that say, 'OK, those things aren't going to be there for you this week,'" Pelini says. "Because later in the game, when I get into my game plan, I don't want to see a couple plays (from the offense). If I can put in their heads, 'OK, let's go away from that stuff,' we're going to be in a better situation as a defense."

■ "I know this: The great defensive football players play with very little or no wasted movement," Pelini says. "They're very efficient."

■ He says a prime objective for a defense should be putting itself in "winnable third-down situations," such as third-and-6-or-more yards.

■ He says defensive coordinators shouldn't show panic, because their players will sense it and react accordingly.

For instance, "I've been around coaches who act like the world came to an end if the offense got a 3-yard gain on first down," Pelini says. "What happens is, you act like that toward your players, they get in there and get more aggressive and boom — you start getting beat on play-action (passes) and ultimately you get beat over the top, and that's how you lose games."

■ The most important statistic a staff charts during a game is an offense's "explosive gains," or passes that gain more than 16 yards and runs that cover more than 12. "If offenses don't get explosive gains and have to execute all the way down the field, we're going to win."

Pelini, of course, speaks with his usual confidence and conviction. In 2005, as his LSU defense struggled early in the season, he held firm to his beliefs. You have to figure he'll use the same approach in 2008 as he guides a Nebraska defense that finished this season ranked 112th nationally in yards allowed.

"It's not about what offenses are doing — it's about us," Pelini told the coaches in his spring speech. "If we execute down after down after down, we're going to be fine. That's the key to playing great defense."

Jan. 8, 2008

" He'll be a great head coach. Nebraska's getting a great head coach, a guy who puts his heart and soul into it. "
— LSU defensive tackle Glenn Dorsey

Bo does his part in title game

By BRIAN CHRISTOPHERSON

NEW ORLEANS — It was an hour before the game and already fans were feverish, full of noise and certainly other things. Bourbon Street was just a few skips away, after all.

The bands blared and, at one point, the entire crowd joined in a chorus. "Heeeey, hey baby. I wanna knoooooow if you'll be my girl."

It was fun and craziness in the Big Easy, and there in the middle of it all, the very middle, was Nebraska's man, Bo Pelini.

As the crowd serenaded, he stood by himself, dressed in typical Bo wear: the light-colored slacks, gray sweat shirt, white ballcap. He crossed his arms, pacing back and forth on the Superdome's midfield logo, giving a piece of gum a serious workout.

Here was Husker fans' dream, their head football coach beneath the hot spotlight of a national championship game.

OK, OK, in the dream Pelini probably doesn't have LSU written across his sweat shirt.

But that's how reality would have it, and Pelini sure wasn't going to apologize for that smile on his face Monday night as the seconds ticked away in LSU's 38-24 win against Ohio State.

He hugged players, slapped their hands. They doused him with water. There is no better goodbye in football than that.

"It's the way to go out," Pelini said. "That's why I came back here, to finish it off, to send these guys out the right way. So we part the way we want to part. It was an emotional day for me and for the players. I'm just going to enjoy it, because they've earned it."

He is Nebraska's today. But Monday was a good night to be a Tiger one last time.

Pelini's double-dip felt awkward

There's no need to consult Giorgio Armani to understand one of life's fundamental truths.

Red and purple typically don't go well together.

I guess it worked out OK, this period during which Bo Pelini remained Louisiana State's defensive coordinator after being hired Dec. 2 as Nebraska's head coach. There was never a doubt Pelini would stay with the Tigers through the Bowl Championship Series title game. And make no mistake — Pelini absolutely did the right thing in fulfilling his commitment to LSU.

His Nebraska boss, Tom Osborne, fully supported Pelini's decision. After all, Osborne says, many coaches never get a chance to capture a national title. Amen to that. Plus, a strong defensive showing by Louisiana State against Ohio State's powerful offensive line obviously would reflect well on the Huskers and perhaps steer a recruit or two toward Big Red.

However, I still think Pelini's double-dip felt awkward at times.

Maybe it's just me, but I'm guessing some Nebraska fans might have cringed a time or two in the past month when Pelini stated, "I'm all about LSU right now," especially considering Pelini has been on NU's payroll since Dec. 2.

Technically, Pelini is no longer on salary at LSU. But terms of his contract mandate that he will receive a $96,000 bowl supplement should LSU win or an $80,000 supplement should it lose, according to USA Today. Bully for Bo. In fairness, coaches being paid by two schools have become fairly common during bowl season.

Pelini worked at Nebraska for two weeks — mostly recruiting — until a recruiting dead period began Dec. 17. He then turned the lion's share of his attention toward Louisiana State.

However, "He's had some time in the mornings and at night when he works Nebraska stuff," says Carl Pelini, Bo's brother and the Huskers' new defensive coordinator. "He gets to his meetings and practice time with LSU and hustles for his game prep. I think it's gone pretty smoothly."

Says Carl: "I'm sure Bo's not sleeping a whole lot. But he's hanging in there just fine."

Even so, it felt awkward in Huskerville last month when Nebraska recruits began decommitting in bushels. All told, nine once-committed prospects reneged on their verbal pledges to the Huskers since Pelini's arrival. So much for momentum generated from the hire. Many of the defections occurred during the dead period, when there essentially was nothing either Bo or his assistants could do about them.

Anyway, no need for panic on the recruiting front, Carl Pelini says.

"We're looking at it as a marathon and to be honest, we're really excited," he says. "You know what, there are a lot of great players out there. We get calls from coaches basically every day. We're just going to keep hammering away, and I think in the end, everybody will be pleasantly surprised."

At any rate, I'm guessing many Nebraska fans will feel better come Tuesday, when Pelini can say, "I'm 100 percent red." After all, Husker fans' passion tends to manifest itself in a year-round sense of urgency. That sense probably was heightened in recent days as Big 12 North rivals Missouri and Kansas posted impressive bowl victories.

One thing we can say with great certainty: Nebraska, with a dozen returning starters, won't be favored to win the Big 12 North in 2008. The Huskers probably ought to be picked, say, fourth.

Yes, sir, it's almost time for Bo Pelini to roll up his Big Red sleeves. Come Tuesday, it might still feel as though he's working two jobs, given the intense stretch of recruiting ahead, the reclamation project he faces with Nebraska's defense, and the stiff competition within the North Division.

"It's a different conference than it was four years ago, just in terms of balance," Carl Pelini says, referring to the Pelinis' one-year stint at Nebraska in 2003. "You just look at Kansas offensively and defensively and Missouri offensively and defensively, and Colorado taking a step forward."

So, should Nebraska fans temper expectations?

"No, you don't temper expectations," Carl Pelini says. "You just have to understand what your obstacles are going to be. But you can never temper expectations. Nebraska's got the fan base and facilities and all of the bullets you need. We should be at the top. But you also know you have to battle every week."

— Steven M. Sipple

About his next step as Nebraska's coach, Pelini said: "I'll worry about that tomorrow. I don't want to talk about that right now. I'm just going to go enjoy this with my family and the players. I'll worry about tomorrow tomorrow."

Nearby stood his three kids and wife, Mary Pat, wiping tears from her eyes.

If anyone would know if Pelini was stressing the last few weeks, taking on two jobs at once, it's her.

So?

"Not really," she said. "No, not really. He's a great multi-tasker. He doesn't let pressure get to him. You guys know how he is. He hasn't changed."

Pelini was as intense as usual in his final game as LSU's defensive coordinator.

The snapshot moment came in the fourth quarter with Ohio State facing a fourth-and-7 from the LSU 35-yard line. The score was 31-17 Tigers, but the Buckeyes had some momentum.

On the critical play, Pelini's defense brought pressure, a vicious hit put on the quarterback by LSU's Ali Highsmith. The ball came loose and the Tigers' Harry Coleman picked it up and returned it about 30 yards.

If you watched the LSU sideline during the play, you saw a gray blur. It was Pelini running just behind Coleman, joyfully screaming. When the play was over, Pelini jumped into the pile of his players, the biggest kid out there.

Pelini takes a sort of linebacker's stance when he's watching his defense — slight crouch, hands on knees. Sometimes he'll remain in that posture throughout the entire play.

Of course, he did not like what he saw early on.

On the third play of the game, a third down, Ohio State completed a slant pass to move the chains. Pelini threw his arms into the air.

He'd like the next play even less, a 65-yard touchdown run by Chris Wells.

When Wells reached the 50-yard line, obviously on his way for a score, Pelini just folded his arms, didn't say a word. He saved his voice until his players got to the sideline.

A talking to his defense didn't stop the storm.

Ohio State's next possession, first play: The Buckeyes found a wide-open receiver on a blown coverage by LSU. The play went for 44 yards. Less than six minutes into the game, the score was 10-0 and the Buckeyes' 133 total yards had already bettered the 82 they had in last year's title game against Florida.

Pelini's star defensive tackle, Glenn Dorsey, said Pelini kept his cool despite the poor start.

"He didn't really say too much, because he knew once we settled down, just get our calls right, put ourselves in the place we're supposed to be, we'd be OK, and we were," Dorsey said.

The night started to turn toward the Tigers.

LSU's defense started to breathe some fire. On a third-and-8 in the second quarter, Pelini brought a safety blitz, leading to an interception by LSU cornerback Chevis Jackson, starting a Louisiana party that is still going.

By halftime, the Tigers had a 24-10 lead.

"Our guys just reacted the way I knew we would," Pelini said.

The Tigers caused three turnovers, the last one an interception by Curtis Taylor that sealed matters with less than six minutes left.

Pelini put both arms in the air and hugged LSU head coach Les Miles.

If there's a better way to leave one job for another, Pelini would sure like to hear about it.

"He'll be a great head coach. I wish I could go play a few snaps for him," Dorsey said. "Nebraska's getting a great head coach, a guy who puts his heart and soul into it."

In his last game as LSU's defensive coordinator, Bo Pelini's charges sent him out on a winning note. The Tigers dominated top-ranked Ohio State 38-24 to win the national championship. (Chuck Burton/Associated Press)

"Every great program sags at some point. This was Nebraska's turn, and I think Pelini will definitely bring it back to where it needs to be. — Tony Barnhart"

Jan. 9, 2008

Media singing Pelini's praises

A quick rundown of Fox commentators Thom Brennaman and Charles Davis' on-air comments regarding Bo Pelini:

■ First mention of Pelini occurred with 10:50 left in the first quarter, as Ohio State was about to make it 10-0. Play-by-play man Brennaman mentioned the fact Pelini had been named head coach at Nebraska.

"Pelini said multi-tasking would not hurt his preparation," said color analyst Davis.

■ "Nice job by Pelini's defense," Davis said after LSU held Ohio State to a field goal.

■ After LSU's Chevis Jackson's second-quarter interception, on which Todd Boeckman was pressured by a safety blitz, Davis noted, "Bo Pelini dials it up."

■ In the second quarter, Davis said Ohio State must avoid abandoning the run "because then you're handing Bo Pelini a blank slate to send blitzers and mix up coverages."

■ On an Ohio State third-and-8, Davis said: "This is Bo Pelini land. He'll dial up something big here." Pelini did, in fact, dial up an overload blitz from the back side, but Boeckman made a first-down throw.

■ Late in the half, the Pelini publicity picked up markedly. Fox twice showed him on camera in the final minutes, the second time flashing up a photograph from his playing days at Ohio State (1987-90). Pretty cool, actually.

■ The pub continued in the second half. On an Ohio State third-and-long, Davis said: "Chances are you'll see Bo Pelini apply pressure on this snap." (Camera cuts to Pelini flashing in signals). "LSU's defensive backs feel, 'Hey, they can't beat us down field, so go beat them up front,'" Davis said. "And that's exactly what's happening."

■ Pelini gets extended on-air time after one of LSU's biggest defensive plays of the night — linebacker Ali Highsmith's forced fumble on a fourth-and-7 early in the fourth quarter. Safety Harry Coleman picked up the pigskin and bolted downfield. Cameras focused on Pelini pacing the sideline for a few seconds right before Fox cut to a commercial break.

■ Said Davis: "Bo Pelini tells his defenders you have to earn the right to rush the passer on third down. Well, third-and-15 gives you that right." Sure enough, Boeckman, under heavy pressure, tossed an interception on the next play.

■ Sideline reporter Chris Myers does a brief report on Pelini in the final moments as cameras show Pelini congratulating his defenders on the sideline. Myers says "it was understood" between Tigers head coach Les Miles and Nebraska officials that Pelini would coach LSU's defense in the BCS title game. Myers says Pelini wanted to say hello to his father, Anthony, who has been fighting an illness but is doing a lot better. Pelini then got the celebratory bath from his players.

— Steven M. Sipple

NEW ORLEANS — The game came with an alarming start to Husker fans. But in the end, Monday night's national title showdown finished exactly as they wished — Bo Pelini on the receiving end of praise from national pundits.

In his last game as LSU's defensive coordinator, Pelini's defense emerged triumphant after a shaky beginning in which it surrendered 10 points and a 65-yard touchdown in the contest's opening six minutes.

But the Tigers responded strongly to their initially failings, the defense coming back to record three turnovers and five sacks in a 38-24 win against Ohio State.

And a day after the victory, the French Quarter still intact despite a massive party that kept the music playing until sunrise, national analysts were looking on Nebraska's hiring of Pelini in a positive light.

"Bo Pelini is the next Bob Stoops," said Tony Barnhart, longtime college football writer for the Atlanta Journal-Constitution. "A guy who is fundamentally sound, who has been around great coaches all his life, who knows what a championship football team is supposed to look like.

"The fact that he was able to come here and have that defense ready to play with all the things going on, I think speaks well of him and his ability to run an organization."

Some Husker fans were rankled recently when Sporting News columnist Matt Hayes gave Nebraska a C-minus grade concerning the hiring of Pelini as its new coach.

Hayes' point was that Nebraska is too established as a football program to hire someone who has never been a head coach before.

Others are more optimistic about Pelini's chances to turn around the Huskers, coming off a 5-7 season.

"I think there's a stability now with Pelini because of an earlier presence, and obviously Tom (Os-

borne) must have a real comfort level," said Malcom Moran, who has covered college football for USA Today, The New York Times, Newsday and the Chicago Tribune.

"I'm looking at this from a distance, but I think the biggest thing Nebraska needs now is to get back to the stability, the comfort level that existed for a long time."

Of Monday night's game, Moran said, "I think (Pelini) impressed a lot of people."

By BRIAN CHRISTOPHERSON

Added Mark Blaudschun of the Boston Globe: "Last night certainly helped him. It was a great game plan by him."

And what do outsiders think of the Nebraska program as a whole? Has missing bowl games in two of the past four seasons caused the program to slide off their radar screen?

Moran: "Oh, no, which is the problem. (The program) was on the map in a way that wasn't much fun to watch. I mean, you saw things that you never thought the Blackshirts would ever experience. (Nebraska) always remains visible, but this season it wasn't for the reason that existed for decades. The struggle became so bad that you couldn't look away."

Blaudschun: "It's not off the map, but we're scratching our heads at the nature of (Nebraska's) decline. It's like Notre Dame this year. People expect dips, but it was so bad at Notre Dame. When you see dips like that, it's like, 'What is going on there?'"

Barnhart: "Nebraska to me is a franchise college football program, like a USC, like an Alabama, like a Notre Dame. They made a philosophical decision to go in another direction. It didn't work out. Every great program sags at some point. This was Nebraska's turn, and I think Pelini will definitely bring it back to where it needs to be."

Chapter 6: Rookie thrown into the fire

Pelini seems to thrive on pressure

STEVEN M. SIPPLE

It's late July as I write this part of the book. For what it's worth, I'm on record predicting Nebraska will finish 8-4 overall and 4-4 in the Big 12 in 2008. I wrote that a couple times during the months following Bo Pelini's hiring as NU's head coach. Let's just say he didn't necessarily agree with my prognostication and leave it at that.

By now we all know Pelini is a tenacious competitor with a bit of an ornery streak. It's his nature to forever believe he can find a way for his team to beat any team at any time. We've had the Pelini-is-confident thing drilled into our collective consciousness, and believe me, it's as real as a punch in the nose.

That said, virtually everyone predicted Missouri to win the Big 12 North Division in 2008, with Kansas the likely runner-up. I envision the Tigers going either 8-0 or 7-1 in conference play. I see them being pushed to the limit Oct. 4 in Lincoln in the conference opener for both teams, but ultimately prevailing for their first win in Memorial Stadium since 1978.

OK, say Nebraska upsets Missouri. It obviously would be a huge shot of momentum for Pelini's Big Red reclamation project. With a win against the Tigers, the Huskers finishing 5-3 in the league, or even 6-2, would become very possible.

If Nebraska gets six wins in the league, Pelini ought to be named Big 12 coach of the year.

Pelini, by the way, embraces Nebraska fans' traditionally lofty expectations. He said he wants it no other way. He seems to thrive on the pressure.

As for Tom Osborne, his expectations for Nebraska in 2008 are

During the news conference announcing his hiring as Nebraska head coach, Bo Pelini had a smile for his wife Mary Pat after being asked about his sideline demeanor. (Ted Kirk)

relatively modest compared to the dominance the Huskers enjoyed during his tenure as head coach. For now, the NU athletic director mostly wants to see Pelini get the program on solid ground. Osborne said he wants to see a team that is well-prepared and plays with great passion every week.

"I pretty much stay away from (predicting) numbers of wins and losses," Osborne said as the early-August start of preseason practice neared. "I generally tell fans I think we'll be better. I think we'll play hard and play with intensity. That's my perception. And I tell them we're not devoid of talent. Certainly some positions are stronger than others. That's true of every team.

"But I think the new coaches generally felt coming in here that the talent level exceeded their expectations."

Pelini inherited 14 starters (six offense, six defense, two specialists) from last year's team that finished 5-7 overall and 2-6 in the

Big 12, good for a last-place tie with Iowa State in the North Division. Nebraska's offensive and defensive fronts are loaded with battle-tested players. The offensive line, with four players who each made at least eight starts in 2007, is arguably the team's strong suit.

"There's a lot that goes into having a good team," said Osborne, pointing to the challenges faced by Nebraska's overhauled coaching staff entering the 2008 season. "You've got coaches getting to know the players, and vice versa. You've got a different scheme on defense that has to be installed and taught. You've got a similar scheme on offense, but there will be some changes, I'm sure. It's all got to come together.

"You can never predict at the start of the year exactly what the team chemistry's going to be, what the leadership's going to be like on the team. It's hard to predict those things even with coaches who have been someplace for a long

time. I really didn't know what was going to happen each year because although you might have a lot of the same players back, the chemistry always changed.

"Just a few people coming and going can make a huge difference."

Pelini's retention of offensive coordinator Shawn Watson and wide receivers coach Ted Gilmore from Bill Callahan's staff should help lead to continued strong play on offense. Of course, Pelini is in charge of the defense, including making the calls during games.

"Bo knows offense from a defensive standpoint, which is very good, because you know what gives you the most trouble," Osborne said. "So I think they (Pelini and Watson) have had a lot of dialogue in terms of how Bo would like to see the offense structured, and I think Shawn has been very good about keeping a lot of the basic nuts and bolts.

"The big thing is, I didn't want to see a lot of new terminology on both sides of the ball, because it would take some time to get all of that taught. I think it's good the offense won't have to go through a whole new learning process."

So, I close with a simple question: Is Bo Pelini ready for his new gig?

Is any first-year Big 12 head coach really prepared for the meat-grinder that is the league schedule, for all those pinpoint passers these days, for all those savvy veteran coaches?

Pelini's one of three new head coaches in the league in 2008. But the other two — Texas A&M's Mike Sherman and Baylor's Art Briles — have had plenty of experience running programs. Pelini, of course, has never been a head coach at any level. But neither had Osborne, Barry Switzer nor Joe Paterno, and they seemed to manage OK.

Bo Pelini brought a new approach to Nebraska's Red-White Spring Game in 2008. Because it truly was just a scrimmage, Pelini (in white), his brother Carl (right), the Huskers' defensive coordinator, and linebackers coach Mike Ekeler (center) spent most of the scrimmage in the backfield watching how the defense responded. (Ted Kirk)

Contract starts at $1.1 million

Completed without agents and apparently free of discord, Husker head football coach Bo Pelini's contract was made public Wednesday.

Pelini will make a guaranteed $1.1 million a year. It's a deal that runs through five seasons, expiring Dec. 31, 2012.

The contract includes incentives where Pelini

 By BRIAN CHRISTOPHERSON

would earn an additional $400,000 for winning the Big 12 Championship Game and another $400,000 for winning the BCS national championship.

"We're very pleased with the process," Nebraska athletic director Tom Osborne said in a statement. "There were no protracted negotiations and no agents. Everything went smoothly."

Breaking down Pelini's bonus opportunities:

■ By getting to the Big 12 Conference title game, he'll earn $150,000.

■ By winning the Big 12 title, he'll get another $250,000.

■ By appearing in the BCS Championship Game, he'll earn $150,000.

■ By winning the BCS title game, he'll get another $250,000.

■ Pelini can also earn a bonus of up to $250,000 for academic success by his players.

In addition, Pelini will earn $91,667 for his work since his hiring on Dec. 2, 2007 to Dec. 31, 2007.

Certainly, it's a raise for the 40-year-old and first-time head coach. Pelini was making $400,000 last year as LSU's defensive coordinator.

Differing from Bill Callahan's contract, Pelini's contract includes a buyout provision where the university would be paid a minimum of $250,000 should

We could all use a few incentives

We could all use a few incentives.

Dangling a dollar or two to keep our brains from addling, bonuses for going above and beyond.

You know, like Bo.

The new Husker head football coach just signed his five-year, $1.1 million contract. That's $1.1 million each year for five years.

Or about nine times what the athletic director who hired him made as a head coach when he got out of the business in 1997.

Not bad.

A touch over the rate of inflation. Perhaps a bit more than our own salaries have gone up in the last decade, but who's being petty and keeping track?

And that's just Bo Pelini's base salary — along with two cars and a membership at the country club of his choice.

Just for getting a "meets expectations" on the ol' annual review.

Seems the Super Size Me world of NCAA Division I football requires the head honcho receive a bit of extra green for going above and beyond mediocrity.

To wit: An extra $400,000 for winning the Big 12 ($150,000 for showing up and losing).

Another $400,000 for winning the national championship.

Then there's the small change, a quarter-million more if he can get the boys to crack the books and outperform the rest of the student body.

There is a catch.

If the chancellor decides to fire him, he only gets half his salary.

Not sure how anyone could manage on $42,000 a month, but that's the cold, cruel reality of mentoring young student-athletes, who, according to those reality-check NCAA commercials, will almost all go on to

"something besides sports."

I understand the concept. I agree with it. If Bo needs some extra motivation, let's give it to him. That's the world we live in.

What self-respecting D-I football coach would demand less?

Perhaps football fans who buy season tickets or funny red T-shirts and official Husker bling could get in on the athletic department cash flow, too?

Or how about the players who abuse their bodies in exchange for a free college education before going onto "something other than sports?" A hundred bucks an interception! Fifty for every sack!

Oh, wait. I've gone too far.

What I meant to say is incentives are good for some people.

They didn't really work out with that Callahan guy.

But, hey, who's keeping track?

— Cindy Lange-Kubick

Pelini take a job elsewhere. The buyout starts at $1 million in its first year and decreases over the term of the contract.

There are also differences in how Pelini would be compensated if he were fired. The contract calls for Nebraska to pay him $41,700 a month for the remainder of the contract, or $500,000 annually. That figure, however, would be reduced by whatever Pelini earns at his next job.

"I thought it was all very straightforward," said Pelini, who signed the contract on Jan. 16. "We were pretty much on the same page from the start. We agreed on the parameters, and

there wasn't much discussion that needed to be done. I just really trust Coach Osborne and his word."

While $1.1 million is an impressive figure, it's modest in comparison with the pay some college football coaches are receiving.

Coacheshotseat.com, which monitors the contracts of college football coaches, says Pelini's guaranteed salary would tie him for 45th nationally, putting him in the company of the head coaches at Tulsa, Hawaii and North Carolina State.

Osborne, who makes the lowest salary of any Big 12 athletic direc-

tor at $250,000 annually, said before Pelini was hired that he did not want to bring aboard a coach who seemed motivated by money.

"That always turns me off a little bit if I feel that their main interest is how much of a salary they can get," Osborne told the Husker Sports Network just before Pelini's hiring.

Fortunately for Osborne, Pelini seems more concerned right now with winning than dollar signs.

As Pelini recently told the Journal Star: "I wasn't really worried about the contract. I figure I'll do a good job here, and it will all take care of itself."

> **If something didn't sound right, if something didn't feel right, Bo would step up and say, "Hey, let's work our way through this."**
> -- 49er safety Tim McDonald

Jan. 27, 2008

Super Bowl experience pays off

You have to appreciate this about Bo Pelini: He's absolutely confident in himself. We're certain of that by now after reading his comments and studying his demeanor. It's not a front, folks.

Tim McDonald experienced Pelini's confidence in 1994, when Pelini was a 27-year-old assistant secondary coach with the San Francisco 49ers. Many of the players were older than Pelini, including McDonald, the six-time Pro Bowl strong safety who was 29 at the time. As you might expect, knowing what we now know about Pelini, the young coach asserted himself in the Niners' meeting rooms and at practice. He didn't hang back, as young coaches tend to do.

"That's why Bo is where he is right now," says McDonald, now 43, referring to Pelini's new gig as Nebraska head coach. "He was never afraid to test the waters. If something didn't sound right, if something didn't feel right, Bo would step up and say, 'Hey, let's work our way through this.'

"He would work with the players and listen to the players. But at the same time, he was strong enough to say, 'This is right and this is the way we should go about it.'"

If you bleed Husker red, you also have to appreciate this about Pelini: He has coached in some gargantuan games, including two of the last four BCS national title games (with Oklahoma in 2005 and Louisiana State this past season). What's more, he coached in Super Bowl XXIX on Jan. 29, 1995, when San Francisco dismantled San Diego 49-26 in Miami.

"I remember it like it was yesterday," Pelini says.

OK, a quick test: So, Bo, do you remember what happened on the third play of the NFC Championship Game against Dallas, the historic contest that set the stage for Super Bowl XXIX.

"It was a pick for a touchdown," Pelini says without hesitation. "We were in cover-2, and (cornerback) Eric Davis baited Dallas into

throwing an option route, and Davis picked it off. Eric was a smart player, and he baited Troy Aikman into making a bad decision.

"That was a huge game."

Essentially every game was huge in 1994 for San Francisco. Then-Niners head coach George Seifert proclaimed: "With this team, nothing short of a Super Bowl was enough." Seifert's team ultimately performed superbly in the bright lights of Miami, jumping to a 14-0 lead and waltzing past the underdog Chargers.

"Playing great, especially in high-pressure situations, it's all about eliminating distractions and staying focused," Pelini says. "That's a huge part of playing good football, period. In a situation like that, in the Super Bowl, I saw it front and center.

"Just watching and learning throughout that 1994 season, at that relatively young age, it gave me a foundation to build upon," Pelini adds. "It's like anything else. If you don't have a foundation, you have nothing."

Pelini's coaching foundation was fortified by teaching the likes of McDonald, free safety Merton Hanks and cornerback Deion Sanders. ("It was easy coaching Deion," Pelini says. "I mean, he obviously was talented, but he came to practice hard every day.") Sanders was among a handful of veteran defenders who joined the Niners in 1994 as free agents with the objective of winning all the marbles.

Pelini, of course, always has embraced such high expectations.

"Everywhere I've been, it's been like that," he says.

Which brings to mind another trait you have to appreciate about Pelini: He seems tough enough and seasoned enough to handle the sometimes unwieldy expectations of fervid Nebraska fans. Any Husker head football coach obviously must be confident and self-assured. After bad losses, he gets skewered by thousands of armchair fans and the media, and he better be prepared to publicly smile and tell everyone how much he appreci-

ates their passion for the program.

In other words, he better be as thick-skinned as a rhinoceros.

Pelini, by the way, had a note on his office desk Friday to call McDonald, now a high school coach in Fresno, Calif., with whom Pelini has stayed in contact over the years.

"Bo's been a definite, definite student of the game," McDonald says. "He's a fiery guy who pretty much every defensive back in our locker room in San Francisco just adored. It was his work ethic. He

By STEVEN M. SIPPLE

worked so hard, and you knew he wanted it so bad. I always knew it was just a matter of time before he put it all together because he always had great ideas. And I think Bo really took off when Pete Carroll came to San Francisco (as defensive coordinator in 1995).

"That really helped Bo realize his potential."

Pelini rattles off a list of names of coaches who had great influence on him, including a few who worked with him in San Francisco. He originally was hired in 1994 to work in the Niners' scouting department, but was immediately promoted to assistant secondary coach. He soon was preparing for the world's biggest football game.

"I remember the firecrackers and stuff going off after the national anthem," Pelini says. "There were all these distractions. Then I remember looking down the sideline and seeing (the Chargers) looking around at everything going on. I looked over at our sideline and our guys were just locked in."

San Diego had steady Stan Humphries at quarterback, big Natrone Means at running back and a nice, controlled passing attack.

"They were a physical team," Pelini says. "But they had some guys who could run, too."

Yep, Bo remembers it all like it was yesterday.

"I'm good at remembering things," he says. "And, hey, that was a special time in my life right there."

Feb. 7, 2008

> **We're committed to getting the walk-on program back on its feet and becoming a huge part of our future.**
>
> -- Nebraska AD Tom Osborne

He's buying into walk-on program

Bo Pelini didn't get it.

At least not at first.

Please flash back to the spring of 2003. He was Nebraska's new defensive coordinator, fresh from the Green Bay Packers. He walked out to his first Husker practice and encountered a sea of red —150-plus players — about three times the size of an NFL roster.

"I was freaked out," Pelini said Wednesday. "There were players everywhere."

By STEVEN M. SIPPLE

That was Huskerville as we once knew it.

"It was just different," Pelini said.

Yes, Nebraska was different than other places in college football. The Huskers had 60-plus walk-ons back in the day, and Pelini admits he didn't exactly understand the walk-on phenomenon in these parts.

As time passed, Pelini talked to people close to the program: Barney Cotton and Ron Brown and Marvin Sanders and Jeff Jamrog and others who had a deep appreciation for Big Red's walk-on program. Pelini observed things on his own and began to understand the culture and tradition of Nebraska football.

Yes, it's different here. Maybe unique is a better word.

Whatever the case, it was crystal clear Wednesday that Bo now gets it. You heard the passion in his voice. That sea of red that freaked him out in 2003 makes perfect sense to him now.

"We're committed to getting the walk-on program back on its feet and becoming a huge part of our future," the first-year Nebraska head coach said as he unveiled his 2008 recruiting class, which includes 30 walk-ons (18 were announced Wednesday, and 12 others will follow when paperwork is complete) to supplement 28 scholarship recruits.

Some people won't buy Nebraska's company line, which goes something like this: Never mind that we didn't crack the top 20 in the national recruiting rankings (No. 21 by Scout.com, No. 30 by Rivals.com), because those services don't measure the impact of a large and proud group of walk-ons who would tar the roof of Abel Hall if you asked them.

Nebraska coaches say they feel great about the 2008 scholarship recruits, and the coaches say they feel even better about the class when the walk-ons are considered.

In announcing his 2008 recruiting class, Bo Pelini said it will include 30 walk-ons. (William Lauer)

All this walk-on talk probably sounds provincial and hokey and maybe even a tad arrogant to non-Nebraska fans. Some will snicker.

But this stuff is of supreme significance to most Husker fans, many of whom simply want their program back. They want that feeling back. To those folks, Pelini's words Wednesday must have been like music to the ears. Yes, Bo now gets it. He didn't need a script when asked about the importance of the Big Red walk-on program.

"Most of the walk-ons are coming from the state of Nebraska," he said. "They come from towns, from areas that have a love for the state, the university and our football program. And the more people you bring into a culture that have strong beliefs about something and have a strong commitment and want-to, it's going to make you stronger in the future."

Jamrog, NU assistant athletic director for football, is heading up the walk-on charge. He said Husker coaches sorted through 175 potential walk-ons and narrowed the list to 31.

Nebraska recruited those 31 players (only one said "No thanks") as if they were five-star scholarship recruits. And therein may be the main difference between Pelini's staff and Bill Callahan's crew. But let's be clear: Callahan didn't get rid of the walk-on program; he just de-emphasized it.

To wit: When the new coaching staff took over in December, Nebraska had 35 walk-ons on the roster. Jamrog spoke Wednesday of the possibility of NU eventually returning to a 150-plus-player roster — 85 scholarship players and 65 walk-ons.

We'll see. For now, the Big Red boss of bosses is happy.

"I didn't know how well it would work this year," Tom Osborne said of Nebraska's walk-on recruiting. "I thought, well, the previous staff had four years where they had walk-ons. True. But they really didn't go after (walk-ons) in the same way we used to here. So, I didn't know what the response out there would be."

And?

"From a casual observer's standpoint, I was really gratified by the number of really good players who still wanted to walk on here. And they will make a difference. It may not show up for a couple of years. But it will definitely show up."

Perhaps the last four years have showed us Nebraska absolutely needs the walk-on factor to show up in a big way. Callahan's program too often lacked energy and passion — on that we can all agree.

In short, Nebraska often didn't feel like Nebraska.

Bottom line: The walk-on program gives the Huskers a unique edge — an advantage warm-weather schools in highly populated areas lack. That's integral for dear old NU. So, recruit a bunch of Joel Makovickas and Derrie Nelsons and John Parrellas and Adam Treus, and have their ungodly energy and want-to rub off on those megastar scholarship recruits. It's a proven formula.

But here's a key: Treat all the players the same, scholarship or no scholarship, like Nebraska used to do.

Skeptics always will snicker about Nebraska's walk-on phenomenon. The world's changed, they say now. It's an instant-gratification society. Most walk-ons need time to develop. Who has the patience?

Can it still work?

"I don't see why not," Osborne said.

Fullback Joel Makovicka (45) was one of four Makovicka brothers to walk on to the Husker football program. They are poster boys for NU's walk-on program, which Bo Pelini says will be emphasized during his tenure. (Journal Star archives)

Sadler, Pelini mix with the masses

As you've probably figured out, Nebraska's new head football coach lacks pretentiousness.

"What you see is what you get," Tom Osborne says of Bo Pelini.

We've been seeing plenty of Pelini lately — at a couple of Husker wrestling duals and basketball games, at NU men's

By STEVEN M. SIPPLE

basketball coach Doc Sadler's luncheon downtown, at the Metro Football Coaches Association banquet in Omaha with his entire coaching staff in tow, despite an ornery snowstorm.

Pardon me if I left out a function or three.

This isn't to say that a coach regularly mixing with the masses will magically translate into victories. And I'd be the last guy to suggest the Nebraska head football and basketball coaches should take on the public persona of a polished politician. Give me Bo Schembechler over Rick Neuheisel any day.

I guess it just feels kind of nice to see Nebraska's two most high-profile coaches rubbing elbows with John and Jane Q. Public, and enjoying it all the while.

Yes, Pelini and Sadler are throwing us a nice change of pace.

"Doc, from the day he got here (Aug. 8, 2006), was out seeing people and connecting," says Osborne, the Husker athletic director. "Bo has been very good that way, too. I think that's a good thing. The fans feel more connected to the coaches and the program.

"It isn't anything I've asked them to do," Osborne adds. "They operate as they see fit."

Says Sadler: "I think it's the responsibility of whoever the head (basketball) coach is at Nebraska

Football coach Bo Pelini attends Husker sporting events and always is a popular figure with the fans. (Gwyneth Roberts)

to make the people of Nebraska feel they're a major part in this program. It's no longer a deal where you can just coach and go home."

Why?

"There are too many other things for people to do," Sadler says, perhaps referring to Americans' propensity to play video games and channel surf.

At any rate, "If you're going to ask people for their support, then you have to do your part and get out and extend yourself," Sadler says.

These observations about Sadler and Pelini should not be construed as an indictment on their predecessors, Barry Collier and Bill Callahan, respectively. Collier and Callahan obviously are fine gentlemen and excellent coaches. They could be charming in public appearances. But both obviously valued privacy to a large degree.

Callahan, in particular, had something of a strained existence in Lincoln. For instance, he generally avoided restaurants be-

cause he thought fans would recount his every move.

Because most people never really got to know Callahan, he failed to build up a lot of good will among NU fans. Good will can come in handy for a coach when losses begin to mount, as we learned this past fall when Callahan endured intense fan and media backlash.

Of course, it's impossible to quantify how much, if any, the impact of creating good will and positive karma in the fan base affects wins and losses. But maybe, just maybe, building good will among the masses can help matters on a fourth-and-1 late in a key game on Stadium Drive, when Big Red needs that extra oomph to close the deal.

In the unruly Big 12, Pelini and Sadler need any edge they can muster.

"I don't really know what's gone on here in the past, and I don't really concern myself with that," Pelini says. "I just enjoy sports. I enjoy a wide variety of things. My kids enjoy being out

and going to things with the family. We'll be out there. That's just who we are."

For what it's worth, former Nebraska head coach Frank Solich tended toward a generally private life away from work, especially during his first four years in charge.

As for Osborne, "Early on as a head coach, I was out and about a lot," he says. "I did all the Touchdown Club luncheons on Mondays and all the Big Red breakfasts (on Fridays). I did a TV show and had radio responsibilities. But after I had my (heart) bypass in 1985, I realized I had to start focusing my energies a little bit."

Pelini obviously has plenty of focus as a coach. But I'll say it again: The guy is going to have fun, and his players are going to have fun. Same goes for Doc's program. After all, it isn't the Pentagon they're leading.

So, perhaps you noticed Pelini sitting next to Sadler at a recent Husker wrestling dual. Then, at Sunday's dual, Pelini was seated with son Patrick on the Husker bench, next to NU wrestling coach Mark Manning.

Pelini showed up for Sadler's basketball luncheon last week, a day after national signing day. The night before signing day, Pelini gathered all of his assistants and they drove to Omaha in a snowstorm — it took them 30 minutes just to reach Interstate 80 from Memorial Stadium — to attend the Metro coaches function.

Perhaps Pelini and Sadler are establishing strong relationships in advance of long careers at Nebraska (assuming they win enough games, of course).

They act like they want to be Nebraska coaches, as opposed to being coaches at Nebraska — an important distinction.

> I tell the players that you're representing this program all of the time — from the time you wake up in the morning until the time you go to bed at night. — Bo Pelini

March 12, 2008

NU coach: Do the right thing

Football players have fun playing for Bo Pelini. You'll seldom hear otherwise. It's integral to his success as a coach.

But Monday night was not a fun night to be a Nebraska football player. After four Huskers ran afoul of the law this past weekend, Pelini conducted a team meeting. Let's just say the players got a good dose of Pelini's fire.

The gist of his message sounded like a Spike Lee movie: Do the right thing.

Or else.

It's often been a smooth ride for Pelini since he took over as Nebraska head coach on Dec. 2. He's still undefeated, except for one thing: The police blotter got the best of Big Red over the weekend, and the new boss is a little surly as a result.

"I tell the players that you're representing this program all of the time — from the time you wake up in the morning until the time you go to bed at night," Pelini said Tuesday. "And every decision you make affects our program. If you make a decision contrary to the overall benefit of the program, there will be repercussions.

"Every situation is different. Every circumstance is different. They'll all be dealt with differently. But they'll be dealt with strictly and severely. It's about accountability. There's not a lot of gray area. It's black and white — do the right thing."

Pelini made the remarks to reporters early Tuesday afternoon. He made it clear that the buck always stops with him. No question who's the boss here. But sometimes even the boss needs a little help.

Tuesday night, Pelini told me that he was open to the idea of reviving the Unity Council, the 17-player leadership entity that be-

Bo Pelini has made it known to his players that they are accountable, not just to themselves, but also to the Husker program. (Journal Star archives)

gan at Nebraska in 1991 before disappearing when Bill Callahan took over as head coach in 2004.

Pelini said he wants to see who emerges as team leaders before making a final decision whether to implement such a council. He noted that such a council worked well at Louisiana State. But he's told me in past interviews he wasn't always wild about player councils.

It says here that a Unity Council can make a huge difference for a program. Peer pressure tends to make players more accountable.

New York Giants coach Tom Coughlin, who instituted a 10-player council last summer, would back that claim.

So would Matt Hoskinson, a former Nebraska offensive lineman (1993-97).

"What's been lacking in the last eight to 10 years at Nebraska is leadership within the team," said Hoskinson, a native of Battle Creek. "I think it's been a huge factor."

Past Unity Councils at Nebraska featured eight players apiece from offense and defense plus a

kicker. Unity Council members, elected by their peers, met on Tuesdays and dealt with a variety of issues. If a player missed classes or was slacking in practice, the Unity Council might issue a stern reprimand.

I know what you're thinking: A few players get into trouble, and now the know-it-all local columnist thinks a Unity Council will solve everything.

By STEVEN M. SIPPLE

Nah, but maybe it'll help.

Maybe a player council would have helped save Andy Christensen from the ugly situation in which he finds himself.

"It's incumbent on a player's buddies to say, 'Man, you're out of control, you should get your butt home,'" Hoskinson said.

Maybe a player council also would have helped a few other Husker players who were indefinitely suspended — one was even dismissed — from the squad Monday (Pelini declined to identify them).

Suggesting the implementation of a Unity Council isn't to say Pelini can't handle team discipline on his own. If you've experienced the Pelini glare, you know what I mean.

Yes, players have fun playing for Pelini. But make no mistake, most players want discipline in their lives. And former players will tell you Pelini can be a stern disciplinarian, as his players learned Monday night.

Accountability and high standards need to become a way of life in the program, Pelini said.

"Until we establish that across our team and establish the culture of this team, then the foundation is not built," he said. "That has to become who this team is and what we are. We're headed in that direction."

March 27, 2008

They're swimming in it mentally a little bit, but physically, these guys are flying around having some fun.

— Bo Pelini

Pelini says first practice 'normal'

The herd of reporters was so great that at one point, a Husker player exiting the first spring practice of 2008 wondered aloud: "Is the president here?"

Well, no, but the beginning of Bo Ball in a football-crazed state draws a crowd — about 25 or so circling Nebraska's head coach with microphones, notebooks, cameras and curiosities aplenty.

By BRIAN CHRISTOPHERSON

He may have been holding a new job title, but Bo Pelini said it felt like just a normal practice to him.

"About what I expected, about what we expected," Pelini said. "You're not going to be game-ready on the first day. There were a lot of mistakes, but the effort was great.

"We taxed them, we challenged them, we challenged them on every play."

Yes, Husker linebacker Phillip Dillard concurred, there was some serious taxing going on out there.

"Very intense" is how he described practice under Pelini.

"He's very hands-on. He's talking to every player. ... If you're messing up, he's talking to you no matter who you are. He's going to correct you because he wants everything done perfect," Dillard said.

"If you're not doing it right, he's going to call you out and that's how it's supposed to be done."

The motivation to not be the guy singled out is apparently quite a powerful thing.

Afterward, offensive players kept remarking about how tenacious the defense was in this first practice.

Said sophomore receiver Niles Paul: "The defense was flying to the ball, picking up fumbles, dropped passes, they were picking them up and taking them to the house."

The team went through mostly first-and-10 situations, focusing on its base defenses.

Pelini's voice was a constant presence at Hawks Championship Center. Dillard heard it every play.

"Out there on defense today, every play he's yelling, 'Run to the ball.' Everybody, D-line and everything. 'I want you running 10 yards to the ball, no matter what, fumbles, draw play, anything. I want everyone sprinting to the ball every single play.'"

And so defensive bodies flew around until

Head coach Bo Pelini tests Phillip Dillard's core muscles as the players stretch before practice in April of 2008. Players described Pelini's workouts as "very intense." (William Lauer)

the final practice horn. Dillard said he could tell guys were trying to do whatever it took to show the new coach that there is talent on this team, even when tired legs began to show up late in the practice.

This is a defense that was severely humbled last season.

But a new coach with a defensive mind has guys oozing with optimism.

Husker junior center Jacob Hickman noticed that right away in the defensive players.

"It's one of those things, almost like having a new toy. You kind of get excited and I think they all really know they have to show themselves because it's kind of open right now," Hickman said.

"I think it's just a positive energy. It caught me off-guard to start. They were a little bit faster than I expected."

Hickman said Pelini was in the offense's meeting Wednesday morning, but probably

devoted more of his time to helping the defense during the practice.

While Pelini said he is obviously a little more involved with the defense, he said he is certainly "in tune" with what's going on with the offense.

"The evaluation goes on every rep. Every guy is being evaluated every time he walks on the field," Pelini said. "I thought it was a good start. They're swimming in it mentally a little bit, but physically, these guys are flying around having some fun."

A good start, but only a start. There are 14 more of these spring practices left.

As his linebackers did an early practice drill Wednesday, assistant coach Mike Ekeler kept reminding them that this was just the beginning.

Players starting to sweat, Ekeler screamed: "It's got to be every day! It's got to be every day!"

> If we can't count on them to do the right things off the field, we can't count on them on the field, either.
> -- Bo Pelini

April 14, 2008

Making the grade is a priority

OK, I'm guilty. Maybe you're guilty, too.

I sometimes scoff at the "student-athlete" tag as it applies to big-time college athletics.

These guys care about school? They go to class regularly? You hear stories that make you wonder.

Actually, I'm guessing the majority of major-college athletes do attend class regularly, if Nebraska is any indication. NU's record of academic achievement in athletics speaks volumes — a nation-leading 255 Academic All-Americans, for instance.

It appears Bo Pelini is trying to maintain, if not improve, Nebraska's sterling academic tradition. Husker football players tell stories of athletic department academic counselors showing up on campus virtually every day to check on players, per Pelini's orders.

Or sometimes it's an assistant coach doing the checking.

Even Pelini himself has been known to turn up in classrooms.

"It's a bigger deal here now," says Nebraska senior linebacker Tyler Wortman. "We have people checking on everybody."

Nebraska long has conducted class checking of football players, but it wasn't as elaborate and extensive as now. For one thing, not every player was checked in the recent past, according to those close to the program.

Former Nebraska head coach Bill Callahan did a nice job emphasizing the academic area. Last spring, the Husker football program was honored as one of 34 in Division I-A that produced a graduation rate of 70 percent or higher.

But several people in the Nebraska program told me Pelini is ramping up the emphasis on academics — especially class attendance.

Pelini's overriding philosophy regarding academics and going to class?

"Everything counts in this program, from the time you wake up in the morning until the time you go to bed at night — we're going to hold you accountable in every aspect of what you do," the first-year head coach says.

The 40-year-old Pelini — a three-time academic All-Big Ten selection as a safety at Ohio State (1988-90) — says players going to class is "part of who they are. If we can't count on them to do the right things off the field, we can't count on them on the field, either."

Wortman, who carries a 3.98 grade-point average in mechanical engineering, says Pelini's strict academic rules "make a lot of sense. I think it's good."

Perhaps this is merely a first-year head coach laying down the law early in his tenure to set the tone. You know how it goes: The boss eventually will relax a bit, right?

Uh, maybe not.

"It's not up for debate," Pelini says. "If you don't want to go to class, turn pro."

When Nebraska's new football coaches first arrived on campus, they carried to classes photos of unfamiliar players on whom they were checking, Wortman says.

Players who get caught skipping class face a rugged 6:30 a.m. workout with their position coach, or perhaps with the head coach.

And if a player leaves a class early?

Well, Nebraska senior linebacker Cody Glenn recently was caught leaving a classroom 10 minutes before the end, necessitating a 6:30 a.m. session with running backs coach Tim Beck (Glenn since has moved to linebacker).

One part of the early workout was called a "pencil roll," Glenn says.

"You lay down on your side and just roll 100 yards," he says. "It doesn't sound all that bad, but it gets you tired. It can make you want to throw up a little bit.

"I shouldn't have left early," Glenn adds. "I knew there were consequences."

Callahan also dished out early morning workouts for wayward students.

"If a teacher e-mailed our academic counselors and told them people were being disruptive or missing class, you had to get up at 6 o'clock and climb stairs for 30 minutes or an hour with Coach K (former NU head strength coach Dave Kennedy)," Glenn said.

"But we didn't have anybody checking classes like we do now."

It's interesting watching Pelini at work in the early stages of his head coaching career. We're getting a good feel for how he wants to run a program.

Several people saw Pelini making surprise visits to at least a couple Lincoln downtown bars on a recent Thursday night, on the lookout for players who might have been violating team rules.

In the wake of a weekend last month that saw four Huskers run afoul of the law, quarterback Joe Ganz said players were barred from visiting various downtown bars for the rest of the semester. Pelini made clear his anger during a team meeting.

"He's really good at getting his point across," Wortman says.

We're getting the picture.

By STEVEN M. SIPPLE

> She is extremely unselfish. It's who she is. I'm lucky, because it's not easy.
> — Bo Pelini about his wife Mary Pat

Faith, family sustain coach's wife

Faith and family sustain coach's wife while living in the public eye.

Right after Mary Pat Pelini moved to Lincoln for the second time in four years, her parents arrived from Ohio to help.

Boxes sat unopened. Furniture hadn't been delivered.

But Dave and Karen Leetch were determined to hang a few things on the walls of their daughter's new home and set up some shelves.

By KATHRYN CATES MOORE

Pictures of smiling faces would make the place seem more like home for Nebraska's new head football coach and his family, they said.

"And they were right," Mary Pat Pelini said. "Everything that's up is because they put it there."

The Leetches drop in to help every time their daughter sets up a new house, her mom said.

Picking up and moving from city to city is not what Karen Leetch envisioned for her oldest daughter, she said. As a child, Mary Pat was the one of her three children that was more of a homebody. She didn't even really like overnights with friends.

As an adult, her mom said, Mary Pat is resilient, organized and independent.

"She adjusts and keeps smiling."

■■■

Macadamia — the color, not the nut — is the hue Mary Pat Pelini has chosen for most rooms in other homes. The family's new home in The Ridge in Lincoln already had oatmeal/taupe walls on the first floor, so no new paint was required.

■■■

Mary Pat Pelini said her family's memories are wrapped up with the cities in which she's lived and the teams her husband has coached.

Her son Patrick, 9, was born in Massachusetts (New England Patriots). Daughter Kate, 7, was born in Wisconsin (Green Bay Packers). Caralyn, almost 5, was born in Nebraska (Nebraska, the first tour).

Before they moved in to make new memories in Lincoln, the Pelinis had a space in the basement reconfigured for a fifth bedroom.

"We have lots of visitors," Mary Pat said. Her father-in-law is here for the Spring Game. And others in the extended family and

Bo and Mary Pat Pelini watch their 9-year-old son Patrick play flag football. Mary Pat says when her husband comes home, they don't talk about football, but family. (Eric Gregory)

coaching "families" from around the country will drop in — especially during football season.

Connections with family and friends have always been important for this couple from Youngstown, Ohio.

Mary Pat was 15 when Bo Pelini, who is 2½ years older, came into her life. Her parents would not let them date, but he was allowed to come to the house and watch television.

He'd sit on the couch with her and her younger sister and brother.

"If he could put up with all of them, he might be something special," Karen Leetch said she thought at the time.

■■■

More scarlet and cream (or is it Husker Red?) needs to be added to Mary Pat's wardrobe. Not Sooner Crimson (been there, done that). Goodbye to Louisiana State purple and gold. College teams take their colors seriously.

■■■

When Bo Pelini was introduced as Nebraska's new head coach, his smiling wife and three children were at the news conference, dressed — naturally — in red.

"It happened so quickly," Mary Pat Pelini said of the flight from Louisiana. "We had just arrived about 30 minutes before walking into that room."

Nancy Osborne can relate. Her own children were similar in age to Pelini's when her husband, Tom, took over the head coaching job. He was 35.

"It's a huge challenge," Nancy Osborne said. "Basically, you become a single mom."

The one thing she wasn't prepared for was the intense "publicness" of the role, she said.

"We were very private people. And I tried to maintain a sense of normalcy throughout it."

She expects the Pelinis will do just fine with all of the hoopla surrounding Nebraska football.

"I sense they are a team. That is important," Osborne said.

Unlike Osborne, Pelini has moved numerous times. She has it down to a fine science.

Once the decision is made, she said, she leaps into action.

In the two days after the Dec. 2 news conference in Lincoln, she looked at homes and began the process of establishing their family in Lincoln.

Again.

That was the great part about this move, she said. She already had a family doctor, dentist, hair stylist and church.

■■■

Another white minivan. With a sunroof. That was the extent of her answer when asked what she wanted for her "company" car in Nebraska. No bells. No whistles. Just white.

■■■

Ask Mary Pat Pelini to describe her daily routine, and she pauses.

"Routine? Hmm."

A lot of her day takes place in that white minivan. If she can save time and use the drive-through at a business, she does. She's a regular in the express lane at Starbucks.

After school, she picks up the kids and hands out snacks in the car — usually granola bars and a drink — before heading home so they can do homework.

Then it's back in the van to gymnastics or flag football or horseback riding lessons or friends' houses.

Her cell phone beeps and vibrates constantly. Her home phone electronically screens unknown callers.

And then there are the text messages. She says she's "not very high-tech," except for her ability to text.

The constants in her life, besides the white minivan and ringing phone: faith and family.

It is what she carries with her during the moves, meeting new friends, reuniting with old ones.

Kate Pieper got to know Pelini in the neighborhood and at church when the Pelinis lived here four years ago. Pieper had just had a new baby girl, Cecilia. Pelini was just about to give birth to Caralyn.

There was the usual new-mom back and forth, Pieper said. And then they were gone.

Now they're back.

Pieper and Pelini kept in touch, and she couldn't wait for the Pelini family to come back. The two women watch each other's kids, talk several times a day and sometimes get together for dinner.

"We look at a lot of things in the same way," she said.

The idea of rejoining the Lincoln parish and enrolling the children in St. Peter's Catholic School, where they attend daily Mass, was a plus, Pelini said.

She and Bo were both raised Catholic, and the church is a central part of their family's life. In every town in which they have lived, it has been a way to connect, spiritually and physically.

Her mother, who has taught for many years in Catholic schools in Youngstown, describes their faith as "something that has always been there. It just was."

Mary Pat and Bo were married in the same church where her

Mary Pat Pelini and her youngest daughter, Caralyn, 4, watch others warm up during the UNL Kids Gymnastics Spectacular at the Devaney Sports Center in the spring of 2008. (Gwyneth Roberts)

parents and grandparents were married.

Her minivan practically drives itself to St. Peter's and then to her children's sports events.

At a recent end-of-year gymnastics program, Minnie Mouse sat on one side of Mary Pat and Bo sat on the other. (Caralyn thought Minnie should come.)

Bo takes time from football coaching duties to shift into dad mode.

It is one of the things Mary Pat appreciates about her husband.

"When he is home, he's here for us," she said. "We don't talk about football."

In fact, he often drives the kids to school in the morning and puts them to bed at night.

"I don't want them to see me as a coach," he said. "I'm their dad."

He credits his wife with a big part of his success in both roles.

"She is extremely unselfish. It's who she is. I'm lucky, because it's not easy."

■ ■ ■

Pink rooms for the girls. Red,

black and orange for Patrick. Pansies in yellow and white on the front porch.

■ ■ ■

Two fire-belly frogs and two leopard geckos share a Husker and Cleveland Indian-themed bedroom with Patrick Pelini.

The arrangement seems to work well for all of them.

Patrick is just beginning to really get into sports, his mother said. He's watching more ESPN.

And he has his own teams to think about — basketball, flag football, baseball.

In fact, asked to recall her favorite football play, Mary Pat Pelini says:"Watching Patrick run 98 yards during a recent flag football game to score."

But he's happy to be a Husker, too. So much so that he wanted the Blackshirts logo painted in his bathroom.

Kate and Caralyn finally got their pink bedrooms, their mom said. Their beds have netting draped down from the ceiling. And different shades of pink dots adorn their walls.

No lizards or frogs, but each girl has a beta fish.

Kate is crazy about horses and takes riding lessons, Pelini said. She also does gymnastics and will play softball this summer, although she always has played baseball with the boys.

Caralyn also did gymnastics this spring, but her pre-school world is occupied by friends, lots of baby dolls and stuffed animals.

When the family's new dining room china cabinet arrived, Caralyn decided it was a perfect place for her dolls and carefully lined them up inside the glass doors.

The dolls did not get to stay there for long. China took their place — right next to a new, round dining room table with enough places for all of their family.

Today, Mary Pat Pelini will take her place as the new head coach's wife at the Spring Game.

"I'll be there at the last minute," she said. "I don't have the game day schedule down yet."

But she will. And she'll be wearing red, with her kids by her side.

April 20, 2008

Team offers first view of new NU

More than 80,000 fans filled Memorial Stadium on April 19, 2008, to get a look at Bo Pelini's Huskers in the Red-White Spring Game. (Ted Kirk)

The Vine Street block party to welcome the new guy was hardly a formal affair.

When Bo Pelini emerged from the tunnel in the moments before Saturday's Red-White Spring Game, he did it wearing shorts and without his players. They'd come a minute later.

By BRIAN CHRISTOPHERSON

You wouldn't know it by the crowd of 80,149 at Memorial Stadium, but this was indeed a practice. Dockers slacks can wait until the fall to be showcased.

There was a running clock in the third quarter and purple pullover jerseys worn on special teams. There were coaches standing on the field during plays.

As is the way with spring games, pretty play did not rule the day. But that seemed to matter little to the fans that filled the stadium for cathartic reasons as much as anything.

After a 5-7 season, putting on a "Bo Big Red" shirt and chanting BO-PE-LI-NI on a cloudless day in April seemed a slice of goodness for the Husker soul.

"I thought it was a pretty special atmosphere," Pelini said.

"That's something I've never been a part of before, and I don't know if any of these coaches have."

There was a score that came with this carnival atmosphere: a 24-14 triumph for the Reds over the Whites.

The score didn't matter to Pelini. Seeing progress did.

"Every day, I see that indecision going away, and confidence is growing. We'll get there, but it's a process. The process is well under way, but it's not nearly finished," Pelini said.

"We're not going to be satisfied until we're up there at the top.

We're going to keep raising our standard. We have a very high standard; we want perfection. That's what we're going to strive for, and the players understand that."

During the scrimmage, Pelini usually stood about 15 yards behind the quarterback, between the hash marks. Defensive coordinator Carl Pelini and linebackers coach Mike Ekeler often were on each side of him.

Bo Pelini worked with the defense, in a linebacker's crouch, during each play. Offensive coordinator Shawn Watson handled

Quarterback Joe Ganz (12) and running back Marlon Lucky (5) lead the Huskers onto the Memorial Stadium field for the 2008 Red-White Spring Game. (William Lauer)

the other side, conservative in what he revealed with his play-calling.

Missteps? You bet. Plenty.

"There was definitely some feeling out," senior receiver Todd Peterson said. "Just when we came out of the tunnel, all the skill-position guys ran out on the field, kind of went to the center of the field and went, 'Now what do we do?'"

There were strong performances, maybe the best by senior linebacker Tyler Wortman, who got started right away by ruining what was supposed to be a statement first play, an option to the right.

Instead of a successful play, there was a disruption by Wortman, a fumble recovery by Wortman, and a sheepish grin by Wortman after the game: "I don't know how happy the coaches are with me about it."

No hard feelings. Not on a feel-good day like this one.

Sophomore running back Roy Helu seemed as good as advertised and Quentin

Castille ran with purpose, though there was a second-quarter fumble. Quarterback Joe Ganz was steady and receiver Curenski Gilleylen showed his capabilities on a 77-yard first-quarter touchdown pass that put the Red up 14-0 less than six minutes into the game.

But it was Pelini's show. No surprise there. It's been his spring.

And you knew that when it was over. He left the field to an ovation from the fans still in the stadium. Pelini waved, signing autographs here and there.

As he walked through the tunnel toward the locker room, he high-fived fans reaching out from behind the ropes.

Hope lives in April, but Pelini knows as well as anyone that all the fanfare will soon give way to the reality of results.

Peterson said Saturday's end of spring practice doesn't mean relaxation for the players anytime soon.

There are workouts scheduled for 6 a.m. Monday, the Grand Island native said.

"One thing Coach Pelini always says is you got to keep your foot on the gas pedal," Peterson said. "We're not letting up. We've only got so much time and we're going to work hard to get ready."

There was enough evidence Saturday to show that this is still very much a work in progress.

But still you could tell Pelini was enjoying the surroundings, full of pep as he led the crowd during a halftime Drug Free Pledge, his intro being: "It's a beautiful day in Husker Nation, isn't it?"

The crowd, the second-largest to see a college football spring game, thundered its approval.

"It's kind of mind-boggling. It's still a practice ... and we've got twice as many (people) as in my hometown," Peterson said.

"It's just a testament to the fans. They're never going to leave us."

April 22, 2008

What we're trying to do is take the gentlemen that are on campus and develop them and try to push them to reach their potential.

-- Bo Pelini

Pelini likes his team's progress

With spring camp concluded and 15 practices in the books, first-year Husker head football coach Bo Pelini is starting to get an idea about the level of personnel he inherited.

A 5-7 season in 2007 certainly has some people curious about Nebraska's talent level.

By BRIAN CHRISTOPHERSON

Pelini assured Monday that the Husker cupboard is not bare.

"You know, it's not like you can go out and make trades or you can go out and draft or anything like that," Pelini said during a Big 12 Conference coaches teleconference. "What we're trying to do is take the gentlemen that are on campus and develop them and try to push them to reach their potential.

"There's talent here. They're eager and they're learning every day. And what I've seen is guys getting better. How that's going to equate to wins and losses, that's not something we're real focused on right now."

The Huskers concluded spring practice Saturday with the annual Red-White Spring Game, which drew 80,149 fans, the second-largest crowd to see a spring game in college football history.

The coach knows there's still plenty of work to do until the season opener on Aug. 30, but Pelini said he was able to identify some players who could potentially emerge as leaders come the fall.

He cited the leadership exhibited this spring that quarterback Joe Ganz and offensive linemen Matt Slauson and Lydon Murtha have shown on offense. On defense, he has liked what he's seen

Bo Pelini opened his first spring as Husker coach with a practice on March 26, 2008. After the spring, he said on the Big 12 coaches teleconference: "There's talent here. They're eager and they're learning every day. And what I've seen is guys getting better." (Journal Star archives)

from defensive end Barry Turner, linebacker Phillip Dillard and safety Larry Asante.

"A lot of guys showed leadership skills, but I think the key is having a culture that runs throughout your football team and finding the right guys to enforce the culture and promote it; and make sure (that) if there's a crack built in the foundation, that they seal it real quick," Pelini said. "I think that's what's happening. I think guys are buying in."

At a team meeting Wednesday, players will choose representatives from each position group to serve as part of a Unity Council, which became a part of Tom Os-

borne-coached teams beginning in 1991. The council met each week to examine issues within the team.

Frank Solich continued to use the Unity Council when he took over as head coach in 1998, though the group's effectiveness waned toward the end of Solich's tenure. It went away during the Bill Callahan era.

Since taking the job in December, Pelini has stressed a desire to have the football program feel like a family to those involved.

"We're developing better relationships and trust that is going to help us be successful and stay together for a long time through

good times and bad," Pelini said. "Because, no matter what, you're going to have rocky times and you're going to have good times, and you need to have leadership to offset the bad times."

Pelini said he was hopeful that all the crowd support from Saturday's Spring Game might provide a lift to the the team as it goes through summer workouts.

"That sends a bolt of energy through your team," Pelini said. "And the more our players are exposed to that, they start feeling that's a responsibility they have when they put that 'N' on the side of their helmets."

> We're going to have a team that plays with tremendous effort and tremendous passion. ... I just hope they're as passionate as you people are. — Bo Pelini

Football 101 draws a crowd

No blinking applause sign was needed. These people did not need extra encouragement to clap, to laugh, to think that better days were around the corner.

And in the process they'd learn a play or two, about the cover-2 defense, that linebacker LaTravis Washington enjoys a bubble bath the day after a game, that Carl Pelini is full of energy but also parenting guidance: "If he spills his milk and cries, he's a quarterback. If he spills his milk and throws the bones, he's a Blackshirt."

The people laughed. Of course they laughed.

Nebraska coach Bo Pelini's first Football 101 class was in session Tuesday and about 1,000 Big Red fans turned out to the Husker football facilities to see what the new professor had to say.

Along with the football talk was support of a good cause, the $80 fee from each participant going to cancer research. In total, more than $40,000 was raised.

Bill Callahan first started these Football 101 events in 2004. Available to women, they were held annually and were quite popular, some good money in the fight against cancer raised along the way.

And so Pelini continued the tradition, the slight modification being that men could also attend.

The crowd, mostly women, gave standing ovations to every speaker, the loudest cheers expectedly going to athletic director Tom Osborne and Bo Pelini.

Pelini had no guaranteed wins to offer the crowd, but he did have this: "I can guarantee one thing. When we have our football team take the field, you're going to have a team that plays with tremendous effort and tremendous passion. ... I just hope they're as passionate as you people are."

There were Husker trivia contests, lunch in Memorial Stadium, on-field interaction with coaches, a tunnel walk, a question-answer session with some of the players.

Who do the players consider the team's biggest rival?

Colorado, Missouri, Texas, Oklahoma. All got mentioned.

Linebacker Blake Lawrence told the crowd he has switched from No. 12 because people kept confusing him with quarterback Joe

Husker assistant Marvin Sanders (left) was in his element teaching the intricacies of pass defense to participants at the Football 101 clinic. Almost 1,000 people attended the event, which raised money for breast cancer research. (Heidi Hoffman)

Ganz.

Holder Jake Wesch told the crowd he'd maybe like to switch to No. 12 so people would confuse him with Joe Ganz.

"He's probably the toughest holder in the Big 12, if not the country," Ganz said of Wesch. "He's one guy you don't want to mess with."

There were plenty of jokes. There was also a video paying tribute to the Blackshirts' tradition. Defensive coaches watched with interest from the back of the room, highlights of great Husker defenses of the past rolling across the screen.

Trev Alberts narrated the video, which featured interviews with guys like Grant Wistrom and Christian Peter about what being a Blackshirt meant to them.

The crowd roared with delight at the footage of each hit and afterward Carl Pelini told them that "you can't be a Blackshirt by default."

He said even starters wouldn't automatically be given Blackshirts. They'd have to put in the maximum effort to earn the black practice jerseys so well-known around these parts.

Carl Pelini recalled a story of a recent day when walk-on recruits were visiting the campus. The recruits were shown a video of Husker highlights, many Blackshirt successes playing on the screen. The coach viewed it from the back of the room.

"As I watched it, I got chills," he said. "And as I watched it, I could just feel the weight on my shoulders."

The defensive coordinator said when

coaches review film, they look at it the second time examining only effort. When coaches see great effort on film, he said they make sure to make a point of it to the kids, telling them, "Here it is. This is how we have to play to win a championship."

Words in June won't help the win-loss column, but they're the kind of words a fan base coming off a 5-7 season full of ugly defensive statistics delights in hearing.

Smartly, Bo Pelini did remind fans that this is a work in progress.

By BRIAN CHRISTOPHERSON

"We've made a lot of progress, but let's face it, we're nowhere near where we need to be," he said.

"It's not about who we're playing and what our schedule's going to be. That will all take care of itself. What we're trying to get our young men to focus on is the process that is going to get us to September."

The first-year head coach said Osborne reminds him often there will be bumps in the road.

"You have to stay grounded. You have to stay pretty even-keeled in this profession," Pelini said.

When introducing Osborne, Pelini said the athletic director is what the University of Nebraska is all about.

"I've said this before. I thought I was in the best assistant coach's job in the United States the last couple years," Pelini said. "I had a great situation. I thought I was in a position where I could wait for the best job available, the best job where my family could grow up and we could move some place and be some place hopefully for a long time.

"You evaluate facilities, you evaluate places, but ultimately when you've been in it as long as I have ... you find out it's all about people.

"When Coach Osborne came back to be the athletic director at the University of Nebraska, that made this the best job in the United States."

The fans thundered their approval. There is not much that didn't bring applause.

When it was Osborne's turn, he brought his humor with him, at one point smiling and telling the gathering: "I hope you're all as enthusiastic in December as you are now."

> If they (expectations) are not reasonable, I don't want to be here.
>
> -- Bo Pelini

Eight wins a reasonable expectation

New Nebraska football coach Bo Pelini received celebrity treatment while making appearances around the state, including throwing out the first pitch at a Husker baseball game. We'll see about his reception after the 2008 football season. (William Lauer)

He traveled the state in recent weeks meeting and greeting Nebraska fans, spreading good will and connecting with the football-starved masses.

But Bo Pelini didn't actively attempt to gauge fans' expectations for his team in 2008. Fan expectations are not his concern, he says. He wants to help fans understand what he's trying to accomplish in his program. He wants fans to be proud of the program. He wants to create optimism and excitement.

By STEVEN M. SIPPLE

As for measuring expectations, "I really can't worry about that," Pelini says flatly.

As for his own expectations, "I want to win them all," he again says flatly.

That, of course, is the essence of Pelini. He's confident, blunt and brutally honest. It's refreshing and concerning all at once. It's not always so much what he says as how he says it. But you get the feeling the first-year head coach believes at his core Nebraska really can "win them all," no matter how preposterous an undefeated season sounds when discussing a team that finished 5-7 last season. Indeed, the Huskers played a level of defense that Big Red fans now avoid discussing as if it were a deep, dark family secret.

Predictions are hokey and meaningless and generally mindless. Predictions typically contain as much nutritional value as a batch of cotton candy. Far be it for me to be above mindless predictions. So, here goes:

I'm solidly in the camp that says Nebraska will finish 8-4. I'm guessing the Huskers will wind up 4-4 in the Big 12, which last season would have been good for third in the North and South divisions. Given last season's ugliness, I'm guessing Big Red fans could live happily with 8-4 and 4-4.

Nine wins and three losses probably would be a best-case scenario.

Seven and five would be acceptable.

Six and six would be a prelude to a brutally long winter of carping around water coolers.

Bottom line is, Nebraska fans want to see the Huskers be competitive in every game. Maybe that's the most important thing — avoiding embarrassment. Big Red rolled over too many times last season. Rolling over is sim-

Husker fans wait to high-five (and low-five) Husker quarterback Joe Ganz after Nebraska's dismal 2007 season came to an end with a 65-51 loss at Colorado. (Eric Gregory)

ply unacceptable unless you're my dog Stitches.

The feeling I get is fans mostly want to see Nebraska show marked improvement in 2008 and get to a decent bowl game. Doing so would establish a nice foundation.

We broach the "expectations" discussion largely because of those glossy preseason magazines. Lindy's and Athlon predict Nebraska will finish fourth in the Big 12 North. Phil Steele picks the Huskers to finish second in the division behind Missouri. However, Steele's credibility diminishes greatly because he ranks NU's defensive line among the top four in the league.

At any rate, offseason predictions and expectations for Nebraska seem surprisingly reasonable.

Bo ought to thank Bill for that.

The Nebraska program, under Bill Callahan, dipped to levels last season that Big Red fans couldn't have imagined, even after finishes of 7-7 in 2002 and 5-6 in 2004. NU allowed Kansas to score 10 touchdowns last November.

That's why Nebraska's first few games next season will be critical. You have to believe the Huskers' confidence on defense is somewhat fragile. Pelini's trademark swagger will help matters greatly. His confidence permeates the program. But his defenders need to see results on the field or else it might be, "Here we go again."

Every bit of Pelini's defensive know-how will be necessary in the nation's highest-scoring league. Even Pelini admits he was "a little blown away" upon seeing the numbers Big 12 teams have been putting up.

The days of going 49-2 in a four-season stretch, as Nebraska did from 1994-97, seem increasingly unlikely considering the changing landscape in the college game. That's a column for another day. For now, Big Red fans hold tightly to the belief that they soon will enjoy the lofty level of preseason expectations that exist nowadays at schools such as Southern Cal, Oklahoma and Louisiana State.

Of course, Pelini embraces such expectations, even if they aren't necessarily reasonable at Nebraska right now. If you listen to Pelini, you can't help but believe such expectations at dear old NU will become reasonable soon enough.

"If they're not reasonable, I don't want to be here," he says, confident as always.

> **If it ever gets to the point where I feel like I'm losing the balance, to me that's when it's time to quit and do something else.**
> — Bo Pelini

Bo balances football, family

As Bo Pelini likes to say, it's not rocket science here.

For someone who's been playing and coaching football for most of his 40 years, he figures he should have a pretty good handle on the game by now.

Nebraska's coach expects to work, and plenty hard at that, but not 18 hours a day like some coaches are doing. He hasn't ever pulled an all-nighter in a coach's office and he doesn't expect to start now.

By BRIAN CHRISTOPHERSON

"Just in my estimation, if you're working that many hours, you're doing something wrong," Pelini said. "When you work you need to be efficient, you need to know what you're after, you have to be zeroed in. There's a difference between putting in hours and putting in efficient hours. But everybody has their own styles. There's a lot of ways to skin a cat."

For some coaches — former Husker coach Bill Callahan seemed to fit in this crowd — it has become a normal enough thing to spend an entire day consumed with football. Go to work in the dark and come home in the dark.

Former Husker Mike Grant, who has been an assistant at the likes of Iowa State, Southern Miss and now Western Michigan, said he's heard and seen the stories of NFL coaches who practically kill themselves with hours, depriving themselves of sleep and sometimes seeing family in the pursuit of gaining a football advantage.

"Being with three or four different programs, I've seen there's more than one way to do it," Grant said. "There are guys who are grinding from 6 a.m. to midnight and expect to do it again the next day. Some guys are family first. If your kid has a recital, they'll tell you to go to the recital."

Bo Pelini makes time to attend his kids' sporting events. (Gwyneth Roberts)

There's no written rule on how to do it. It's a pressure-packed gig and people want wins. So if a guy sees an advantage in watching replays of last Saturday's game while the rest of the city sleeps, so be it.

In Pelini's case, he said he wants to make sure he's giving as much attention to what he considers his top job — being a husband and father — as he does to coaching.

"I try not to get consumed with this. Honestly, I don't watch a lot of football when I go home. I don't talk about it much. When I go home, I'm not coaching, I'm Dad. That's the way it is. That's the way it's always going to be. If it ever gets to the point where I feel like I'm losing the balance, to me that's when it's time to quit and do something else.

"... I don't know where this perception ever came out that when you become a football coach that being a father and being a husband take a back seat. I believe in balance. I talk the same thing with our players and our staff: 'You need balance in your life to have success at what you do.'"

Fellow Youngstown, Ohio, native and Oklahoma coach Bob Stoops has much the same approach. Perhaps contributing some to it is that both Pelini and Stoops have younger kids and they certainly don't want to miss important things in their lives.

"It's a family atmosphere, no question," Oklahoma offensive coordinator Jay Norvell said of Stoops' work environment philosophy.

Pelini has children aged 9, 7 and 5. All are heavily involved in activities.

"I try to expose them to everything and encourage them to do whatever they want," Pelini said.

Baseball, softball, piano, horse riding, tennis — the kids are trying all that stuff.

"Playing tennis I don't know anything about," Pelini said. "But I just try to hit the ball back to them."

Pelini has set no magic number of hours he expects his coaches to work. The number of hours, he said, simply depends on how long it takes to be fully prepared.

"No, I'm not going to sleep here, but there are going to be some days during the season (where) I'll be here as long as I need to get the job done," Pelini said. "We don't have a lot of set hours around here. When you're done, go home. But there are certain things you have to accomplish. That is why you have to hire good people and hire people you trust, people that believe in the same things you do."

Bo Pelini and his family on the day of his hiring as Nebraska's head football coach: Wife Mary Pat and children Patrick (left), Caralyn and Kate. (Ted Kirk)

> I think that's what makes the University of Nebraska unique over any place I've been coaching — how much it means to the state. It's like one big family, and that's what I want it to be.
>
> — Bo Pelini

Mark "Bo" Pelini

Born

Dec. 13, 1967, Youngstown, Ohio

Family

Wife, Mary Pat; son, Patrick; daughters, Kathryn and Caralyn.

Education

Graduated from Ohio State in 1990 with a bachelor's degree in business marketing. Earned a master's degree in sports administration from Ohio University in 1992.

Playing career

Free safety at Ohio State (1987-90).

Coaching career

1991	Graduate assistant, Iowa
1993	QB coach, Cardinal Mooney High School, Youngstown, Ohio
1994-96	Defensive backs coach, San Francisco 49ers
1997-99	Linebackers coach, New England Patriots
2000-02	Linebackers coach, Green Bay Packers
2003	Defensive coordinator, interim head coach, Nebraska
2004	Co-defensive coordinator, Oklahoma
2005-07	Defensive coordinator, LSU